Competition Law on the Global Stage: David Gerber's Global Competition Law in Perspective

Editors
Nicolas Charbit
Elisa Ramundo

60 Broad Street, Suite 3502, NY 10004
www.concurrences.com
contact@concurrences.com

Printed in the United States of America
First Printing, 2014
ISBN 978-1-939007-20-9

Publisher's Cataloging-in-Publication
(Provided by Quality Books, Inc.)

Competition law on the global stage: David Gerber's global
competition law in perspective / editors,
Nicolas Charbit, Elisa Ramundo.
pages cm
LCCN 2013947670
ISBN 978-1-939007-20-9
ISBN 978-1-939007-21-6

1. Antitrust law (International law) 2. Gerber,
David J. 3. Restraint of trade. 4. Antitrust law.
I. Charbit, Nicolas, editor. II. Ramundo, Elisa,
editor.

K3850.C66 2013 343.07'21
QBI13-600165

Cover and book design by Yves Buliard, www.ybgraphic.fr

Editors' Note

Nicolas Charbit
Elisa Ramundo

Since 2004, the *Institute of Competition Law* has focused its attention and devoted its efforts on stimulating antitrust dialogue across the world through publications and conferences.

With over 120 competition regimes worldwide, the challenge to narrow the gap and enable the antitrust community to communicate efficiently and resourcefully becomes increasingly more important.

Platforms like the International Competition Network, the Organization for the Economic Cooperation and Development, and the United Nations Conference for Trade and Development—just to mention the most important—have put in place the institutional framework to favor dialogue, analysis, and discussion in the antitrust area.

The *Institute of Competition Law* parallels the above-mentioned institutional efforts with the aim of being at the cutting edge of antitrust publications for experts around the globe. The *e-Competitions Bulletin* database features over 2,000 authors and more than 9,000 case-summaries covering 55 jurisdictions. The *Concurrences Journal* quarterly provides readers with peer reviewed academic contributions.

In addition to these publications, the *Institute* has become over the years one of the leading antitrust events' organizers, having held conferences, lunch meetings, in-house seminars, private dinners in Brussels, London, Paris, New York, and Washington, DC.

Yet, the *Institute*'s role of antitrust publisher on the global scale could not be fully achieved without publishing books in both print and electronic format.

The *Institute of Competition Law* had the privilege to collect contributions of the "Global Competition Law Conference," organized by Professors David Gerber and Sungjoon Cho, held on October 28, 2011 at Chicago-Kent College of Law. The Conference's goals to expand the discussion on the future of competition law on the global level fully embody the *Institute*'s mission as described above.

This collating volume includes ten contributions signed by prominent antitrust practitioners and academics. Readers will be offered the opportunity to explore the various views on the current and future developments of competition law on the global level as enlightened by David J. Gerber, Eleanor M. Fox, William E. Kovacic, David A. Hyman, Xiaoye Wang, Laurence Idot, Spencer Weber Waller, André Fiebig, Javier Cortázar-Mora, Wentong Zheng, and Mor Bakhoum. Contributors' short bios appear at the end of the book.

The editors would like to express their gratitude to all authors and, in particular, to Professors Gerber and Cho for their invaluable contribution to this editorial project.

Institute of Competition Law Publications

WILLIAM E. KOVACIC: AN ANTITRUST TRIBUTE
LIBER AMICORUM (Vol. I)

Nicolas Charbit - Elisa Ramundo - Anna Chehtova - Abigail Slater (Eds.)

January 2013
431 pages (Hardcover and e-Book)

WILLIAM E. KOVACIC: AN ANTITRUST TRIBUTE
LIBER AMICORUM (Vol. II)

Nicolas Charbit - Elisa Ramundo (Eds.)
Anna M. Pavlik - Jessica Rebarber (Asst. Eds.)

March 2014
(Hardcover and e-Book)

2013 COMPETITION DIGEST
A SYNTHESIS OF EU AND NATIONAL LEADING CASES

Foreword by Frédéric Jenny
Nicolas Charbit - Elisa Ramundo - Maly Op-Courtaigne (Eds.)

January 2013
672 pages (Paperback and e-Book)

2014 COMPETITION DIGEST
A SYNTHESIS OF EU AND NATIONAL LEADING CASES

Foreword by Frédéric Jenny
Nicolas Charbit - Elisa Ramundo - Maly Op-Courtaigne (Eds.)

September 2014
(Paperback and e-Book)

COMPETITION LAW ON THE GLOBAL STAGE:
DAVID GERBER'S GLOBAL COMPETITION LAW IN PERSPECTIVE

Nicolas Charbit - Elisa Ramundo (Eds.)

January 2014
173 pages (Hardcover and e-Book)

EU LAW AND LIFE SCIENCES

Peter Bogaert - Damien Geradin (Eds.)

January 2014
274 pages (Hardcover and e-Book)

Preface

The recent global financial crisis and in particular governments' responses to the crisis raise many concerns for the global competition law community. Bailouts and other emergency measures ironically tend to create various market distortions, such as crisis cartels. After all, in an era of globalization, one nation's response to an international crisis might affect other nations' policy goals.

Against this turbulent yet academically inspiring background, my colleague and dear friend David Gerber has recently published *"Global Competition: Law, Markets and Globalization"* (Oxford University Press, 2010, pbk., 2012). Needless to say, this is a very timely endeavor. As a crystallization of his decade-long research in the field, this book has made an enormous contribution in helping us understand competition law on the global level and its complex dynamics with regard to domestic legal regimes. David's book, not surprisingly, has received rave reviews from a number of prestigious journals, including the American Journal of International Law and the European Journal of International Law.

In tandem with David's stellar achievement, I had the honor and privilege of organizing a conference at Chicago-Kent College of Law in late October of 2011. The main goal of this conference was not just to revisit David's brilliant work but more to expand the discussion to the next stage in a way which would prov ide the global competition law community with critical thinking and rich narratives.

Fortunately, we had a gathering of excellent academics and practitioners in the area. The Honorable Diane Wood, judge of the United States Court of Appeals for the Seventh Circuit, delivered opening remarks. Speakers included William Kovacic, former chairman of the United States Federal Trade Commission, Eleanor Fox, Walter J. Derenberg Professor of Trade Regulation at New York Law School whose name is synonymous with global competition law, Wang Xiaoye, Professor of Law at Hunan University in China and formerly Professor of Law at the Chinese Academy of Social Science, who is the "mother" of the Chinese Anti-Monopoly Law, and Laurence Idot, professor at University of Paris II (Pantheon) who is one of the most preeminent competition law scholars in Europe.

Other distinguished speakers included Professor Andrew Guzman (University of California Berkeley School of Law), Professor Michal Gal (Haifa University Law Faculty), Professor Seung Wha Chang (Seoul National University School of Law, and a member of the WTO Appellate Body), Professor Spencer Waller (Loyola University, Chicago, School of Law), André Fiebig (Partner, Baker & McKenzie), and Professor Javier Cortázar-Mora (Javeriana University, Bogota, Colombia). We also had impressive and rapidly rising junior scholars in the field, such as Professor Wentong Zheng (University of Florida School of Law) and Mor Bakhoum (Max Planck Institute, Munich).

We had truly rich and vibrant discussions at the conference. We first analyzed the global competition law dynamics in general. And then, we investigated the subtle interplay between national and transnational dynamics. Finally, we attempted to conceive the way forward by relating convergence to commitment.

After the conference, a firm consensus emerged among participants that we should share this valuable outcome of the conference with the rest of the global competition law community. We initially published some of the conference proceedings online at *Concurrences* (www.concurrences.com). After further editorial efforts, we now publish those proceedings in a bounded volume.

We hope this volume will stimulate further debates and discussions in this increasingly important area.

In closing, I would like to express my deep gratitude to contributors of the volume. Also, I thank Nicolas Charbit, Editor-in-Chief of *Concurrences* for his support of this publication project. My thanks also go to Elisa Ramundo of *Concurrences* and Laura Caringella of Chicago-Kent College of Law for their valuable editorial contributions. Finally, special thanks to David Gerber himself for writing such an excellent book, which made all these wonderful projects possible.

Sincerely,

Sungjoon CHO
Professor of Law

Contributors

Mor BAKHOUM
Max Planck Institute for Intellectual Property and Competition Law

Javier CORTÁZAR-MORA
CESA University, Bogota

André FIEBIG
Baker & McKenzie - Northwestern University School of Law

Eleanor M. FOX
New York University School of Law

David A. HYMAN
University of Illinois, College of Law

Laurence IDOT
University Paris II Panthéon-Assas - Concurrences Journal

David J. GERBER
Chicago-Kent College of Law

William E. KOVACIC
George Washington University Law School

Spencer WEBER WALLER
Institute for Consumer Antitrust Studies,
Loyola University Chicago, School of Law

Xiaoye WANG
Hunan University and Chinese Academy of Social Sciences
Chinese Antimonopoly Commission

Wentong ZHENG
University of Florida Levin College of Law

Table of Contents

Competition Law and Globalization: Where Do We Go from Here?

David J. GERBER

dgerber@kentlaw.iit.edu

Distinguished Professor of Law, Chicago-Kent College of Law

Global Competition: Law, Markets and Globalization addresses a problem that in one way or another affects almost every aspect of life in almost all corners of the world—the strained relationship between national laws and global economic forces.[1] As so often, the problem also creates opportunities. National institutions—legislatures, courts and administrators—provide norms for economic conduct within their territory, but their markets are increasingly interwoven with much broader, often global, economic relationships. National institutions have their own interests, but increasingly the global dimensions of economic conduct frustrate and confuse their efforts to advance those interests. Increasingly, the forces of globalization create interests that are shared across national borders. Yet many thinkers and decision makers either fail to recognize the extent to which these interests are shared or pay little, if any, attention to this shared dimension of their interests. The legal regimes designed to establish the boundaries of competitive conduct—i.e., competition law or "antitrust law"—are at the center of this dilemma.

Effective competition law responses to this set of issues may, therefore, be of much value to many. Unfortunately, however, discussions in the area are often distorted, sometimes false, and frequently misleading, which means that the decisions based on them may not be well supported. These weaknesses are to some extent inevitable. The issues are often relatively new, and there are many obstacles to developing effective responses. It is critically important, however, to improve the factual and intellectual bases for decision making in this area of law, and Global Competition pursues that objective.

In writing the book I saw three main challenges. One is the thin and often distorted factual basis for both thought and decisions relating to global competition law. Commentators and policy makers often make claims about competition law experience that are wrong, incomplete or highly misleading. Sometimes the claims result from simple lack of knowledge, but often they are also distorted by ideologies and biases. Second, the intellectual tools that are being used for analysis and decision making in this area are often either inappropriate or poorly developed or both. A key role for analysis is to raise questions that need to be asked, and often the questions asked in this area are far too narrow. A third challenge is the narrow and fragmented discussion of potential responses to

1 David J. Gerber, Global Competition: Law, Markets and Globalization (Oxford University Press 2010).

the current problems. Again, ideology, interests, and limited vision combine to restrict and distort available policy options. Lack of depth and clarity in discussions of convergence combine with narrow assumptions about the potential for coordination to present a skewed view of policy options.

The book addresses these three goals. First, It broadens the canvas of discussion, revealing important elements of the dynamics of competition law in the context of globalization, and it identifies aspects of those dynamics that had been and continue to be ignored or misunderstood. Second, it develops a methodological focus on the dynamics of decision making in the international domain, focusing, in particular, on the interrelationships between national and international dimensions of competition law, often including economic, political, legal and technological factors. Finally, it relates these factual and intellectual tools to the task of developing more effective policies for the future.

The mini-symposium on the book that was held in Chicago in October of 2011 further advanced this project. An extraordinary group of scholars gave their views on the book and on some of the issues raised in it. More importantly, they offered perspectives on the future of competition law on the global level. I am grateful to all who participated in the discussions there, and especially to those who agreed to publish some of their thoughts in this format.

The three central challenges that first encouraged me to write the book are likely to remain with us for a very long time. This brief essay outlines some of my own views on the book and on its place in discussions of competition law issues today. I look briefly at the book's contributions and as well as at reactions to the book in the literature as well as in countless meetings and presentations around the world. I draw from these discussions some conclusions about where we are and some suggestions about how we can move from here toward a more valuable and useful basis for analysis and decision making in the area.

I. Responses, Receptions & Lessons

The book's contributions focus on these challenges. First, it provides a wider and deeper view of the global dimensions of competition law. The value of placing competition law s in their historical, economic and political contexts is difficult to overstate, but apparently easy to overlook. Moreover, the extraordinary speed of change in global economic, political and legal conditions since the 1990s has left a veil of superficiality over many discussions in the area.

The book broadens the context of discussion in both time and space. The temporal dimension is critical to many current discussions and decisions, because it determines the kinds of experience that are considered relevant. For example, it is common to assume that efforts to deal with transborder competition law issues are very recent, but the book reveals that such efforts began much earlier than most discussions recognize—in the 1920s, not the 1990s. It then shows how these earlier episodes fit together with each other and shaped later developments, including the evolution of European integration and twenty-first century treatment of transnational competition law issues. At the very least, this broadening of the context suggests that, if appropriately structured, coordination strategies might garner more support than some are tempted to suppose.

Global Competition deepens the context of decisions by emphasizing the close and often overlooked or underappreciated interweaving of national, regional and international domains of decision making. These domains are often treated quite separately, but to do so is to exclude from view central pieces of experience and critical issues. Each piece of the system can influence and interact with every other piece of the system, and these interactions constitute the dynamics of transnational competition law. U.S. antitrust, EU competition law, the competition laws of newer players in Asia and elsewhere—all influence decisions in other parts of the system, and developments on the international level often profoundly influence what appear to be purely domestic decisions. Sometimes these relationships involve influence alone, while at other times they create elements of conflict. Many commentators have claimed that the book's focus on these issues has been particularly valuable.

The book also responds to the "tools" challenge, illustrating the need for additional and more sharply refined intellectual tools in thinking about transnational competition law. The central concept here is "decisions" and the factors that influence decisions—that is, the dynamics of the relationships that constitute the cross-border dimension of competition law. The book shows how this approach can shed light on causal relationships among events, decisions, and other elements of the picture that are generally seen as unrelated. This approach also allows us to more effectively organize the overwhelming amount of data that is now available relating to competition law around the globe. In *Global Competition* I use this methodological perspective throughout, although I do not dwell on its intellectual underpinnings. I am currently engaged in developing those aspects more fully.

third set of contributions in the book is based on the first two and developed from them. Here the focus is on the current and future development of competition law on the transnational level. The book looks with care at discussions of the issue and seeks to clarify the language used in referring to the two main strategies for solving some of the problems created by the limitations and weaknesses of the current jurisdictional framework—i.e., the concepts of convergence and coordination. Attention is today focused primarily on convergence as a strategy, but discussions on the subject often reveal confusion and a degree of obfuscation that impedes thought, communication and, ultimately, effective decision making. What does "convergence" even mean? The term is very often used in contradictory and often vapid ways without any clarity as to its content. This nebulous term has the political advantage of allowing each observer to believe and/or claim that it means what they want it to mean. This makes it potentially valuable as rhetoric, but also as invitation to mistakes, misunderstandings and worse as a basis for analysis and policy decisions. The book tries to bring further clarity to the discussions by analyzing its uses, its potential meanings, and some of its consequences for particular groups.

"Coordination" represents another approach to the problem. Here the idea is that states, international organizations and other institutions can work together to find ways of responding to the problems and opportunities of global competition. The book looks at some of the reasons why many assume that this approach has limited prospects for success. It also looks at some of the potential forms of coordination and their potential advantages and pitfalls for various states, organizations and interest group. It concludes that traditional forms of coordination have limited prospects in the context of globalization, but it goes on to suggest a new approach to coordination that may have significant benefits and perhaps even prospects. I refer to this as a "commitment pathway" or "coordination pathway" approach. It takes into account the much changed contexts of decision making on the global level, including the impact of new technologies of communication and transportation. The book outlines this approach. I am currently developing it more thoroughly.

1. Receptions

Many audiences have received the book warmly. Interest has been particularly strong outside the United States, especially in Europe and in Asia, and international organizations such as UNCTAD have also welcomed it and helped to make it better known. Translations have appeared in Spanish and Chinese, and others are either underway or under discussion. Europeans have often been particularly interested in the interrelationships among competition law systems around the world and in the potential for improved global relationships. As expected, participants from newer competition law countries have shown special interest in the comparative aspects of the work and the lessons they can draw from U.S. and European experience.

Two groups have shown more limited interest in the book. One includes those U.S. antitrust scholars who are primarily or exclusively concerned with U.S. antitrust law. This is not surprising, given that many in the group assume that transnational aspects of competition law have little to do with domestic antitrust law. This often combines with the belief that the basic substantive provisions of U.S. antitrust law should be the model for all competition laws, and that therefore there is little reason to be particularly interested in what is happening elsewhere. The second group includes economists who deal with competition law. For many in this group, the main focus of attention is on economic theory and its application. Moreover, economists are typically and understandably interested primarily in the work of other economists. This tends to limit interest in the legal and political contexts in which economics is used. Nevertheless, I think there is much in the book that can be of value to both of these groups, and I hope to do more to bring this type of work to their attention. Some of the recent changes in U.S. antitrust law and in its relationship to the rest of the world may also lead in this direction.

2. Notes and Lessons

These discussions have provided two main forms of value for me. One comes from the perspectives, insights and experiences of the participants. Their contributions are far too numerous even to mention, but the Chicago mini-symposium itself offers a few examples (chosen from among the participants whose prior commitments and or publications prevented them from including their remarks in writing here)—Michal Gal's insights into the specific needs of competition law in smaller economies, Seong Wha Chaeng's discussion of the potential for competition law at the WTO, and Andrew Guzman's discussions of the potential roles of social science analysis in analyzing transnational competition law issues.

The discussions have also revealed or highlighted important factors that influence thought and decisions in the area. Noting what the participants pay attention to (or fail to pay attention to) in their comments on the book and how they interpret the material in the book can tell us much about the shape of thought in this area. Brief mention of some of these response patterns may, therefore, be of value to others seeking to identify and understand those factors. Personal objectives and relationships necessarily also influence these reactions, but they are not our concern here.

One set of factors that is prominent in shaping these perspectives derives from traditional ways of thinking. Despite the obvious fact that the many forms of globalization impact competition law in fundamental ways and present many new issues, problems and challenges, responses to the current situation continue to rely heavily on categories and ways of thinking that were developed to deal with other issues and problems. One of the book's main objectives was to take as a fresh look as possible at the material, but some commentators simply preferred to place new information, insights and suggestions into old categories and disregard what is new about them. It is, of course, always difficult to accept new information and new ways of thinking, but, in my opinion, the obvious "disconnect" between the current legal, political and economic situation and what existed even twenty years ago calls for openness to dealing with these issues. Some participants did espouse such openness, but the hold of traditional thinking was often stronger than one might hope.

This distorting influence is sometimes intertwined with and exacerbated by the hold of current institutional and national agendas. I note a growing tendency toward polarized thinking about the issues. At one pole are those who believe that the law and economics approach to competition law developed primarily in the United States should be followed everywhere, that it is "correct," "modern," "mature," and so on. Members of this group often promote their views with missionary-like zeal. At the other pole are those who have doubts about the relevance of this approach for their countries or regions and who therefore react strongly to what they see as efforts to impose this model. This polarization can obscure constructive thinking that focuses on adapting some of the basic ideas of the economics model to differing needs in different systems. I hope this polarization can be overcome through creative thinking about alternatives and by increased awareness among members of each group of these differing needs and concerns.

One example of the effects of this polarization can be seen in some comments on the book. Some conference participants have assumed that because I am a U.S.-based writer the book naturally promotes a U.S. "agenda." The book specifically eschews any such identification and emphasizes instead the need for a more nuanced and accurate picture of differing views and experiences of competition law. Any serious reading of the book should, therefore, quickly dispel any concern that it has a particular national agenda, but polarization can blind readers and stifle thought.

Another example of this type of polarization relates to the book's discussion of current transnational policy. Those who favor the U.S.-based economics model typically favor convergence toward that model as a solution to the weaknesses of the current transnational legal regime, while those on the other side are generally wary of convergence as a solution and more often open to other forms of response. As noted above, the book's main objective in this area is to clarify the concepts and to identify some of the factors that influence their use as well and their potential consequences. Nevertheless, the book's effort to reveal problems with current discussions of convergence claims has led some commentators to see this as opposition to convergence as policy. To clarify concepts and identify consequences is not, however, to oppose (or favor) a particular policy. Similarly, the book suggests that some forms of coordination may be valuable in dealing with these issues, but some have read the discussion as an argument for traditional forms of coordination such as a transnational competition code. This, despite the fact that the book explicitly rejects the idea of a binding code and emphasizes an approach that is new and specifically designed for the globalization context. Clearly, polarization can stand in the way of more effective thought and decision making.

In addition to these polarizing factors, numerous assumptions appear frequently in the discussions—sometimes near the surface and sometimes more submerged. I mention only a few. One is the assumption that competition law systems develop in linear and uniform ways and thus that some systems are more "mature" than others and that the "immature" systems must simply learn to follow the mature ones if they wish to be "mature." Experience in one competition law system can, of course, bring practical knowledge that can be of great value to those less experienced. Experience in one environment with one set of problems may, however, be less useful when the environment in which it is to be applied is significantly different. The lens that views competition law development solely as a matter of "maturity" can, therefore, mislead and should be used with care.

Some assumptions are associated with particular groups, reflecting national experience or professional interests or both. For example, economists and commentators favoring an economics-based system often tend to assume that competition law is just about economics and that in general the more a system relies on economics to set its norms, the "better" the system is. For other groups this assumption may be difficult to recognize and/or understand. Moreover, it is likely to be inconsistent with their experience and perceived as contrary to their interests. When this assumption shapes the views and responses of participants, but in contradictory ways, it can significantly cloud and impede discussions of the issues.

Similarly, commentators from newer competition regimes sometimes assume that competition law is primarily a matter of "power"—i.e., that powerful governments and dominant firms from the United States and Europe will simply force decision makers in other countries to pursue a particular competition law agenda and that national institutions have little or no choice in shaping their competition laws. Few in the United States or Europe view the discussions through these lenses, and, as a result, the assumption can create misunderstanding and even rancor. Uncovering assumptions of this kind can thus be an important tool for improving interactions among competition law scholars and officials.

These and other "lessons" from the discussions draw attention to deficiencies in the intellectual tools being used to deal with the issues. Three aspects of the problem call for particular mention. One is the general lack of attention to issues of method—that is, there is little evidence that people engaged in the process have thought very seriously about HOW they are viewing decisions and discussions in the area. All are aware that globalization creates new and complex issues, but, participants are often content to rely on conceptual lenses fashioned under very different circumstances from very different materials. References to globalization are common, but they seldom seem to engender sustained efforts to understand globalization on its own terms—as a set of interrelated processes with specific characteristics. The discussions reflect limited attention to key factors in the development of competition law such as the relationships between national, international and civil society institutions and organizations, not to mention the emerging roles of administrative, scholarly and other types of networks.

Also striking has been the lack of attention to basic issues of comparative and international law. Many of the issues revolve around analyzing differences and similarities between legal systems, but discussion of these issues seldom uses methods or insights from comparative law scholarship. Similarly, the role of public international law is in some ways central to the entire discussion, but even basic knowledge of international law and its roles is often lacking. For example, some commentators seem unaware that "jurisdiction" is at its core an issue of public international law. Failure to recognize that fact can and does lead to misunderstanding the issues.

Discussions surrounding the book suggest the need for significantly increased attention to these issues. Polarization, national and groups of interests and the hold of traditional ways of thinking—each may interfere with effective development of competition law around the globe. This kind of attention is very likely to enhance effective competition law development. I hope to take these lessons into account in future work in the area.

II. Toward a Deeper Understanding of the Dynamics of Transnational Competition Law

These insights and lessons are valuable in thinking about the central question we started with: "Where Do We Go from Here?" I note in the following sections a few specific aspects of these challenges that I believe deserve particular attention. Again, discussions of the book have helped to highlight many of them, but this is just the beginning.

The challenge of expanding and enriching the factual base for competition law thought and decisions is fundamental to the entire enterprise. Decision makers in all parts of the system are likely to perform their tasks more effectively if they have a better understanding of the consequences they can expect their decisions to have, and the firmer the factual base for decisions, the more capable they are likely to be to assess those consequences. At one level, this means more data. It also means more focused and valuable data, and that, in turn, means gathering and analyzing data in ways that are informed by appropriate conceptual and theoretical guidance.

Discussions (and the literature) often reveal the thinness of the data. We simply do not know very much about many of the issues and questions that should be relevant to decision making in the area. Improved data-gathering should, therefore, be a major focus of attention in the field. Here the need to understand causal relations and influences seems particularly obvious. If, as I believe, it is generally important for decision makers to recognize the factors that can influence their decisions as well as the consequences of those decisions, then providing data about these issues should be a foremost task.

Recent experience suggests three potential focus areas. One is the temporal dimension. Serious work has been done recently on the evolution of competition law in a few systems—notably, the United States and some parts of European experience, but even here there are often enormous gaps in historical understanding—analysis of what has happened and what factors have influenced competition law development. Outside these jurisdictions there is often little or no available data relating to these factors. Moreover, little attention has been paid to the evolution of the transnational "global" dimensions of the system itself—i.e., the interactions that constitute the system as it evolves.

The "what" question also demands more attention. What kind of data can provide value? It is common enough to gather and analyze formal data—how many cases have been brought, how many economists are on the payroll, etc., and this is important. Its utility is, however, limited by the difficulties of evaluating and interpreting such formal data. For example, formal actions may be primarily intended to achieve recognition or approval from foreign institutions or observers. In such cases, formal data can be highly misleading. Cases can be initiated without any expectation of effect on conduct. Economists can be employed without any expectation that they will significantly influence decision making. This kind of formal data needs to be accompanied by data that explores the extent to which decisions actually influence conduct.

This points to at least two more specific directions for study. One is the need to provide data about relationships among decision makers. This is the domain in which influences move—people and institutions deal with each other, influence each other, and respond to each other. It includes the formation and operation of formal relationships, but also informal relationships such as transnational legal, administrative and economic networks that today often involve public and private actors and that often play major and as yet little studied roles. The other is the need to identify the incentives and interests at play within these relationships. Which ideas and personalities and power levers have operated in particular kinds of relationships and what have been the consequences? This type of socio-legal research has great potential value.

Finally, systematic data-gathering and analysis should focus far more heavily on countries outside the United States and the European Union. The data gathering and analysis has so far centered on U.S. and European experience, paying limited attention to experience that is now rapidly accumulating among newer players such as China. This is neither surprising nor negative. In the United States and Europe information is comparatively available, and there are many academics with incentives to do research in the area. In other regimes, especially in Africa and Southeast Asia, information is more difficult to find, and there are fewer incentives for investigators there to engage in this type of research. Research through international organizations and civil society organizations may be particularly important, therefore, in enabling investigators to gather and analyze data from these systems.

In each of these areas a key criterion for evaluating research projects should be the accessibility of the data. In order for the data to be effectively used, it must be organized and analyzed in ways that make it accessible not only to scholars, but also to decision makers. "Accessibility" here refers not only to publication and dissemination of results, but also to the manner of presentation of data and its organization—what I call "cognitive accessibility." Where the results of investigation are presented in ways that are difficult for decision makers to understand or trust, they tend to pay limited attention to the information. If, for example, data appears to be presented to support a particular political or ideological agenda or if it is presented in overly technical language designed only for scientists, it may have limited influence on thought and decisions outside very narrow circles.

III. Toward Improved Analytical Tools

We have only begun to understand the "tools" challenge. Discussions of the book and responses to it underline three aspects of this challenge. Information (data) is shaped by the tools that are used in gathering and interpreting it, and thus the tools challenge is not only important in itself, but central to the tasks of both creating a more effective factual base for decisions and developing effective policies.

One aspect of this challenge is the basic but often overlooked task of clarifying and sharpening the concepts used in the area. Discussions tend to be replete with loose concepts that can mean many things to many audiences. Terms such as "economics-based," "mature system," "effects-based," "European approach," "more economic approach," "ordoliberal," and many others often carry many different meanings. As a result, participants in transnational discussions often use words that are interpreted in many different ways by others in the discussions, thereby creating misunderstandings and confusion. It will be difficult, if not impossible, to make significant progress on an international level without more attention to clarifying the concepts used.

A second task is to develop an analytical approach that is specifically adapted to the contexts of competition law today and the problems and issues associated with them. Those contexts are characterized by many varying forms of interconnection between thinkers and decision makers in different legal systems and in differing transnational groups. This calls for an analytical approach based on interconnectedness. Discussions in the area repeatedly go "off-track" when participants are unable or unwilling to transcend traditional ways of thinking about the issues and are limited by the compartmentalized and cantonized approaches that have characterized the discussion in the past. For example, many legal scholars, practicing lawyers and many competition law officials focus primarily on formal legal material and pay little attention to how these issues fit into the larger picture. Formal legal material often loses much of its relevance when applied, for example, to unstable and minimally funded competition law regimes. Similarly, economists often see the issues solely in terms of economics and the role of the economic profession. As a consequence, they fail to give sufficient attention to the factors that influence how economics is used and to political and other factors that influence how competition law decisions are made. Approaches are needed that tie these factors together and relate them to each other.

A third, and related, component of the tools challenge is the importance of interdisciplinary scholarship. A more integrated analytical approach calls for more work across academic disciplines. This type of work can provide the needed information and insights on which more integrated analysis can be built. New work in the social sciences, esp., political science, is beginning to take related issues more seriously. Work in global governance, economic sociology, complexity science and other areas can be of much value for developing such an approach. This does not mean that specialization is itself a problem, but the lack of synthesis is, in my opinion, a serious problem.

The analytical approach of the book is based on what I call "system dynamics." This analysis focuses on the ways in which decisions are embedded in legal systems and in relationships among legal systems. These systems have formal elements as well as less formal elements based on patterns of relationship that have sufficient stability to influence decisions.[2] The main objective in this form of analysis is to identify factors that influence decisions in these contexts and to relate these influences to each other. I have so far only sketched the underlying theoretical component of the approach, but I am currently preparing materials that give additional depth to this analysis.

2 *See* David J. Gerber, *System Dynamics : Toward a Language of Comparative Law*, 46 Am. J. Comparative Law 719 (1998).

IV. Toward More Effective Policies: What to Do?

Where then does that lead—i.e., what are the policy implications of knowing more and analyzing more effectively? The problems and costs of the current jurisdictional system weigh heavily on global economic development, and thus the issue of what to do about it should always be central. Discussions of the book demonstrate that participants are concerned about the issue, but that there is extensive confusion and misunderstanding concerning the choices and their consequences. It is critical, therefore, to develop more effective ways of thinking about both choices and consequences, and—in doing this—the tasks outlined above are likely to be central.

1. Convergence

The confusion and uncertainty surrounding the concept of convergence are particularly troublesome. Analysts and commentators often speak and write about convergence of competition law systems without having a clear idea of what the term means or how it is likely to be understood by others. The term is often just used to refer to increasing similarities of some kind, but used this way—i.e., without indicating what is similar to what—it has virtually no useful content. Further work is necessary not only to clarify the concepts, but also to develop some degree of consistency in their use.

Central to effective analysis of convergence as a strategy is or should be questions such as "How different are the systems, in what ways? What kinds of differences exist—procedural, substantive, institutional? How do we think about the differences and measure them?" There has been little systematic study of these fundamental issues, but without careful comparison the strategy operates in a kind of phantom world. Here the lenses and methods of comparative law can be especially useful.

Knowing and evaluating the differences and similarities is not, however, enough. Convergence is a "process," so it is also necessary to understand the factors that influence decisions that are part of that process. What factors can be expected to reduce the differences or increase them or impede movement in one direction or another? Convergence as a strategy is based on the idea that independent decision makers will decide to make particular kinds of "moves" or decisions, but we currently have limited understanding of its dynamics. There is no lack of general suppositions about what might influence such moves, but there is surprisingly little serious analysis or firm data.

2. Coordination

The other main strategy of response to the problems of the current jurisdictional system involves the coordination of decisions. I use the term to refer to interactions among decision makers that are related to a particular goal or set of goals. As with convergence, however, there is much confusion and uncertainty relating to this form of response, and thus clarification of concepts and alternatives is a necessary basis for thinking about these issues. This may be even more important in relation to coordination strategies than it is in relation to convergence, because coordination strategies must necessarily be based on communication, and thus they require for effectiveness at least a shared understanding of what the goals and obligations of participants involve. If participants seeking to coordinate their activities are not "on the same page," effective coordination is likely to be virtually impossible.

The identification, analysis and measurement of differences and similarities, is also critical here. In this context, they are central because they are, in effect, the basis for coordination. For example, decision makers are unlikely to seek coordination to achieve a particular goal unless they have some basis for believing that the strategy can be effective, and this, in turn, depends, at least in part, on each participant's evaluation of existing differences among the participants and of the factors that are likely to influence decisions in the area.

For purposes of coordination, however, additional factors need to be added to the picture. Actually achieving effective coordination depends on interactions, which means that the processes of transnational and transcultural knowledge transfer, communication and negotiation will be central. This calls for increased attention to behavioral components of the process and thus to both social science and practice-based forms of analysis. Each of these issues deserves far more attention than it has received so far.

These comments suggest the need for relating and integrating the two approaches—i.e., convergence and coordination. Remarkably little work has been done in this regard. The polarization of views on the future of global competition law seems to have obscured the need for thinking about how the two relate to each other. Coordination and convergence are in one sense closely related. Both involve differences among system, and both involve ways of dealing with those differences. They may have different objectives and modalities, but creative thinking is needed to develop ways in which the advantages and benefits of each can be combined.

The book describes briefly the idea of a commitment pathway as one form of coordination that is specifically designed for global legal issues, in general, and the global competition law context, in particular, and many have asked me to develop the idea more fully. I hope soon to deliver a fuller analysis, but for our purposes here I note only that the factors just mentioned are critical to developing the analysis.

V. Ways Forward: Perspectives & Audiences

Global Competition and the many discussions of the book have contributed to shaping the ways that at least some scholars, officials and lawyers think, talk and make competition law decisions. The book's central aim has been to expand our understanding of competition law in relation to the processes we call "globalization." It seeks to improve analysis of the costs and problems of the current system, to sharpen perspectives on options for responding to these costs and problems, and to identify opportunities for improving the current system.

Progress toward these goals is likely to be shaped by two sets of factors. One is a "who" question: Who is talking and who is listening? Discussions of competition law on the transnational level still tend to feature voices from the United States and Europe. Others are more likely to listen than to contribute. This may be appropriate in the early stages of the discussion, when those who have extensive experience with competition law are dealing with those who have limited experience in the area. This tends inevitably, however, to narrow the discussion, leaving unexpressed and unexplored perspectives from the many other areas of the world that need to be part of the discussion if effective responses are to be found to the problems and costs of the current system. As these newer players develop experience with competition law, it is important that their voices be an important part of the discussions, which means that Asian, Latin American and African voices will have to play much larger roles in the discussions. When they do, they will inevitably bring their own perspectives and needs to these discussions. How those who currently lead the discussions respond will be a key to determining where competition law goes at all levels—national, regional and global. Will they listen? With what degrees of openness? How will they respond? The answers to these questions will be crucial.

A second set of key factors involves what the participants see and hear. The relative lack of experience with competition law issues among many participants and the largely unidirectional flow that has characterized most such discussions has led many to view transnational competition law issues in ways that are narrow and that tend to impair understanding and discussion. For example, viewing these issues as solely a matter of economics or of power distorts the picture, eliminating or marginalizing many forces that will shape progress in this area. Broadening and sharpening the lenses available to these and other groups for viewing and discussing competition law experiences and opportunities will be a key to the future of global competition law. If combined with expanding participation in the dialogue, it can lead to more effective competition law development around the globe and to the potential benefits that this dares to promise.

The "Alternative World-Antitrust Framework" in the Light of the Twenty-First Century

Eleanor M. FOX

eleanor.fox@nyu.edu

Walter J. Derenberg Professor of Trade Regulation, New York University School of Law

From 1991 to 1993 I was a member of the Munich-centered project, chaired by Wolfgang Fikentscher, that produced the Draft International Antitrust Code (DIAC) of 1993.[1] That document responded to the globalization of markets and the perceived need for a world concept of competition principles and modalities of enforcement fitting for a world without parochial borders. The work product was not expected to be politically correct or necessarily politically acceptable. Rather, our charge was (led by Professor Fikentscher): Imagine the best that world antitrust law and institutions could be. If politically infeasible (as it was sure to be), at least it could be a guiding light for serious reformers.

The group did indeed write a Draft International Antitrust Code, limited to transactions or conduct of world dimension. The DIAC articulated "minimum" rules in virtually all areas of antitrust law—horizontal restraints, vertical restraints, abuse of dominance, intellectual property-related restraints, mergers, joint ventures, and state enterprises. DIAC contemplated a plurilateral agreement pursuant to which each participating nation would agree to establish a national competition authority. To aid in national enforcement, particularly where restraints in one nation had anticompetitive effects abroad, DIAC proposed a system of positive comity backed by the power of a transnational authority (International Antitrust Authority), much like an ombudsman with standing to sue, to initiate enforcement at national level in the home institutions of a member who failed or refused to enforce its law. Also it contemplated a dispute resolution panel (International Antitrust Panel) comprised of experts, appointed by consensus of the nations involved in the dispute. The panel would be subject to WTO panel rules and constraints. Disputes would be brought to the panel by any contracting party that believed another party was violating obligations under the agreement.

An example of the generality of the proposed minimum rules can be found under the heading "Horizontal Restraints" (Art. 4). Hard core cartels would be illegal. Art. 4 §1. The prohibition would

1 International Antitrust Code Working Group, Draft International Antitrust Code as a GATT-MTO-Plurilateral Trade Agreement (published and released on July 10, 1993), BNA Antitrust & Trade Reg. Rep., Special Supplement, Vol. 64, no. 1628 (Aug. 19, 1993).

apply to all import, export and international cartels. Other agreements between or among competitors would be illegal if they unreasonably restricted competition. An agreement with the purpose or effect to harm competition would be presumed to unreasonably restrict competition unless the agreement was justified by outbalancing pro-competitive effects, efficiencies, increase in rivalry or inventiveness, or otherwise by "increase [in] the firms' responsiveness to the needs or wants of people." Art. 4 § 2.

Certain proposed rules were more proscriptive than others (e.g., vertical restraints, Art. 5), although almost all potentially proscribed behavior would be subject to market justifications of the sort specified directly above.

Two of the members of the Munich Group—Professor Lawrence Sullivan and I—took issue with the code as proposed and presented an alternative "DIAC." We proposed 15 principles, which are printed in the DIAC document itself at point VIII. We argued that DIAC's substantive rules were too specific and too prohibitory; nations might choose to formulate antitrust rules differently. In our view, specific formulations of law were not necessary to achieve the principal objective of DIAC, with which we agreed; namely, providing an integrating, non-parochial antitrust-and-trade framework copious and flexible enough to fit a world of global competition. Indeed, we feared that the very specificity of the DIAC formulations could undermine the basic purpose, providing—as it later did—fodder for critics who rejected an international framework.

On the tenth anniversary of DIAC, I revisited the alternative proposal in a festschrift for our fellow member of the group, Ulrich Immenga.[2] I examined each of the 15 principles and assessed how well they withstood the test of time. I concluded that they did so fairly well; indeed some had been implemented over the years. Others, however meritorious, posed serious problems of adoption and implementation, practically and politically (although as I have noted, DIAC was not written with an eye to political acceptability).

Now, nearly another decade has passed. On the occasion of celebrating David Gerber's excellent and provocative book, GLOBAL COMPETITION: LAW, MARKETS AND GLOBALIZATION, I revisited once again The Alternative DIAC.[3]

What is my reaction today to The Alternative DIAC? First, it was exactly what was called for in response to DIAC, which was an excellent idea but was too intrusive. The Alternative DIAC was a more liberal, more national-choice regarding version of a coherent non-discriminatory world framework. In theory, the 15 principles make good sense. But as a practical matter, it would be very hard to implement the scheme, and hard to implement it with transparency and legitimacy. As a political matter, the set of 15 principles would be impossible to adopt, and that impossibility is clearer now than in the heady years of imagining international antitrust in the early 1990s. In today's inward-looking environment, there is surely no will of nations to deepen world linkages and forsake negative externalities. In some respects, there is less urgency today for a global framework, because convergence of substantive antitrust law and practices of deep cooperation have dimin-

---

2 Eleanor M. Fox, *The Alternative DIAC in the Twenty First Century*, *in* WIRTSCHAFTS UND PRIVATRECHTI M SPANNUNGFELD VON PRIVATAUTONOMIE, WETTBEWERB UND REGULIERUNG (Verlag C.H. Beck München 2004) [hereinafter *The Alternative DIAC*].

3 This article is adapted from *The Alternative DIAC*, *supra* note 2.

ished the realm of conflict. But in other respects there is more need for this unifying vision, in view of the contemporary trend towards nationalism and no progress towards integrating trade and competition. The Alternative DIAC serves two functions today: 1) as an identifier of the largely unsolved market issues of the world, and 2) as a blueprint of aspirations towards which world trade-and-competition might be usefully nudged over time.

Below is an updated version of my essay in the festschrift volume for Ulrich Immenga.

The essay sets forth and then comments upon each of the 15 principles. Before reproducing the 15 principles, let me give background and a summary.

The early 1990s were a period of thinking and debating about an integral world view of trade and competition, and indeed trade and environment, trade and investment, trade and intellectual property, and other subjects of "trade and . . . ." The Uruguay round was drawing to a successful close. Many barriers, previously impenetrable, had been negotiated away. The issues that were soon to emerge as "the Singapore issues" were being groomed for presentation to the WTO nations, and one of those four issues—the interaction between trade and competition—was soon to become the basis of a working group of the WTO. When the Singapore Ministerial Declaration was adopted in December 1996, it reflected the aspiration for "the continuing liberalization of trade within a rule-based system"; it applauded the economic growth and integration that had been spurred by liberalization while noting that the "scope and pace of change" "require adjustment by economies and societies"; and it expressed the need for multilateral review of policies to "address the challenges of an evolving world economy."

In this earlier window of time it was not out of bounds to suggest that there were links between trade and competition, and that rules of trade and rules of competition could and should be adjusted to one another in the interests of a fairer and more efficient world. This usually meant: fairness and efficiency gained at the expense of the vested interests.

It was in this environment that Professor Fikentscher called together the group of 12 experts from around the world (Germany, Switzerland, Poland, Japan, and the United States), and gave us the charge, in effect: Imagine an international antitrust code fitting for a global regime that will bridge the gaps of the world.

Thus, the group wrote the DIAC. But while the DIAC has many rules and procedures, Larry Sullivan and I thought it better to have only a few, which would operate as a framework within which nations should write their own rules. Our 15 principles are divided into three parts. Part I includes principles 1 to 6. It contains substantive principles and requirements of national law. Thus, a rule against cartels, a rule for market access, two rules of legality contingent on disclosure, "freedom" principles—e.g., to engage in R&D, and a rule bringing anti-dumping rules into line with price predation rules. Part II concerns implementation; it comprises principles 7-11, and is largely drawn from DIAC itself. For example, each nation should adopt the "consensus rules" identified in principles 1-6 into their national law in their own words; they should extend the reach of their law to protect all victims of the consensus wrongs wherever they may be; and positive comity should be multilateralized. In view of a need for an enforcement mechanism that would not have the drawbacks of a centralized bureaucracy and also would not have the flaws of unilateralism, an International Antitrust Authority (IAA) would be empowered to bring enforcement actions at a national level if a nation unjustifiably refused to enforce its law against nationals who hurt outsiders (e.g., enforcing against import cartels or boycotts). Part III (principles 12-15) concerns IAA as a forum for various consultations to develop convergence and common policies. Thus, IAA as a forum for exploration of a common merger notification scheme; IAA as a forum for consultations and exchanges of information that might lead to convergence in process and in substance; and IAA as a forum to develop and agree upon permissible and impermissible uses of national law against actors and acts abroad.

I now proceed by setting forth each passage of the text of the Alternative Proposal, and then by providing comments from a vantage of 10 or 20 years. The DIAC contains much that is included in the 15 principles, but the overlap comprises a small part of the text of DIAC.

The Fox/Sullivan Alternative Proposal begins with the following statement of concept:

The concept: . . . [N]ational law is inadequate to the task of dealing with transactions of an international dimension [because of limits of national law and nations' lack of a "view from the top" of effects of global transactions]. Moreover, national law in a vacuum tends to be parochial and can be protectionist, leading to counter-protectionist moves and isolated rather than integrated markets. To smooth the flow of trade and competition, to deflect trade disputes, and to increase the welfare of all people, fundamental international principles that are market-opening and that produce more nearly integrated markets should be developed. At the same time, however, national experimentation and choices should normally be accepted, both out of respect for each nation's choices and in view of the value of diversity. Therefore one should leave a wide berth for differences in national law. The following scheme is grounded on a few clear and strong framework principles: subsidiarity, transparency, extension of the competence of national systems to take account of consensus harms caused abroad, national enforcement with opportunity for appeal to an independent arbiter with a "vision from the top," and facilitation of further cooperation and convergence.

The Fox/Sullivan text continues:

The following fifteen principles should be applied to transactions and conduct with an international dimension:

1) The contracting nations should adopt and enforce a strong anti-cartel rule forbidding conduct that has the purpose or clear effect of reducing output and raising prices, including prohibitions of hard core export, import and other transnational cartels, divisions of world markets, bid rigging, and boycotts in aid thereof. Nations should have the freedom, however, to maintain narrow, tailored exceptions for crisis or depression when important to the economic viability of their internal markets, as long as such approved cartels are time-limited and transparent.

Comment. This first principle continues to be the central prohibition of antitrust, and indeed, it is the principle on which virtually all antitrust jurisdictions agree. Cartels are harmful; they are emanations of raw power; they have no efficiency or pro-competitive justifications. The controversy among nations centers not on the rule against cartels but on permissible derogations, including nationalistic reluctance to commit not to harm outsiders. The OECD Hard Core Cartel Recommendation[4] substantially reflects principle 1, but allows a broader scope for derogations, as long as the derogation is transparent and its need is continually reviewed.

4 Recommendation of the Council Concerning Effective Action Against Hard Core Cartels, OECD, Paris, 27-28 April 1998 [C(98) 35/FINAL].

A similar principle, but without hint of extraterritoriality, was contemplated as the first substantive principle of a possible future world competition agreement in the context of the WTO, in the now failed Doha trade round.[5]

2) The contracting nations should adopt and enforce law requiring prior notification and disclosure to buyers/suppliers and governments of all export collaborations among competitors, and they should prohibit all non-disclosed export collaborations among competitors.

Comment. This principle backs up principle 1, by information and transparency. Information is normally helpful and the onus and notoriety of filing might discourage export cartels. Filing and information requirements have costs, administrative and practical. Some collaborators might wish to keep their enterprises confidential, and export cartelists would not file. Still, the principle is sound and progressive.

3) The contracting nations should deny availability of a sovereign compulsion defense unless the fact of sovereign compulsion is disclosed to buyers/suppliers in advance of the conduct.

Comment. This requirement could helpfully smoke out true instances of sovereign compulsion, and prevent non-grounded defenses from being asserted strategically.

4) The contracting nations should adopt and enforce free access, non-discrimination principles, according national treatment to foreign goods and services. Tailored derogations would be permissible as in (1) above.

Comment. Non-discrimination and national treatment are internationally required and respected principles. They are hallmarks of the world trading regime. Their primacy is recognized in the Doha Declaration[6] and in virtually all GATT trade agreements. They are world norms. "Free access" is a concept in need of elaboration. The idea stems from the antitrust market access debate of the early 1990s. Antitrust market access was conceived as a counterpart to trade market access. The concept was elaborated in Department of Justice amendments (footnote 159, later withdrawn) to the 1988 International Operations Guidelines under Assistant Attorney General Jim Rill, announced on April 3, 1992. The 15 principles contemplated formulation of an antitrust rule of market access, which could have been, for example: Nations agree to prohibit firms from engaging in anticompetitive, unjustified market blockage if the restraint would be illegal in their domestic commerce.[7]

---

5 Ministerial Conference, Ministerial Declaration at Doha, Qatar, WT/MIN(01)/DEC/1, para. 25 (Nov. 14, 2001), at http://www.wto.org/english/thewto_e/minist_e/min01_e/mindecl_e.htm. The agenda was potentially before the ministerial body in Cancun in October 2003 but was jettisoned in view of the failure of the nations to agree to an acceptable reduction in agricultural subsidies.

6 *See* note 42 *supra*.

7 The U.S. Justice Department rule applied the law of the exporting country; the above suggestion would apply the law of the importing country and institutionally apply a safeguard for non-enforcement. *See, e.g.*, Eleanor M. Fox, *Competition Law and the Millennium Round*, 2 J. Int'l Econ. L. 665 (1999). Thus, if Fuji-Film enlisted the few expert distributors in Japan to boycott Kodak in its attempt to build a presence in the Japanese consumer film market and such a boycott was illegal under Japanese law but Japan refused to sue, the boycott would also be a market access offense under The Alternative DIAC.

5) The contracting nations should recognize a freedom principle for certain consensus "rights" such as the freedom to collaborate with competitors on basic research and development if other significant sources of similar R&D efforts remain.

Comment. This principle brings home the fact that an international scheme based on prohibitory principles alone is incomplete. Competition also requires freedoms. Freedom to invent is a basic freedom. A principle recognizing the right to undertake joint research and development in a context of competition could usefully be adopted. There is a problem, however: the problem is the specificity of such a principle when there are many other practices that are or should be per se legal. The particular freedom principle is therefore more usefully regarded as a symbol and a marker, not a proposal for a rule.

6) The contracting nations should harmonize or accommodate antitrust price-predation rules and trade law dumping rules with a view towards protecting the freedom of sustainable, unsubsidized low pricing that does not threaten to create or increase market power, with limited permissible exceptions such as time-limited safeguards for surges in imports that threaten to destroy a domestic industry.

Comment. Principle 6 was the second "freedom principle." Principle 6 is much more controversial than principle 5, even if much more needed. It would take on the politically sensitive problem of the overbreadth and perversity of anti-dumping laws, which prevent low-priced imports from entering markets, often markets of industrialized nations. Anti-dumping laws work particular harms on developing countries, and may deprive the poorest peoples of the world of their livelihoods. Principle 6 remains not only sound but both urgent and politically impractical.

7) The contracting nations should adopt all consensus principles (1 to 6 above) into their national law, each nation having the freedom to formulate its own legal rules that incorporate the principles.

Comment. The substantive consensus principles are: no cartels, and freedom of research and sustainable low pricing. The procedural consensus principles assure non-discrimination, national treatment, and safeguards against false assertions that "my government made me do it." Principle 7 would require nations to adopt these principles. Principle 7 is an application of the general concept of DIAC, but it narrows the scope of consensus principles and allows more flexibility in their formulation.

8) The contracting nations should extend the coverage of their national law so that consensus wrongs done on their territory and causing injury in or to another contracting nation are prohibited by their law. "Consensus wrongs" shall include prohibitions pursuant to this agreement and prohibitions common to the law of both the injuring and injured nation. In adjudicating legality the national court should be obliged to treat consensus harms in another contracting nation's territory or to its commerce with the same seriousness as it treats harms in its own territory or to its own commerce.

Comment. Respect for harmed individuals outside of the territorial bounds of a jurisdiction is of the essence of a global perspective. Those who support a continued nationalistic perspective argue that nations should not be required to protect foreigners on foreign soil whom they have harmed; that is not their problem. This perspective is both inefficient and unjust. It is, effectively, a denial of the globalized world.

9) A contracting nation whose economy, nationals or residents are injured by another nation's nationals or residents should be entitled to request enforcement by that other nation ("the injuring nation"). The injuring nation should be obliged to enforce its law or give reasons for declining to do so. In the event of unjustified refusal to enforce, the injured nation should have a right of appeal to a panel of an International Antitrust Authority, which should have the power to order enforcement by the injuring nation.

Comment. Principle 9 is a principle of positive comity. Lack of recourse at the home of the perpetrators is a quintessential problem of global markets, global impacts, and the confinement of law to its national level. The first two sentences mirror the 1998 EU-U.S. cooperation agreement on positive comity.[8] Principle 9 would multilaterize this obligation. The third sentence underscores the seriousness of the obligation by providing governance "from above" if the injuring nation shirks its obligations. The dispute resolution panel would have the power to affirm (or in clearly erroneous cases overrule) the exercise of discretion of the regulating nation to choose not to bring proceedings if none are warranted. The availability of an impartial panel to address their minds to the subject of conflict would help to legitimize the system.

10) Upon request by the antitrust authority of an injured nation, the International Antitrust Authority should be obliged to examine the global impacts of transactions or conduct of international dimension, and to report conclusions to the national authority or to a national court regarding impacts beyond its borders. The national court should be obliged to give deference to the conclusions of the International Antitrust Authority.

Comment. Principle 10 bolsters the obligation to take account of the harms one causes outside of its own geographic borders. On request by an injured nation (which could be a developing country without sufficient resources or expertise to protect itself), the IAA would perform an investigative function to document extraterritorial harms, which the national court would then be obliged to take into account, presumably in adjudicating violations or ordering relief. This is a wise principle but would face two hurdles: 1) The IAA would need to be adequately funded and to have expert investigative capabilities; 2) Where the conduct does not harm a nation's domestic economy, revision of law may be necessary to expand coverage (a requirement also for proscription of export cartels in principle 1 and accounting for external impacts in principle 8).

11) Contracting nations should be invited to assert, in a proper case, that another nation's enforcement will impair competition, efficiency or technological progress so as to undermine an important national or world interest. If the complaining nation has been unable to obtain satisfaction from the enforcing nation, it should be entitled to seek an order of non-interference from a panel of the International Antitrust Authority. The enforcing nation should be obliged to respect an order of non-interference. (The proposed relief by the European Commission against IBM-Europe requiring disclosure of IBM's interface designs as a remedy for alleged abuse of dominance in Europe is an example of a situation in which a nation (the United States) might seek an order of non-interference from an enforcing authority.)

---

8 *See* Agreement between the European Communities and the Government of the United States of American on the Application of Positive Comity Principles in the Enforcement of their Competition Laws, June 4, 1998, 37 I.L.M. 1070.

Comment. Principle 11 complements the "freedoms" aspect of principles 5 and 6. It underscores the point that competition policy is not a one-way ratchet. The main aspect of competition policy is: people have the freedom to compete and invent. Overbroad prohibitions can undermine competition. If proscribing jurisdictions always win out over authorizing jurisdictions, competition is impaired. If one jurisdiction proscribes conduct that another determines is good for competition, progress, markets and consumers, this constitutes a clash. There is thus a problem that could, and in a globalized world should, profit from reasoned resolution—rather than be left to self-help remedies such as trade wars. The proposal is that the IAA resolves the clash, one way or the other, by reasoned analysis of whether the transaction, practice or relief is anticompetitive. Legitimate and respected resolution will require a panel with expertise, impartiality and credibility. This is a tall order.

12) Within the context of the International Antitrust Authority, the contracting nations should explore development of common merger notification and reporting forms and common pre-merger waiting periods. If standardization proves feasible, provision should be made for merging parties to file a master form with the International Antitrust Authority, and at the merging parties' option (exercise of which assumes a decision by the parties to waive confidentiality) the International Antitrust Authority should be obliged to provide the document to all interested national authorities, which in turn would be obliged to accept the document in satisfaction of their notification and reporting requirements. The European Patent Convention might provide a procedural model.

Comment. The need for convergence, harmonization, or common clearing house for merger filings has become more and more palpable as merger-notification jurisdictions have multiplied to more than 85. Many businesses and antitrust authorities agree. The initiative has been seized by the International Competition Network, which has adopted principles and recommended practices for convergence in merger notification requirements; and the Japan Fair Trade Commission has offered to facilitate an international cooperative framework for merger review. A central clearing house has not yet been the chosen vehicle, although it has some superior qualities; it may, however, require a "body" with funding.

13) The International Antitrust Authority should be a forum for consultations and information exchanges regarding the exercise of jurisdiction, deference in the exercise of jurisdiction, and reciprocal aid in discovery and enforcement, along lines of the 1991 U.S./EC Executive Agreement. It should be a forum, also, for further convergence of process, enforcement, and relief.

Comment. The IAA, here, resembles the Competition Committee of the WTO once proposed by the European Union and reflected in the Doha Declaration. With respect to cross-fertilization and convergence, the ICN has since undertaken this mission. The OECD has engaged in supportive research over the years.

14) The International Antitrust Authority should be a forum for promoting further convergence of substantive law, e.g., on principles of abuse of dominance, merger control, joint ventures, distribution restraints, and technology licensing. As an early project, the International Antitrust Authority should consider formulating principles on transparency of subsidies and elimination of unjustified subsidies not now caught by the GATT but which distort terms of international competition, using as a guide Articles 92 to 94 of the EC Treaty of Rome. The International Antitrust Authority should coordinate its legislative activity with the work of the Organization for Economic Cooperation and Development and with the work of the United Nations.

Comment. Here, again, the IAA resembles the ICN and aspects of the proposed WTO Competition Committee. There is a major exception: Antitrust authorities have studiously avoided the delicate but vital enterprise of advocacy to eliminate subsidies—as well as anti-dumping duties. On the run up to the notorious Cancun meeting in the Doha trade round, the industrialized nations' subsidies and anti-dumping duties were well documented as measures that devastate millions of people in developing countries who would otherwise be well equipped to compete on their merits. The world competition picture is not complete without measures to break these barriers, which advantage the industrialized countries and lower world welfare.

15) Within the context of the International Antitrust Authority, the contracting nations should develop and agree to principles of permissible and impermissible use of national law to reprehend acts of citizens/residents of another contracting nation performed solely or largely on the territory of the other contracting nations. At the outset, the nations should develop principles of clearly permissible reach and clearly impermissible reach of national law. It should be clearly permissible to reprehend such acts/transactions if they are consensus wrongs under this agreement or per se wrongs under the domestic law of both the injuring and the injured nation and they have a perceptible effect in the regulating nation or on its international or foreign commerce. It should be clearly impermissible to reprehend such acts/transactions if they are neither consensus wrongs or per se wrongs under the domestic law of both nations and they are essentially internal market transactions within the actors' nation; unless, however, the act or transaction has a substantial anticompetitive effect in or on the regulating nation and the relief desired by the regulating nation can be limited to its own territory (*e.g.*, injunction against a combination of domestic subsidiaries of foreign merging parents).

Comment. In the absence of harmonization and in the presence of increasingly frequent exercises of extraterritoriality, there are and will be conflicts. It is important that jurisdictions agree to principles that will channel resolution of those conflicts. Principle 15 can help to forge this path.

[Below is the final paragraph of the 1993 Fox/Sullivan DIAC statement.]

These fifteen principles would comprise the minimal market-opening, world-integrating agreement, functioning largely as national systems bridged by consensus principles enforced in national courts. By breaking down frontiers and enlarging the vision of national authorities, [adoption of the principles] would shrink the purview for extraterritoriality . . . and substitute as a touchstone the common interests of the community of contracting nations.

Comment. The 15 principles would indeed bridge the competition moats and integrate trade and competition principles, eliminating negative externalities and increasing fairness and efficiency. The Alternative DIAC remains, in my view, a progressive guiding light for an integral conception of antitrust.

At the points where The Alternative DIAC touched no raw nerve (e.g., conversations on coordination of merger process; deeper cooperation and convergence), similar recommendations have been favorably received, and cooperation and convergence are progressing. But The Alternative DIAC does touch raw nerves—of vested interests—on a litany of issues that matter and that stubbornly resist reform: antidumping, subsidies, export cartels, and freedom to harm one's neighbors even when they cannot fend for themselves.

The Alternative DIAC was both bold and naïve in 1993, and it would be even more naïve to make such a proposal today. There is little will for global solutions. Much good work has been done to bridge some of the gaps by nation-to-nation antitrust cooperation; but not the gaps that lie at the borders of nations. Perhaps someday it will be second nature to observe that global markets demand global solutions.[9] But not so today.

9 *See* DAVID J. GERBER, GLOBAL COMPETITION: LAW, MARKETS AND GLOBALIZATION (Oxford University Press 2010); Eleanor M. Fox, *International Antitrust and the Doha Dome*, 43 VA. J. INT'L L. 911 (2003).

Competition Agencies with Complex Policy Portfolios: Divide or Conquer?

David A. HYMAN

dhyman@illinois.edu

Professor, University of Illinois, College of Law[*]

William E. KOVACIC

wkovacic@law.gwu.edu

Professor, George Washington University Law School[*]

The worldwide adoption of competition law is a remarkable development in economic regulation. More than 120 jurisdictions have enacted competition laws, and roughly 90 of these have come into being since 1990.[1] Companies accustomed to regarding antitrust rules as the sum of commands issued by the European Union and the United States now must account for policies set in countries such as Brazil, China, and India. In only the past five years, major additions have included the establishment of a new antimonopoly law in China and a thorough overhaul of India's system.[2]

The attention now given to the formation of antitrust laws globally has obscured an important characteristic of the institutions entrusted with their implementation. The agencies established to enforce competition laws often have mandates that encompass other policy responsibilities. The U.S. Federal Trade Commission (FTC) is an informative example. The FTC is a policy conglomerate, a body whose mandate combines antitrust, a wide range of consumer protection functions (most notably, oversight of commercial advertising and marketing practices), and an increasingly important role as the principal U.S. data protection and privacy agency.[3]

---

* Hyman is H. Ross & Helen Workman Chair in Law and Professor of Medicine, University of Illinois. From 2001-2004, he served as Special Counsel at the Federal Trade Commission. Kovacic is Professor at the George Washington University School of Law. From 2001-2011, he was, at various points, the General Counsel, Commissioner, and Chairman of the Federal Trade Commission.

1 On patterns in the adoption of competition laws, *see* William E. Kovacic, *The Institutions of Antitrust Law: How Structure Shapes Substance*, 110 Mich. L. Rev. 1019, 1042-43 & n. 82 (2012). One excellent repository of information on the establishment of new systems is the International Competition Network, whose members include the competition agencies of roughly 100 jurisdictions. Modern developments in the creation and implementation of competition systems can be followed on the ICN website, which is http://www.internationalcompetitionnetwork.org.

2 On the modern competition law reforms in China and India, *see* Competition Law in the BRICS Countries (Vassily Rudomino et al. eds., 2012).

3 On the FTC's diverse mandate, *see* Federal Trade Commission, The FTC in 2012 (Mar. 2012), *available at* http://www.ftc.gov/os/highlights/2012/ftc-highlights.pdf.

The FTC's multi-dimension policy portfolio is the norm among jurisdictions with competition laws. Over half of the jurisdictions with competition laws assign to what often is called a "competition agency" important economic policy functions beyond competition law. For example, more than thirty jurisdictions rely on a single agency to enforce antitrust laws and to implement consumer protection statutes (especially measures that ban false advertising).[4] Other countries employ still more elaborate combinations such as Peru's INDECOPI (antitrust, consumer protection, trade, intellectual property, and bankruptcy), Russia's Federal Antimonopoly Service (antitrust, advertising, and public procurement), and the Australian Competition and Consumer Commission (antitrust, consumer protection, and regulatory matters involving the telecommunications sector). Still other countries, such as the Netherlands and Spain, are considering the formation of new government bodies that would merge the competition agency with various other regulatory authorities

The specific amalgamation of policy tasks within a single government body has important consequences for how competition agencies define their goals, allocate resources, and select programs to fulfill their duties. The assignment of multiple regulatory tasks can deeply affect a competition agency's performance, just as it affects the performance of other agencies. This issue has attracted little attention in competition policy circles,[5] although public administration scholars (and, to a far more limited extent, legal academics) have done important work on such issues in other areas.[6]

Despite this gap, there is growing interest among government agencies in the links between institutional design and agency behavior. In scholarly commentary and in the work of multilateral orga-

---

4 Some of the world's best known competition policy bodies share this design characteristic, including the United Kingdom's Office of Fair Trading (OFT) and Canada's Competition Bureau.

5 Noteworthy recent exceptions have examined the combination of competition and consumer protection duties in a single agency. *See, e.g.*, Competition Committee of the Organization for Economic Cooperation and Development, Background Documentation for the Global Forum on Competition (Feb. 21-22, 2008) (collecting materials on "the interface between competition and consumer policies"); Katalin J. Cseres, Integrate or Separate—Institutional Design for the Enforcement of Competition Law and Consumer Law (Amsterdam Centre for European Law and Governance, Working Paper Series 2013-01, Jan. 2013).

6 An abbreviated list of articles on the subject by legal scholars would include Jody Freeman & James Rossi, *Agency Coordination in Shared Regulatory Space,* 125 Harvard L. Rev. 1131 (2012); Keith Bradley, *The Design of Agency Interactions,* 111 Columbia L. Rev. 746 (2011); Jason Marisam, *Duplicative Delegations,* 63 Admin. L. Rev. 181 (2011); Rachel Barkow, *Insulating Agencies: Avoiding Capture Through Institutional Design,* 89 Texas L. Rev. 15 (2010); Jacob Gersen, *Designing Agencies: Public Choice and Public Law,* in Research Handbook in Public Law and Public Choice (D. Farber & A. O'Connell eds., 2010); Eric Biber, *Too Many Things to Do: How to Deal with the Dysfunctions of Multiple-Goal Agencies,* 33 Harv. Envtl. L. Rev. 1 (2009); Dara K. Cohen, Mariano-Florentino Cuéllar, and Barry R. Weingast, *Crisis Bureaucracy: Homeland Security and the Political Design of Legal Mandates,* 59 Stan. L. Rev. (2006); Jacob E. Gersen, *Overlapping and Underlapping Jurisdiction in Administrative Law,* 2006 Sup. Ct. Rev. 201; Anne Joseph O'Connell, *The Architecture of Smart Intelligence: Structuring and Overseeing Agencies in the Post-9/11 World,* 94 Cal. L. Rev. 1655 (2006); David A. Weisbach & Jacob Nussim, *The Integration of Tax and Spending Programs,* 113 Yale L. J. 955 (2004); Jonathan Macey, *Organizational Design and Political Control of Administrative Agencies,* 8 J. L. Econ. & Org. 93 (1992). Public administration scholars and political scientists have spent decades on these issues. *See, e.g.*, Karen M. Hult, Agency Merger and Bureaucratic Redesign (1987); Beryl A. Radin & Willis D. Hawley, The Politics of Federal Reorganization: Creating the U.S. Department of Education (1988); James Q. Wilson, Bureaucracy: What Government Agencies Do And Why They Do It 212 (2000); Amy B. Zegert, Spying Blind: The CIA, the FBI, and the Origins of 9/11 (2007); David E. Lewis, Presidents and the Politics of Agency Design: Political Insulation in the United States Government Bureaucracy, 1946-1997 (2003). The literature on the organization of private firms is, of course, vast. *See, e.g.*, Harold Demsetz, Ownership, Control, and the Firm (Blackwell 1990).

nizations such as the International Competition Network (ICN), there is greater recognition that the quality of a nation's competition policy depends crucially on the effectiveness of the institutions entrusted with the formulation and implementation of that policy.[7] There is little point in discussing what substantive programs the world's competition agencies should pursue without a more careful examination of how they agencies will carry them out. As we have suggested in other works, the latter inquiry inevitably and necessarily involves an assessment of institutional design.[8]

In this article, we continue our analysis of the relationship between agency design and performance. We illuminate the dynamics that influence the assignment of regulatory duties to an agency, how those dynamics (and the allocation of responsibilities) can change over time, and how the specific combination of regulatory functions and purposes can affect agency performance. We focus on the organization of public competition agencies, but our analysis has obvious implications for agency design at other governmental levels (i.e., both trans-national, and sub-national),[9] and to the design of public and private universities,[10] and other nonprofit entities.

Part II provides a historical perspective on the complexities of designing a public agency. Part III spells out a basic analytical framework for analyzing the problem of agency design. It then identifies seven factors that have proven significant in predicting the success and failure (judging by both durability and popular and academic regard) of any given combination of functions. Part IV applies our analysis to the FTC and its combination of competition, consumer protection, and privacy responsibilities. Part V poses the question whether the correct solution is to "divide or conquer." Part VI concludes.

---

7 *See* Daniel A. Crane, *The Institutional Structure of Antitrust Enforcement (2011); Daniel A. Crane, Antitrust Anti-Federalism*, 96 Calif. L. Rev. 1 (2008) (studying impact of institutional arrangements in shaping outcomes in U.S. antitrust system); William E. Kovacic, *The Digital Broadband Migration and the Federal Trade Commission: Building the Competition and Consumer Protection Agency of the Future*, 8 J. Telecom. & High Tech. L. (2010) (describing institutional elements for successful competition and consumer protection programs).

8 William E. Kovacic & David A. Hyman, *Competition Agency Design: What's on the Menu?*, 8 European Competition Journal 527 (Dec. 2012). David A. Hyman & William E. Kovacic, *Institutional Design, Agency Life-cycle and The Goals of Competition Law*, Fordham L. Rev. (forthcoming, 2013).

9 *See, e.g.*, Nicholas Confessore, *Cuomo's Deep Reach Into Regulatory Territory Could Provoke Clash in Albany*, N.Y. Times Feb. 15, 2011, *available at* http://www.nytimes.com/2011/02/16/nyregion/16cuomo.html?hp (describing proposal to merge "the state's Insurance and Banking Departments, along with the Consumer Protection Board, into a new Department of Financial Regulation . . . [aides] said a single regulator with broad jurisdiction would be more effective than the patchwork of agencies charged with protecting New Yorkers from financial fraud . . . It could have the effect of transforming the superintendent of the new agency into a second "sheriff of Wall Street," forcing [Attorney General] Schneiderman, a fellow Democrat with whom Mr. Cuomo has clashed in the past, to compete for high-profile cases.").

10 For example, at the University of Illinois, physics is in the College of Engineering, but chemistry and chemical engineering are in the College of Liberal Arts & Sciences. Agricultural economics is in the College of Agricultural, Consumer & Environmental Sciences, but the economics department is in the College of Liberal Arts & Sciences. And, there are a series of smaller units, institutes, and centers, whose independent status remains an open issue. *See* Stewarding Excellence @ Illinois, *Academic Unit Reviews*, at http://oc.illinois.edu/budget/projectteams.html#unitreviews and *Initiatives and Small Centers,* at http://oc.illinois.edu/budget/projectteams.html#smallcenters. Similar issues are also raised within individual units. Should the law librarian be a member of the law faculty; the library faculty, or both?

I. Public Agency Design

1. First Principles

To create a public agency, one must specify at least five major institutional characteristics: (1) the agency's relationship to the political process (the autonomy/accountability tradeoff), (2) the governance mechanism (management by a single executive or a multi-member board), (3) location within the government (stand-alone institution or sub-unit of a larger body), (4) exclusive or shared policy responsibilities, (5) single- or multi-purpose mandate, and (5) the policy instruments the agency may use in carrying out its duties (e.g., data collection and reporting, law enforcement, business and consumer education, rulemaking, administrative adjudication, civil and/or criminal authority).[11]

Our analysis focuses on the fifth of these questions: the assignment of policy tasks. In a rough sense, we are taking a step toward sketching out the public administration equivalent of Ronald Coase's *Nature of the Firm*.[12] Post-Coase, scholarship has recognized the complex issues raised by the specification of the boundaries of the firm, and the linkage between organizational and institutional choices and firm "outputs." When do firms carry out some functions themselves, and when do they contract with others? How do firms decide between contract, acquisition, and joint venture, when they are not able to do something themselves? Why do firms enter some product lines and geographic areas, and not others? Are conglomerates, which participate in multiple independent and unrelated lines of business, a good idea or not? How important are transaction costs (i.e., the relative costs of out-sourcing versus internal production) and product complementarities (i.e., should a manufacturer of mobile phones also make apps?) in specifying the boundaries of the firm?

How then should we think about the "optimal" boundaries for a government agency's substantive responsibility? [13] The polar solutions are obviously unacceptable: no one creates an agency and fails to give it something to do, and there are no takers in a modern nation state for a "Department of Everything." In between, the dividing lines are less obvious: how does one decide whether an administrative agency should have N or (N+1) or (N+10) areas of responsibility? What counts as a distinct area of responsibility? Does it depend on whether the areas involve separate substantive bodies of law—and how are the boundaries to be set? Should the same agency enforce both civil and criminal laws? Should the agency combine legislative, judicial, and executive functions, or just amalgamate two of the three—and which two? What arrangement minimizes the possibility of capture by those being regulated?[14] What arrangement will be most appealing to the legislators who create the agency in the first place—as well as those charged with oversight and budgetary

11 These and other important institutional choices are set out in Kovacic & Hyman, *supra* note 8.

12 Ronald Coase, *The Nature of the Firm*, 4 ECONOMICA 286 (1937).

13 Some of these parallels are explored in Oliver E. Williamson, *Public and Private Bureaucracies: A Transaction Cost Economics Perspective,* 17 J. LAW, ECON. & ORG. 306 (1999). *See also* Jonathan Klick, Francesco Parisi & Schulz, *The Two Dimensions of Regulatory Competition*, 26 INT'L REV. L. ECON. 56 (2006).

14 *Cf.* Barkow, *supra* note 6.

authority? If another agency already occupies part of the field, is it better to expand capacity at the existing agency, add responsibility to the existing agency without expanding capacity, or create an entirely new agency? Should we have multiple agencies responsible for the same general area—and if so, how should their jurisdiction be defined and enforced? If we want closer coordination of policy and implementation, should we combine two (or more) agencies into one, or are other strategies (e.g., creating a coordinating council or a "czar") more effective? What are the differing consequences of creating a new agency, adding new functions to an existing agency, and reorganizing governmental functions? And so on.

To address these questions, we first examine the forces that historically have shaped the assignment of regulatory tasks to agencies.

2. Constructing the Regulatory Portfolio

Unlike business firms, which set their boundaries through acquisitions, contracts, expansion and contraction, government agencies acquire substantive responsibilities through one of four paths. The simplest case is the assignment of specific functions to a particular agency by *deliberate legislative choice*. Congress created the FTC in 1914 as an alternative to the Sherman Act's prosecutorial model, which vested public enforcement in an executive body (the Department of Justice) and relied on the federal courts to adjudicate cases and shape doctrine.[15] Congress intended Section 5 of the FTC Act, which authorized the Commission to address "unfair methods of competition," to enable the FTC to follow a more activist path in enforcing antitrust law and doctrine.[16] The agency was to apply this authority to develop norms of business conduct.

When it is allocated explicitly by statute, regulatory authority may be shared, concurrent, or exclusive. There are numerous instances where regulatory authority is shared between a sector-specific agency (e.g., the Federal Communications Commission in telecommunications) and a government body with a broader generic mandate to address certain categories of business transactions (e.g., the Department of Justice Antitrust Division and the control of mergers). Alternatively, Congress can grant concurrent authority to two agencies, as is the case with the grant of merger control authority under the Clayton Act to the DOJ and the FTC.

Agencies can also acquire regulatory or operational authority by *accident or fortuity*. As noted above, the original ambit of the FTC was antitrust law, and there is no evidence that Congress intended for it to play a role in consumer protection. However, from its first years the FTC used Section 5 of the FTC Act to respond to complaints from business firms about their rivals' deceitful marketing campaigns, Congress explicitly expanded the FTC's authority so it could challenge "unfair" and "deceptive" business practices.[17]

---

15 *See* Crane, *supra* note 7, at 13-26 (describing institutional choices underpinning adoption of the Sherman Act).

16 15 U.S.C. Section 45. The establishment of the FTC is examined in detail in Marc Winerman, *The Origins of the Federal Trade Commission: Concentration, Cooperation, Control, and Competition,* 71 Antitrust L.J. 1 (2003).

17 The formative legislation is the Wheeler-Lea Act, 52 Stat. 111 (1938). This evolution is described in Marc Winerman & William E. Kovacic, *Outpost Years for a Start-Up Agency: The FTC from 1921-1925,* 77 Antitrust L.J. 145, 193-95 (2010).

More broadly, an agency with capabilities originally designed to serve one purpose may find those capabilities suitable for other analogous purposes—e.g., "if you've got a hammer, why not help other agencies with nails that need pounding?" Thus, helicopters and warships used to deliver troops into combat also can be used to assist civilians suffering from natural disasters, such as earthquakes or floods—explaining why the humanitarian programs of the Department of Defense have expanded considerably in recent years.

An agency's regulatory jurisdiction may also be affected by agency action in response to *changes in business products or technology*.[18] Consider privacy and data protection policies. Modern advances in communications and information services technology have dramatically expanded the ability of firms to collect and use information about consumer behavior and preferences. The United States does not have an omnibus privacy and data protection statute. Instead, the U.S. regime consists of federal and state statutes that regulate specific sectors (e.g., data collection and use by health care providers) or specific types of transactions (e.g., financial services), with regulatory authority dispersed among the agencies responsible for administering each of these statutes.

The resulting policy vacuum allowed the FTC to emerge as the leading federal privacy agency, by virtue of several cases it brought against firms that failed to fulfill promises concerning data protection.[19] The FTC also issued reports in December 2010 and March 2012 which proposed a policy framework for handling privacy issues.[20] The Department of Commerce has sought to play a role into the same policy space, triggering a behind-the-scenes contest for regulatory primacy, which Congress has not yet settled.[21] In like fashion, the development of broadband networks has similarly sparked a dispute between the FTC and the FCC over which agency will oversee this element of the communications sector.

The same dynamic has played out in operational terms within the DOD on several occasions. Technological development invariably triggers intense contests to determine which of the uniformed services will control the deployment of weapons based on the new technology. Consider nuclear weapons. The Air Force, Army, and Navy all sought to occupy the relevant policy terrain, devising solutions that were based exclusively on each service's area of primary expertise. The Air Force emphasized long-range

18 We exclude technological developments that cause Congress to act. So, the emergence of powered flight resulted in a new branch in the Department of Commerce, which ultimately became the FAA.

19 *See, e.g.*, Federal Trade Commission, Consumer Electronics Company Agrees to Settle Data Security Charges; Breach Compromised Data of Hundreds of Consumers, Feb. 5, 2009, *available at* http://www.ftc.gov/opa/2009/02/compgeeks.shtm; Federal Trade Commission, Iconix Brand Group Settles Charges Its Apparel Web Sites Violated Children's Online Privacy Protection Act, Oct. 20, 2009, at http://www.ftc.gov/opa/2009/10/iconix.shtm; Federal Trade Commission, CVS Caremark Settles FTC Charges: Failed to Protect Medical and Financial Privacy of Customers and Employees; CVS Pharmacy Also Pays $2.25 Million to Settle Allegations of HIPAA Violations, Feb. 18, 2009, *available at* http://www.ftc.gov/opa/2009/02/cvs.shtm; Federal Trade Commission, FTC Says Mortgage Broker Broke Data Security Laws: Dumpster Wrong Place for Consumers' Personal Information, Jan. 21, 2009, *available at* http://www.ftc.gov/opa/2009/01/navone.shtm.

20 Federal Trade Commission, Protecting Consumer Privacy in an Era of Rapid Change (Mar. 2012), at http://www.ftc.gov/os.2012/03/130326/privacyreport.pdf; Federal Trade Commission, FTC Staff Issues Privacy Report, Offers Framework for Consumers, Businesses, and Policymakers, Dec. 1, 2010, *available at* http://www.ftc.gov/opa/2010/12/privacyreport.shtm.

21 *See* Press Release, Commerce Department Unveils Policy Framework for Protecting Consumer Privacy Online While Supporting Innovation, Dec. 16, 2010, at http://www.commerce.gov/news/press-releases/2010/12/16/commerce-department-unveils-policy-framework-protecting-consumer-priv.

bombers and intercontinental ballistic missiles.[22] The Army developed intermediate range ballistic missiles and nuclear-capable artillery pieces. The Navy built ballistic missile submarines and acquired carrier-based aircraft with the capacity to deliver nuclear weapons. Congressional appropriations to each service and allocations to particular weapon systems functioned to indicate the winners and losers of the fight for operational dominance.

Finally, there is *legislative divestiture*. Perceived failure (especially catastrophic failure) can spur Congress to divest some of an agency's functions, or fold the entire agency into another institution. So, as detailed below, the Deepwater Horizon oil spill in the Gulf of Mexico resulted in a fundamental reorganization of the Minerals Management Service (MMS) in the Department of Interior. The melt-down of the financial markets resulted in the shuttering of the OTS, and transfer of its functions to the OCC. The devastation of New Orleans in the wake of Hurricane Katrina resulted in a reorganization of the Department of Homeland Security.[23]

In some instances, divestiture is the result of a planned incubation of a new regulatory function, and does not necessarily indicate dissatisfaction with the agency. This was the case with federal securities regulation in the United States. In the 1920s and early 1930s, the FTC used its consumer protection authority to challenge deception in the sale of securities. These cases made the FTC the principal federal entity ensuring honesty in the securities market. The FTC bolstered this role through hearings and reports involving the securities industry and the establishment and operation of public utility holding companies. Although Congress considered assigning responsibility for securities regulation to the FTC, it ultimately used the FTC as a transitional platform for the implementation of the 1933 and 1934 securities statutes, until the Securities and Exchange Commission (SEC) was set up. As part of this plan, James Landis served a short tenure with the FTC before moving to the new SEC as a commissioner.

The different ways by which agencies acquire (and sometimes lose) portions of their regulatory portfolio have two distinct implications. First, agencies seem inevitably to acquire multiple functions and purposes, with their precise portfolio of responsibilities changing over time. Whether this multiplicity is the result of deliberate legislative assignment, inadvertence, seizure of newly created policy terrain that emerges as a result of technological dynamism and other forms of industry change, or the periodic divestiture and reallocation of tasks, the reality is that purely single function/purpose agencies are the exception rather than the rule.

Second, agencies will often have actual or potential rivals for control of specific policy making functions. Some agencies share policy areas with other government bodies. In other instances, there is a common boundary, and agencies periodically contest the location of the property line. In still other cases (such as when technological change transforms an industry and its products), the property line shifts. The process is no different than when a deed defines real estate ownership according to the course of a river.

---

22 The Air Force was originally unenthusiastic about ballistic missiles, since they threatened the supremacy of the bomber, which dominated the Air Force culture. When it became clear that DOD was going to acquire the missiles, the Air Force "faced an awkward choice: either preserve the culture at the cost of letting the army and navy have what may turn out to be the weapon of the century, or get on the bandwagon at the cost of modifying the culture." WILSON, *supra* note 6, at 105.

23 Congressional Research Service, Federal Emergency Management Policy Changes After Hurricane Katrina: A Summary of Statutory Provisions, Nov. 15, 2006, *available at* http://training.fema.gov/EMIWeb/edu/docs/Federal%20EM%20Policy%20Changes%20After%20Katrina.pdf.

A change in the course of the river creates predictable disputes over who owns what.[24] Finally, agencies sometimes approach legislators to request ownership of a previously uninhabited policy area or simply seek to expropriate another agency's portfolio. Secretary of Interior Harold Ickes was notorious for his raids on the territory (both real and regulatory) of other Departments.

Given these dynamics, it would be very useful to know which factors contribute to the success or failure of particular combinations, and the associated trade-offs. Part III turns to this issue.

II. Who Should Do What: Seven Criteria

How should we decide who should do what? We offer seven criteria that reflect our reading of the mix of factors that have historically influenced agency design, location, and performance.[25] We note at the outset that the factors are "squishy," inter-related, and are framed at a high level of generality. We offer them in the spirit of Professors David Weisbach and Jacob Nissim: even "relatively crude ideas . . . can help policymakers muddle through the problems they face."[26]

---

24 In property, the boundary either moves along with the river (if the change is the recent of accretion) or remains where it was originally (if the change is the result of avulsion). This rule explains why although the Mississippi River generally forms the border between Tennessee and Arkansas (with Arkansas on the east bank, and Tennessee on the West bank), some of the land on the west bank is in Tennessee, and other land on the eastern bank is in Arkansas. *See* State of Arkansas v. State of Tennessee, 246 U.S. 158 (1918).

25 Importantly, each factor should be assessed at the level of the agency/department, rather than any subdivision or bureau within the agency/department. Otherwise, the entire debate becomes moot, since even facially absurd combinations can look sensible if you drill down far enough into each agency/department's organizational chart. *See* Weisbach & Nissim, *supra* note 6, at 958-959 ("Consider, for example, a proposal to have the IRS run the country's defense system, replacing the Department of Defense. The proposal is not as silly as it sounds. It would not mean that bespectacled revenue agents would be parachuting into the Hindu Kush wearing night goggles, camouflage, and pocket protectors. Instead, an intelligent Commissioner of Internal Revenue would allow his employees to specialize. Revenue agents would specialize in reading financial statements and soldiers would specialize in fighting. Policies under such a proposal might very well continue much as they do today."). With all due respect to Weisbach & Nissim, we think the proposal is exactly as silly as it sounds. Weisbach & Nissim suggest that the main impediments to the proposal are the absence of benefits to coordinating tax administration and defense, and the additional costs of administration and oversight of two dramatically different functions. *Id.* We suspect that cultural differences between operators who perform these disparate functions have far more explanatory power for why we do not observe the imagined combination. Indeed, the FBI's repeated failures in the area of domestic intelligence provide an ideal case study of what happens when one ignores operator culture. *See generally* Richard Posner, Remaking Domestic Intelligence 10, 14-34 (2005). *See also* Luis Garicano & Richard Posner, *Intelligence Failures: An Organizational Economics Perspective,* 19 J. Econ. Persp. 151, 166 (2005) ("If crime fighting requires a geographically decentralized organization with limited sharing of information and strong individual incentives based on outputs, but national-security intelligence requires a geographically centralized organization with extensive sharing of information and careful screening of inputs but low-powered incentives, the organization's geographical, incentive, and information-sharing structure will either be an unhappy compromise or assure poor performance of one of the two missions."). The Air Force is currently facing similar difficulties, in trying to adapt its longstanding officer-pilot based culture to the increasing use of unmanned aerial vehicles. Mark Mazzetti, *The Drone Zone,* N.Y. Times M32 (July 8, 2012); David Zucchino, *Drone pilots have a front-row seat on war, from half a world away,* L. A. Times (Feb. 21, 2010); Rachel Martin, *Drone Pilots: The Future of Aerial Warfare,* NPR Nov. 29, 2011 at http://www.npr.org/2011/11/29/142858358/drone-pilots-the-future-of-aerial-warfare.

26 Weisbach & Nissim, *supra* note 6, at 997.

1. Evaluative Criteria

1.1. Policy Coherence

A fundamental question posed by a combination of policy duties is policy coherence: how related and consistent are the functions that will reside in the same agency? Do the functions engage the agency in the pursuit of a single set of internally consistent goals, or do the multiple functions command the agency to accomplish inconsistent or unrelated objectives?

In economic terms, one can ask whether are the functions to be combined are complements or substitutes. If they are complements, the combination has the potential to result in synergies and efficiencies; if they are substitutes, the combination is unlikely to result in synergies and efficiencies, and may actually degrade overall performance if it gives rise to internal disagreements over which function should be given primacy. Stated broadly, synergies and efficiencies are more likely to result if there are commonalities among the functions, whether they are derived from a common client population or type of regulated entity, temporal or physical commonalities (including but not limited to common inputs and/or outputs), or even just a shared intellectual framework regarding means and ends.

To be sure, the level of generality at which policy coherence is assessed can result in radically different organizational outcomes. For example, in 1930, the Veterans Administration (VA) was created by uniting three bureaus—the Veterans' Bureau (which was itself created in 1921 by combining programs offered by the Bureau of War Risk Insurance, the Public Health Service and the Federal Board of Vocational Education), the Bureau of Pensions (located in the Department of the Interior) and the National Homes for Disabled Volunteer Soldiers. The common element of these combinations was the nature of the client population (veterans), even though the nature of the services being delivered to the client population varied tremendously (e.g., pensions, health care services, education, and housing/nursing home care). But the VA does not run all programs for which veterans qualify; if a veteran is homeless and also has substance abuse problems, the Department of Housing and Urban Development (HUD) is responsible for the veteran's housing issues, and the VA is responsible for the substance abuse issues.[27]

Further, Congress need not organize services around client populations. For Native Americans, Congress focused instead on the nature of the underlying services being delivered. Accordingly, it allocated responsibility for native lands and native education to the Bureau of Indian Affairs (in the Department of Interior), while responsibility for health care services rendered to the same population was vested in the Indian Health Service (in the Department of Health & Human Services).

Of course, policy coherence is not necessarily of the highest priority—which explains why some Departments are little more than a collection of odds and ends. Consider the Department of Interior, which was created in 1849 by combining the General Land Office (from the Department of the Treasury), the Patent Office (from the Department of State), the Indian Affairs Office (from the

27 David Brooks, *What Government Does*, N.Y. Times, Apr. 28, 2011.

War Department) and the military pension offices in the War and Navy Departments.[28] Interior's authority subsequently expanded to cover such functions as the census, regulation of territorial governments, exploration of the western United States, management of the jail and water systems in the District of Columbia, management of hospitals, universities, and public parks, and the colonization of freed slaves in Haiti.[29] Not surprisingly, "serious observers and satirists alike regularly decried an absence of unifying purpose in the seemingly disparate collection of offices,"[30] and Interior was widely described as "the Department of Everything Else" and the "Great Miscellany."[31] Less kindly disposed commentators described it as "a slop bucket for executive fragments," and a "hydra-headed monster."[32] John C. Calhoun predicted that "everything upon the face of God's earth will go into the Home Department."[33]

The Department of Commerce, which houses bureaus responsible for the census, patents and trademarks, weather forecasts, and weights and standards, has many of the same difficulties. Former Secretary of Commerce William Daley observed that because the Department of Commerce includes the National Oceanic and Atmospheric Administration, the secretary of Commerce "spent 60 percent of his time dealing with fish."[34]

This dynamic can also become self-reinforcing; the less coherent the combination of functions in a Department to begin with, the easier it becomes to add the next unrelated function or functions. Not surprisingly, some departments have become little more than a dumping ground (or less charitably, a rubbish bin) for bureaus with dissimilar portfolios.

Even if the purposes are related, if they are at odds with one another the combination can lead to schizophrenia, if not outright paralysis.[35] Combining the proposed Department of Peace and Nonviolence and the Department of Defense is unlikely to be a good strategy, regardless of ones position on the optimal budget for either department.[36] An agency responsible for both antitrust and trade will have to reconcile the belief that low prices are generally good (antitrust) with the belief that low prices of imported goods are generally bad (anti-dumping authority). An agency charged with the promotion of trade (U.S. Trade Representative) will not be a good partner for

---

28 Department of Interior History, *available at* http://www.doi.gov/archive/history.html.

29 *Id.*

30 Robert M. Utley & Barry Mackintosh, The Department of Everything Else: Highlights of Interior History (1989), *available at* http://www.nps.gov/history/history/online_books/utley-mackintosh/interior2.htm.

31 *Id.*

32 Horace S. Merrill, William Freeman Vilas, Doctrinaire Democrat (Madison, Wisc., 1954), pp. 134,139.

33 Henry B. Learned, *The Establishment of the Secretaryship of the Interior,* 16 AM. HISTORICAL REV. 751, 768 (1911).

34 Jim Kuhnhnen, *Commerce Cuts Coming in Obama's Reorganization,* AP, Jan, 29, 2011, at http://abcnews.go.com/US/wireStory?id=12792513.

35 We focus on inconsistencies in ends or goals, but there can also be inconsistencies in preferred means, even when there is agreement on ends, at least at a high level of generality.

36 *See* Department of Peace and Nonviolence Act, H.R. 808, 110th Cong. (2007). The Department of Peace was to include offices of peace education and training, domestic and international peace activities, technology, arms control and disarmament, peaceful coexistence and nonviolent conflict resolution, and human and economic rights. *But see* P.J. O'ROURKE, GIVE WAR A CHANCE (2002) "the Marine Corps does more to promote world peace than all the Ben & Jerry's ice cream ever made."

an agency predisposed to regard trade as dumping (International Trade Commission). An agency charged with the protection of workers (i.e., the Department of Labor) is unlikely to be a good combination with an agency charged with the promotion of business (i.e., the Department of Commerce)—making it understandable why this particular combination only lasted a few years, after which the Department of Commerce and Labor was split in two. When President Johnson proposed to recombine these two departments in 1963 and again in 1964, the proposal went nowhere.

Other examples of such difficulties are easy to find. Between 1967 and 1974, the National Transportation Safety Board (NTSB) was part of the Department of Transportation (DOT). NTSB was charged with investigating every civil aviation accident and all significant highway, marine, railroad, pipeline, and hazardous-materials accidents. In 1974, Congress spun NTSB off from DOT in 1974 because it concluded NTSB could not perform its investigatory functions properly if it was part of a department also responsible for regulating and promoting transportation.[37] A similar dynamic explains the separation in 1974 of the Atomic Energy Commission (responsible for encouraging the use of nuclear power and regulating safety) into the Energy Research and Development Administration (ultimately merged into the Department of Energy, and charged with promoting the use of nuclear power) and the Nuclear Regulatory Commission (regulating safety).[38]

Similarly, until it was reorganized in the wake of the Deepwater Horizon oil spill, the Minerals Management Service in the Department of Interior was "charged both with collecting revenue generated by oil and gas drilling to fund the government, and with approving the permits that generate that revenue . . . [leaving the MMS] torn between whether to be a regulator or friend to industry."[39] The Bureau of Land Management (in the Department of Interior) is responsible for mining and grazing on federal lands, but it also houses the National Landscape Conservation System, whose priorities are, to say the least, quite different.

When Congress created the Federal Reserve in 1913, its original mandate was to maintain price stability (i.e., to combat inflation and deflation). Congress subsequently added to this mandate. Since 1977 the Federal Reserve is charged with "promot[ing] effectively the goals of maximum employment, stable prices and moderate long-term interest rates." There is an obvious inconsis-

---

37 This background is recounted in National Transportation Safety Board, *History of the National Transportation Safety Board*, *available at* http://ntsb.gov/about/history.html.

38 This split solved one problem but created another. The NRC is now far more susceptible to capture than was the case when it was part of a larger entity with a more diversified portfolio. *See* Mark Seidenfeld, *Bending the Rules: Flexible Regulation and Constraints on Agency Discretion,* 51 ADMIN. L. REV. 429, 465 (1999); Barkow, *supra* note 6.

39 Mark Jaffee & David Olinger, *Tracking down Minerals Management Service's dysfunctional history of drilling oversight,* DENVER POST, June 6, 2010, at http://www.denverpost.com/headlines/ci_15236764. In response to these criticisms, and the firestorm of Congressional disapproval that followed the Deepwater Horizon disaster, Secretary of the Interior Salazar reorganized MMS into three separate entities: the Bureau of Ocean Energy Management, which is responsible for "the sustainable development of the Outer Continental Shelf's conventional and renewable energy resources, including resource evaluation, planning, and other activities related to leasing"; the Bureau of Safety and Environmental Enforcement, which is "responsible for ensuring comprehensive oversight, safety, and environmental protection in all offshore energy activities;" and the Office of Natural Resources Revenue, which is "responsible for the royalty and revenue management function including the collection and distribution of revenue, auditing and compliance, and asset management." Press Release, Salazar Divides MMS's Three Conflicting Missions, May 19, 2010, at http://www.doi.gov/news/pressreleases/Salazar-Divides-MMSs-Three-Conflicting-Missions.cfm.

tency between these goals; if price stability were the only priority, a zero interest rate would be the relevant target, but maximum employment might require a higher interest rate.[40] The dual mandate also makes the actions of the Federal Reserve less predictable, harder to assess critically, and more susceptible to political interference.[41]

The Federal Aviation Administration (FAA) has encountered similar difficulties, since it is charged with "fostering air commerce," as well as safety.[42] According to a former DOT Inspector General, the FAA has generally responded by favoring commerce at the expense of safety.[43] When the issue attracted public attention, Congress responded by modifying the dual mandate, but the change had limited impact on the culture of the FAA.[44]

Similar conflicting mandates also help explain why the problems with Fannie Mae and Freddie Mac got as bad as they did. As former-Treasury Secretary Lawrence Summers noted, "the illusion that the companies were doing virtuous work made it impossible to build a political case for serious regulation. When there were social failures the companies always blamed their need to perform for the shareholders. When there were business failures it was always the result of their social obligations."[45] Stated more broadly, a department with multiple mandates can come up with a plausible justification for almost any decision under the sun.

One should not overstate the necessity for consistency within a single department or agency, since sound policy-making usually requires the balancing of competing interests. Consider banking regulation, where solvency must be balanced against consumer protection. If solvency and consumer protection are handled by distinct agencies, each will focus on the areas within their respective domains, and either discount or ignore entirely the other's area of responsibility. Yet, that approach is a recipe for regular battles between the agencies as to which should prevail on an issue that implicates both sets of interests. A decision balancing the relevant considerations will eventually have to be made by someone—either within a single agency, if both functions are combined, or at a higher level if the two (or more) involved agencies are unable to agree amongst themselves. Obviously, the mission and location of the Consumer Financial Protection Bureau (CFPB), and the

---

40 Ben Bernanke, Federal Reserve Communications, Nov. 14, 2007, at http://www.federalreserve.gov/newsevents/speech/bernanke20071114a.htm ("Were price stability the only objective mandated for the Federal Reserve, the FOMC presumably would strive to achieve zero inflation. . . . But under the Federal Reserve's dual mandate, the determination of the appropriate long-run inflation rate must take account of factors that may affect the efficient functioning of the economy at very low rates of inflation . . . [t]hus, the (properly measured) long-run inflation rate that best promotes the dual mandate is likely to be low but not zero.").

41 George F. Will, *The Trap of the Federal Reserve's Dual Mandate,* WASH. POST, Nov. 18, 2010 ("The Fed cannot perform such a fundamentally political function and forever remain insulated from politics. Only repeal of the dual mandate can rescue the Fed from the ruinous—immediately to its reputation; eventually to its independence—role as the savior of the economy, or of any distressed sector (e.g., housing) that clamors for lower interest rates.").

42 MARY SCHIAVO FLYING BLIND, FLYING SAFE 51 (1997).

43 *Id.* at 65 ("If outsiders viewed the FAA as encumbered by a divided loyalty and hamstrung by its dual mandate, the FAA didn't seem to share that confusion. The tombstone mindset made plain its loyalty to the cost-conscious interests of the aviation industry.").

44 *Id.* at 203, 206.

45 LAWRENCE SUMMERS, *You Want Creative Capitalism? Try This,* 195, 196 in CREATIVE CAPITALISM: A CONVERSATION WITH BILL GATES, WARREN BUFFETT, AND OTHER ECONOMIC LEADERS (Michael Kinsley & Conor Clarke eds., 2008).

reorganization of MMS raise these issues in a very concrete way.[46]

The problem gets stickier when the interests that must be balanced fall in different legal domains, or are incommensurable. Consider the risks (whether real or hypothetical) posed to endangered species and the general population by military training and technology.[47] If DOD is put in charge of deciding whether military training/technology is more important than the risks created by such training/technology, it will predictably focus on the benefits, and decide accordingly. If Interior or EPA get to decide the same dispute, they will predictably focus on the risks of training/technology, and decide accordingly. Similarly, if there is an environmental issue on a military base, DOD and EPA are likely to have very different assessments of the seriousness of the problem.[48] The dispute over the Keystone XL pipeline provides another example of this phenomenon; the Department of State found no material environmental problems with the project, and Secretary of State Clinton stated that she was "inclined" to approve it—but EPA had a dramatically different perspective on the environmental risks, and was viewed by project supporters as a "*de facto* ally of environmentalists."[49] Similar dynamics play out across other domains, including the balancing of environmental protection against nuclear energy, balancing industrial development (and the asso-

---

46 The press release announcing the reorganization of MMS highlights the benefits of avoiding agencies with conflicting missions—but it says nothing about the necessity of integrating the conflicting decisions that will result from separate agencies. *See* Press Release, *supra* note 39 ("The Minerals Management Service has three distinct and conflicting missions that—for the benefit of effective enforcement, energy development, and revenue collection—must be divided,' said Secretary Salazar. 'The reorganization I am ordering today is the next step in our reform agenda and will enable us to carry out these three separate and equally-important missions with greater effectiveness and transparency.").

47 *See, e.g.*, State of Wisconsin v. Weinberger, 736 F.2nd 438 (7th Cir. 1984) (dispute over whether the Department of Defense was required to prepare a supplemental environmental impact statement pursuant to the National Environmental Policy Act with respect to construction of a new extremely low frequency (ELF) submarine communications system based in Michigan and upgrading of ELF system in Wisconsin when new information was available on the biological effects of ELF). A similar dispute raged over the use of Vieques Island as a bombing range by the U.S. Navy. *See, e.g.*, Edward Walsh, *Despite protest, Navy resumes bombing exercises on Vieques/Training interrupted briefly—14 arrests,* WASH. POST, Apr. 28, 2001 ("The Navy resumed practice bombing on the small Puerto Rican island of Vieques yesterday, intensifying a debate that has pitted what the Navy says is the vital need for realistic training exercises against the health concerns of the island's population and the Puerto Rican government.").

48 Lyndsey Layton, *Pentagon Fights EPA on Pollution Cleanup*, WASH. POST, June 30, 2008, *available at* http://www.washingtonpost.com/wp-dyn/content/article/2008/06/29/AR2008062901977.html.

49 *See* Secretary Clinton speaks about Innovation and American Leadership, http://newsblaze.com/story/20101017130926stat.nb/topstory.html ("[W]e've not yet signed off on it. But we are inclined to do so and we are for several reasons—going back....original questions—we're either going to be dependent on dirty oil from the Gulf or dirty oil from Canada."); Elana Schor, *Canada-U.S. Oil Pipeline Poses Few Environmental Risks—State Dept.*, N.Y. TIMES, Aug. 26, 2011 ("Among the entities that now could scrutinize the document during a 90-day comment period are other federal agencies—including EPA, which called for more in-depth review of the project's footprint in June comments that called an earlier EIS 'insufficient.' That stance has led some green groups to look to EPA to expose any potential flaws they might see in the final EIS, while some of the pipeline's supporters view the agency as a *de facto* ally of environmentalists. Robert Jones, vice president of the Keystone pipeline system at TransCanada, said earlier this month that 'I want to be responsive' to EPA's concerns, but 'the frustration I have is that I might as well be talking to NRDC or the Sierra Club.'").

ciated employment) against population health and environmental justice claims, and so on.[50]

Thus, which agency is the "decider" will significantly affect the outcome of any given dispute, as well as whether particular circumstances count as "disputes." Stated differently, despite the rhetoric that typically surrounds reorganization, the issue is not just about process efficiencies—it is also about outcomes.

1.2. Credibility/Branding

A public agency's "brand" conveys a message about the agency's priorities and aims to both internal and external constituencies. The brand can become diluted and/or confused if the agency has too many responsibilities, or if the responsibilities are not complementary and consistent. For agency insiders, a diluted/confused brand can create confusion about what projects ought to be selected, what theory ought to motivate the pursuit of individual matters, and the relative priority and seriousness of particular projects/matters.[51] A diluted/confused brand can also affect the agency's decision rules: personnel working for an agency with a diluted/confused brand will find it easier to adopt amorphous standards and employ ad hoc reasoning when justifying their decisions.[52] A diluted/confused brand can also distract the agency from its core mission, and may even affect the culture of the agency. Those who interact with an agency with a diluted/confused brand are more likely to complain that it operates inconsistently and unreliably.

These branding dynamics also influence agency credibility. The better the reputation an agency has with Congress and congressional staffers, the more likely it is to receive adequate funding, and not be subjected to routine second-guessing/reversal. The better the reputation an agency has with courts, the greater the deference it is likely to receive for its decisions. The better the reputation an agency has with the parties it regulates, the more likely it is to be able to work out a cost-effective solution in a timely way, without resorting to full-blown adversarial proceedings.

---

50 *See* Howard Seidman, Politics, Positions and Power: The Dynamics of Federal Organization (5th ed. 1998) ("If agencies are to work together harmoniously, they must share at least some community of interests about basic goals. . . . Senator Frank Moss ascribed the conflict between the National Park Service and the Army Corps of Engineers over the Florida Everglades to 'uncoordinated activities. Park service officials complained that the engineers drained the Everglades National Park almost *dry* in their efforts to halt wetlands flooding and reclaim glade country for agriculture. The Army Corps of Engineers argued that wetlands were 'for the birds' and flood control for the people.").

51 *Cf.* Wilson, *supra* note 6, at 55-59 (describing how the Economic Cooperation Administration and the Central Intelligence Agency were profoundly affected by the personnel they acquired from other agencies, given the open-ended nature of the original mandate (i.e. the brand) for each agency). Indeed, as Wilson concisely observes, "if a new agency has ambiguous goals, the employees' prior experience will influence how its tasks get defined."). *Id.* at 55.

52 *See* Summers, *supra* note 45; Janice Revell, *Interview with John Taylor*, Money Magazine 93, 96 (Aug. 2012) ("The Fed needs to focus on a single goal of long-run price stability. We should remove the Fed's dual mandate of maximum employment and stable prices, which was put into effect in the 1970s. From 2003 to 2005, the Fed held interests rates too low for too long. A primary reason was its concern that raising rates would increase unemployment. . . . More recently, the Fed has cited concerns over employment to to justify its interventions, including quantitatitive easing. *Removing the dual mandate would take away that excuse.*") (emphasis supplied).

Although credibility obviously depends on multiple factors, including the particulars of the involved agencies, and their respective histories and past decisions, the bundling of functions influences an agency's reservoir of political capital. Regulatory bodies are continually engaged in a process of accumulating and spending political capital. Combining a function that generates political capital surpluses with a function that runs political capital deficits may give an agency greater ability to perform deficit-prone functions that are important to the larger economy. Conversely, an agency whose portfolio of responsibilities ensures that it always runs a political deficit is an agency that has no constituency. The Office of Information and Regulatory Affairs (OIRA) is a case study of precisely this phenomenon.[53]

Such considerations help explain why agencies sometimes resist the addition of new responsibilities, even when acceptance would result in a greater budget and more visibility. For several decades, the FBI vigorously resisted attempts to expand its jurisdiction to encompass federal drug laws.[54] The State Department did not want the United States Information Agency and the Agency for International Development.[55] On at least two occasions, the Secret Service declined requests from the CIA to spy on visiting foreign dignitaries.[56]

A similar dynamic explains why agencies sometimes try to get rid of responsibilities that senior agency personnel believe detract from the agency's core mission. In 1973 and again in 1974, the Department of Agriculture tried to get rid of responsibility for the Food Stamp program, since it viewed itself as being in the "food business"—not the "welfare business."[57] As these examples indicate, agency personnel have complex interests and incentives, and do not simply seek to grow their domains and budgets.

Another factor affecting an agency's brand and credibility is its susceptibility to capture. In general, the broader an agency's portfolio, the harder it is to capture, since all of the covered industries must bid against one another to capture the regulator. This dynamic may raise the price of capture so high as to make it no longer cost-effective for any given industry or market participant to attempt to do so. Thus, the Interstate Commerce Commission (ICC) was much harder for a single industry to capture, because it covered both trucking and railroads, compared to the dynamic in financial services, where Congress allocated responsibility for regulating insurers, banks, and securities to entirely separate regulators. (We leave to the side the question of whether the ICC performed well or poorly; our point is simply about the relative likelihood of capture). The EPA presents a similar dynamic; because it is responsible for pollution of the air, water, and land, it is harder for polluters in a single industry to capture the agency. To be sure, the prospect of capture may be the whole point of creating an agency in the first place.

---

53 *See* Susan E. Dudley, *Lessons Learned, Challenges Ahead: Is There a Constituency for OIRA*, Regulation 7-8 (Summer, 2009) ("OIRA's mandate is to advance the general public interest. . . . Hence there is no concentrated constituency for OIRA.").

54 Wilson, *supra* note 6, at 180 ("For years members of Congress tried to persuade J. Edgar Hoover that the FBI should take over federal responsibility for investigating drug trafficking.").

55 *Id.*

56 Marc Ambinder, *Inside the Secret Service*, Harpers, Mar. 2011, *available at* http://www.theatlantic.com/magazine/archive/2011/03/inside-the-secret-service/8390/ ("over the past 10 years, the CIA had asked the service on at least two occasions to help develop intelligence on a visiting foreign leader—that is, essentially, to spy on the very person it was assigned to protect. Both times, the service refused.").

57 Wilson, *supra* note 6, at 108-109.

1.3. Capacity/Capability

Agency resources are scarce, just like everything else. Assigning N +1 functions to an agency that only has the resources (whether measured by headcount, band-width, or credibility) to handle N responsibilities is asking for trouble. Stated differently, an agency with multiple discrete functions can easily find itself with too many things to do, relative to the pool of talent that it has available. One needs a critical mass of talent to do any one thing well; to do multiple things well requires both sufficient capacity and continuous fine-tuning of the agency's allocation of resources.[58] Absent such conditions, agencies will necessarily give superficial treatment to areas that, at any particular point in time, are deemed less central to the agency's mission. Agency employees are not stupid, and will respond accordingly, sorting themselves to work in particular areas—with their choices dictated by their ambition and enthusiasm. The result is that some areas will flourish and others will languish—even if budgets keep pace with new responsibilities (which they almost never do).

Congress already has a tendency to assign new responsibilities to existing agencies without providing much in the way of additional funding. For example, expansions in the responsibilities of the Food and Drug Administration (FDA) have not been accompanied by similar expansions in funding.[59] To be sure, there will always be competition for resources, regardless of how many functions an agency performs. But, combining functions within a single department does not eliminate the problem. Instead, it is merely shifted to a less transparent setting for resolution.

The funding/resource allocation problem noted above will necessarily be less visible if it is resolved within a single agency. The agency will present a funding request that reflects its internal resolution of the budgetary fight, and its assessment of its overall priorities. The same dynamic applies to the allocation of effort within the agency. Barring a whistle-blower, external constituencies will never learn the details of who wanted what—and what is no longer being done with the same enthusiasm, if at all. If the funding debate involved multiple agencies, there would be a higher degree of transparency, since each agency would be required to make its case individually.[60]

Capacity is not the same thing as capability. Capability determines whether an agency has the tools to make good decisions, and does so. An agency with enforcement responsibilities first needs the statutory authority to exercise its will, and an adequate set of remedies with which to enforce compliance. Once it is so armed, it will predictably make two types of errors: Type I (intervening when it should not, or a false-positive), and Type II (not intervening when it should, or a false negative).

---

58 Wilson, *supra* note 6, at 378 ("[W]e live in a country that despite its baffling array of rules and regulations and the insatiable desire of some people to use government to rationalize society still makes it possible to get drinkable water instantly, put through a telephone call in seconds, deliver a letter in a day, and obtain a passport in a week. . . . One can stand on the deck of an aircraft carrier during night flight operations and watch two thousand nineteen-year-old boys faultlessly operate one of the most complex organizational systems ever created. There are not many places where all this happens. It is astonishing that it can be made to happen at all.").

59 *See, e.g.*, Ladd Wiley & Steven A. Grossman, *Does FDA Have Enough Funding to Fulfill its Critical Role in Protecting the Public Health?* 1 FDLI Food and Drug Policy Forum (2011).

60 To be sure, the budgeting process is not fully transparent. If the Administration decides not to include funding for an initiative that agency personnel would like to pursue, Congress may never learn of that fact. Agency personnel are not allowed to request from Congress a budgetary allocation in excess of the amount in the Administration's budget—which can lead to considerable frustration during Congressional hearings, if the recent fight over the funding of the Consumer Product Safety Commission is any indication.

The institutional design question is whether an agency with multiple (and potentially competing) functions and purposes is likely to make more or fewer mistakes—and perhaps, of which type. In principle, both types of error are equally problematic; it is the overall frequency of error that matters. In practice, false positives are viewed as more problematic than false negatives, since they are more visible, and the aggrieved constituency can readily mobilize in opposition. Such issues should be considered in deciding how to allocate regulatory authority.

A related point concerns the agency's own ambitions. Expansion of the agency's substantive mandate can degrade capability. As the agency's authority grows, its leadership and staff may acquire an exaggerated sense of the institution's ability to perform effectively, and pay less attention to whether the agency's commitments match its capabilities. These circumstances can result in agency leadership "over-promising and under-delivering."

A second problem arises from legislative perceptions that the breadth of an agency's mandate gives it the capability to address all troublesome phenomena. The more expansive an agency's mandate, the more likely it is that Congress will turn to the agency to address developments that do not fit neatly elsewhere—even if those problems do not actually play to an agency's strengths. Thus, an agency with expansive powers becomes a default option for handling the latest problem, regardless of whether the agency's actual capacity and capabilities supply effective means for achieving a good solution.

More broadly, inadequate capacity forces a bureau or agency to set priorities (and accordingly, triage the issues in its regulatory portfolio). Some issues will receive close attention, while others will only get attention in response to complaints or crises. Such triage is necessary if the agency is to keep its head above water, but it means that "law in action" is quite different than "law on the books." It is also a recipe for recriminations and oversight hearings when an issue on the losing end of the triage process blows up in the face of the agency. The FDA's attempts to do both food and drug safety provide an obvious example of how this sequence can play out.[61]

Capability is also influenced by the degree to which agency personnel self-critically assess both means and ends. When multiple agencies share responsibility for a particular area, there is a feedback loop for surfacing and resolving disagreements regarding such matters. When a single agency has sole responsibility, and seeks to handle such matters internally, the risks of groupthink and tunnel vision increase. Conversely, the increased transparency that results from two agencies disagreeing on such matters lowers these risks—particularly if those on the "losing" side of the dispute are willing to leak the information, as is often the case.

For example, the Departments of State and the CIA have been at odds over the use of drones in Pakistan. In one recent incident, the ambassador sought to postpone a strike for what he believed to be good reasons, but was overruled by the CIA director, for what he believed to be good reasons.[62] Reasonable people can disagree as to whether the CIA or the Department of State had the better

61 AP, *Risks of tainted food rise as inspections drop*, NBC News, Feb. 26, 2007, at http://www.msnbc.msn.com/id/17349427/ns/health-infectious_diseases/t/risks-tainted-food-rise-inspections-drop/.

62 Adam Entous, Siobhan Gorman & Julian E. Barnes, *U.S. Tightens Drone Rules,* Wall St. J., Nov. 4, 2011, at http://online.wsj.com/article/SB10001424052970204621904577013982672973836.html?mod=WSJ_hp_LEFTTopStories.

of the argument in this particular case, but it seems clear that the dispute was much less likely to come to light if the issue was being decided by (and within) a single entity than when two agencies/ departments with different views were involved.

1.4. Resilience: Is the Assignment of Functions Adaptable and Sustainable?

Statutes routinely allocate jurisdiction according to the technology used to supply a product or the status of the organization that provides the service. What happens when the character of the industry is altered by technological change or the emergence of new categories of suppliers of the sector's goods or services? As suggested earlier, regulatory jurisdictional boundaries can shift over time in much the way that the movement of a river will sometimes alter rights in real property.[63] When such changes take place, multiple agencies may seek to exercise authority by arguing that the reconfigured industry falls within their purview. A sustainable assignment of functions will be able to adapt to such changes; a non-sustainable assignment will not—making bureaucratic warfare between the rival agencies a very real possibility.[64]

One obvious example is the almost decade-long dispute between the SEC and the Commodity Futures Trading Commission (CFTC) over products that arose at the interface of regulatory authority of these two agencies. The SEC regulates securities; the CFTC regulates futures contracts. But what happens when a futures contract is for the delivery of securities? The SEC took the logical (and self-interested) position that a futures contract involving a security was subject to its jurisdiction. The CFTC took the logical (and self-interested) position that it had exclusive jurisdiction over all futures contracts. Both agencies pointed to their enabling legislation. When the CFTC approved the Chicago Board of Trade's trading of futures contracts on GNMA certifications and the Chicago Mercantile Exchange's trading of futures contracts on T-bills, the SEC took the position that it might view such trading as illegal, notwithstanding the CFTC's approval. The Chicago Board of Trade brought a lawsuit against the SEC, challenging its assertion of jurisdiction.[65] The SEC also brought several lawsuits challenging the CFTC's assertion of exclusive jurisdiction.[66] The dispute was finally settled with a negotiated agreement between the two agencies, which was ultimately enacted into formal law.

The regulation of financial services routinely raises this problem, because regulatory authority is generally tied to the type of entity being regulated, rather than the type of product being offered. Consider the comments of a Federal Deposition Insurance Corporation (FDIC)

---

63 Whether the property right moves with the course of the water depends on whether the movement was the result of avulsion (no change in property right) or accretion (change in property right).

64 *Cf.* David C. King, Turf Wars: How Congressional Committees Claim Jurisdiction 2 (1997) ("As with nations and hunting groups, poorly defined boundaries lead to wasteful skirmishes.").

65 Board of Trade v. SEC, 677 F.2d 1137 (7th Cir. 1982), vacated as moot, 459 U.S. 1026 (1982).

66 SEC v. American Commodity Exchange, 546 F.2d 1361 (10th Cir. 1976); SEC v. Univest, Inc., 410 F. Supp. 1029 (D. Ill. 1976).

associate director, noting the complexities of determining whether a particular depository institution was indeed a bank:

> First, you have to figure out, what in the hell is a bank? And what is the intent of deposit insurance? It's a far cry from when they set it up. A typical commercial bank was one that made agricultural loans, commercial loans, and held demand deposits. . . . Congress had in mind what a bank was. . . . Now you may have a furniture company and they may say "we will sell a lot of couches on credit, and we borrow money to do that. We could [finance the credit] with commercial paper, but by and large we use a commercial bank for our needs. . . . Why don't I establish a bank and get insurance. . . I could go out and sell CDs. . . . Then I've got back up and my financing rates go way down. . . . Now I am a lender for couches; instead of selling the loans to the bank or borrowing, I just put the loans on my books." Well that isn't what anyone was thinking of or imagined at first. . . . They get deposit insurance and they play on the federal guarantee to reduce interest costs and financing.[67]

Such border disputes can easily trigger a turf war between agencies. These dynamics are also affected by the demand side, as firms maneuver to "choose" their regulator.

An adaptive regulatory framework would have clearly allocated regulatory authority over a particular area to a specific regulatory agency—instead of forcing personnel at multiple agencies to spend considerable time and effort disputing the allocation of responsibility. Various strategies are available to proactively address adaptability, but to a considerable degree, Congress only examines such matters in response to train wrecks and crises, in which perceived and/or real failures in the regulatory process give rise to reassessment. Dodd-Frank presents an obvious example of the end game of this dynamic—albeit one that did not provide a resilient solution to the broader problem it sought to address, with the exception of creating the CFPB.

Resilience is obviously not as important as some of the other factors, because problems will emerge, if at all, over time. But, the absence of properly defined jurisdictional boundaries will eventually lead to border wars between agencies/departments, and turf wars among congressional committees. Creating an adaptable and sustainable grant of regulatory authority helps reduce the amount of time spent on such activities.

1.5. Internal Organizational Cohesion

When discrete functions are combined in a single agency or department, the result is usually the creation of separate operating units for each function. As individual operating units become more specialized and autonomous, they quickly develop norms, goals, and priorities that predictably differ from other units in the same agency or department. Over time, this process results in units being staffed by personnel whose interests, training, and abilities focus narrowly on the work of their unit and have little understanding of the backgrounds and activities of other units underneath the same

67 Anne M. Khademian, Checking on Banks: Autonomy and Accountability in Three Federal Agencies 126-127 (1996).

institutional roof. Predictably enough, each individual operating unit starts to see the other units as rivals for prestige, headcount, and budgetary resources.

This rivalry can be beneficial if it results in synergies that serve the larger aims of the agency. Conversely, the rivalry will be destructive if it manifests itself in credit-claiming or other measures designed to enhance the visibility of the operating unit as an end in itself. The third possibility is there will be neither beneficial nor destructive rivalry; individual units will simply not acknowledge the existence of the other units. Issues of culture and history loom large in determining which of these three outcomes will result.

To be sure, such difficulties are likely to arise whether we are dealing with a single agency or multiple agencies that are expected to coordinate their efforts. And, such difficulties can exist within a single department: consider the intra-service rivalries in the U.S. Air Force (bomber v. fighter pilots) and the U.S. Navy (surface navy v. aviators v. submarines).[68] But, matters are often much worse across divisions within a single agency or department, such as the legendary conflicts between the rival military services contained within a single Department of Defense:

> It was the late 1950s and General Curtis LeMay was the Chief of Staff of the Air Force. The Air Force and the Navy at that time were vying for who would have the primary mission of the strategic defense of the country. The Air Force was advocating its land based strategic bombers and intercontinental ballistic missiles. The Navy was advocating its ballistic missile submarines and putting nuclear capable aircraft aboard aircraft carriers. The debate was heated and there was not enough money to do both. The future missions of both services were at stake. An Air Force Colonel was briefing General LeMay on the Soviet threat versus the strategic requirements funded in the budget. The Colonel told General LeMay that the Russians, our enemy, were capable of . . . and at that point General LeMay stopped him. LeMay was quoted as saying, "The Russians are our adversary. The Navy is our enemy."[69]

LeMay's assessment echoes in another story of institutional narrow-mindedness that circulates in the folklore of World War II. In this story, a journalist interviews a Marine Corps pilot after VJ Day in 1945. The exchange goes like this:

> **Journalist:** "What was the enemy like in the Pacific?"
> **Marine Corps pilot:** "Terrible."
> **Journalist:** "What do you mean, terrible?"
> **Marine Corps pilot:** "They were savage, merciless, and relentless. Every time we thought we had them beat, they'd do something despicable and underhanded, and we'd have to start over again."
> **Journalist:** "It must have been a relief to hear that Japan had surrendered."
> **Marine Corps pilot:** "Japan? I was talking about the U.S. Navy!"

---

68 More colloquially, these are referred to as the brown shoe, black shoe, and felt shoe Navy. WILSON, *supra* note 6, at 106.

69 John Melchner, *Managing the Budget Process*, J. PUB. INTEGRITY 11, 13 (Fall/Winter, 1998), *available at* http://www.ignet.gov/randp/jpifw98.pdf.

Other examples of inter-service attitudes (and their consequences) are not hard to find. The Air Force is responsible for close air support of ground operations, but, air force culture is "based on flying high-performance fighters and long-range bombers, especially the latter."[70] Not surprisingly, the Air Force historically gave "minimal attention to close air support and buys just enough attack aircraft to protect its claim to the close air support mission. Meanwhile, the Army, unsure that it can rely on Air Force support when it is needed, purchases a vast fleet of attack helicopters which, while more expensive than attack planes and potentially far more vulnerable, can be placed under direct Army command."[71] When U.S. armed forces invaded Grenada in 1983, there were problems with the interoperability of communications systems between Marines in the north and Army Rangers in the south: "since their radios could not communicate with the ships of the Independence battle group, Army radiomen were forced to send their request for fire support to Fort Bragg which in turn relayed them by satellite to the ships."[72]

Stated more broadly, the coordination of functions and responsibilities will not happen merely because previously separate bureaus are combined into a single department.[73] Indeed, the more each bureau attempts to build esprit de corps and signal that it is truly elite, the less likely "joint-ness" will result. Such dynamics have long complicated attempts to deploy "special ops" teams from different branches of the military in an integrated fashion—particularly when one adds in that special ops has collectively been long regarded with collective suspicion by the "regular" military. When one adds the CIA into the mix, it is easy to understand why joint-ness has been such a challenge—although there have been significant improvements in recent years.[74]

---

70 WILSON, *supra* note 6, at 186.

71 RICHARD A. STUBBING, THE DEFENSE GAME 142 (1986).

72 *See* http://www.dtic.mil/doctrine/jel/history/urgfury.pdf. In the Hollywood version, a Marine squad was in danger of being overrun, and was unable to request air support because its radio had been destroyed. A young Marine (played by Mario Van Peebles) patched together a phone line, and placed a call to Camp Lejeune in North Carolina, using a credit card that he had carried into battle. The call was relayed to a Navy ship stationed off Grenada, which coordinated the necessary close air support. *See* Heartbreak Ridge (1986).

73 *See, e.g.*, DENNIS D. RILEY & BRYAN E. BROPHY-BAERMANN, BUREAUCRACY AND THE POLICY-MAKING PROCESS 71 (2006) ("A specialist in marine biology may in some sense work for the Department of Commerce, but in his or her mind, the job is not with the Commerce Department or even with the NOAA, but with the National Marine Fisheries Service.").

74 Marc Ambinder, *The Secret Team that Killed Bin Laden*, NATIONAL J. (May 3, 2011), at http://www.nationaljournal.com/whitehouse/the-secret-team-that-killed-bin-laden-20110502 ("Sunday's operation provides strong evidence that the CIA and JSOC work well together. . . . In an interview at CIA headquarters two weeks ago, a senior intelligence official said the two proud groups of American secret warriors had been "deconflicted and basically integrated"—finally—10 years after 9/11."); Greg Miller & Julie Tate, *CIA Shifts Focus to Killing Targets*, WASH. POST, Sep 1, 2011 at A1 ("The CIA was heavily involved in the raid by U.S. Special Operations troops on a compound in Abbottabad, Pakistan, in May. Osama bin Laden was killed by U.S. Navy SEALs, but the operation was carried out under CIA authority, planned in a room at agency headquarters and based on intelligence gathered over a period of years by the CTC. The assault was the most high-profile example of an expanding collaboration between the CIA and the U.S. Joint Special Operations Command, which oversees the nation's elite military teams. Their comingling at remote bases is so complete that U.S. officials ranging from congressional staffers to high-ranking CIA officers said they often find it difficult to distinguish agency from military personnel. "You couldn't tell the difference between CIA officers, Special Forces guys and contractors," said a senior U.S. official after a recent tour through Afghanistan. "They're all three blended together. All under the command of the CIA.").

In like fashion, the CIA has had a long-standing cultural conflict between analysts and field agents, as well as ongoing debates between internal communities that favor either reliance on high technology monitoring systems (e.g., reconnaissance satellites) or "Humint" (on the ground in-person collection of intelligence). Those who design and manage intelligence gathering through advanced technology systems tend to have backgrounds in science and engineering. The human intelligence community tends to be drawn from individuals with skills in the social sciences. Not surprisingly, each individual unit believes it has a monopoly (or near-monopoly) on the optimal approach to intelligence gathering and analysis, and the efforts of other units are viewed with disdain.

The problem is not limited to the uniformed services: the U.S. Forest Service has experienced similar difficulties as it has expanded from an agency staffed solely by foresters to a more diversified ecosystem. As James Q. Wilson observed, "today foresters have to contend with engineers, biologists, and economists, among others. The foresters dislike the tendency of engineers to elevate mechanical soundness over natural beauty, of biologists to worry more about endangered species than about big game, and of economists to put a price on things foresters regard as priceless."[75]

As these examples illustrate, the combination of related functions within a single department or agency does not mean that good things will inevitably result. Indeed, destructive rivalry can mean that 2+2 = 1, instead of 4.

1.6. Collateral Effects on the Regulatory Ecosystem

The government is already thickly planted with bureaus, agencies and inter-agency working groups, departments and commissions. Many of these institutions have overlapping authority—sometimes by reason of deliberate legislative choice and sometimes by accident. As noted previously, in some instances shared authority stems from conscious congressional decisions to dedicate policymaking responsibilities to two or more public bodies. Sometimes the deliberate duplication of responsibility stems from Congressional desire to test alternative institutional means of delivering a desired policy result.[76] On other occasions it reflects an explicit desire to use interagency rivalry to spur performance improvements.[77] Finally, as we describe below, technological change and market developments can give rise to regulatory overlaps "by accident."

Whatever the origins, the fact of overlapping authority typically elicits effort by the agencies with shared jurisdiction to coordinate their efforts. These efforts do not arise because the agencies in

---

75 Wilson, *supra* note 6, at 65.

76 This is probably the best interpretation of the decision of Congress in 1914 to establish the FTC and to give the Commission concurrent authority with the Department of Justice over the Clayton Act. The decision permitted a test of the relative efficacy of competition policymaking through administrative elaboration by a multimember commission (the FTC model) versus litigation in the federal courts by a single-headed executive branch body (the Justice Department model). *See* William E. Kovacic, *Downsizing Antitrust: Is It Time to End Dual Federal Enforcement?* 41 Antitrust Bulletin 505 (1996).

77 *See* William E. Kovacic, *Procurement Reform and the Choice of Forum in Bid Protest Disputes,* 9 Admin. Law J. Am. Univ. 461 (1995) (discussing congressional decision in 1980s to give General Services Board of Contract Appeals broader bid protest authority and create an alternative to protest oversight by the General Accounting Office).

question like each other. In many circumstances, rivalry among agencies to be seen as the lead institution in a given field of regulation is inevitable, as perceptions of primacy influence congressional decisions about budgets, affect the recruitment of skilled staff, and generally shape the agency's self-image. In analyzing the conduct of public institutions, one rarely goes wrong by overestimating the power of parochialism and self-interest to warp behavior.

Even though agencies with contested or contestable functions compete aggressively with each other, they often come to realize the need, at least on some level, to avoid destructive duplication and to invest in joint activities to deliver better policy results. The means of cooperation and coordination are myriad, and range from formal exchange of written instruments (e.g., memoranda of understanding) to the creation of interagency working groups to less formal (but still important) personal interaction among agency heads, senior managers, and case handlers. In ways that are sometimes visible but more often invisible to external observers, agencies with overlapping authority and responsibilities routinely create a vibrant and interlocking ecosystem of cooperation.

When regulatory tasks are reallocated, or a new agency is inserted into the mix, or new powers are given to an existing agency, there is a significant potential to disrupt this regulatory ecosystem. Disruption can take a variety of forms. The new entrant may siphon off money and personnel, making it difficult for incumbent agencies to perform their existing responsibilities. Reallocation of authority may also upset long-standing understandings that formed the basis for fruitful inter-agency collaboration. The entrant may receive a substantive mandate whose formal commands resemble the language that appears in the statutes of other regulatory authorities. The interpretation of the new entrant's mandate in one judicial could spill over into the interpretation of the mandates of other agencies in separate cases.

To be sure, Congress certainly has the authority to close down an agency entirely, or substantially limit its jurisdiction and authority—and it knows how to do that when it wants to. But, the kinds of regulatory reorganizations we have been describing usually do not reflect that objective—meaning that the damage to the regulatory ecosystem is often an unintended consequence of Congressional failure to understand that personnel would migrate to the new and more glamorous and higher paying outpost—leaving other parts of the regulatory ecosystem permanently blighted. To summarize, the wisdom and net functional benefits of any specific realignment of regulatory authority will depend heavily upon whether the changes build upon a sophisticated understanding of the existing regulatory ecology.

1.7. Political Implications

Politics is a major factor in the design and location of government agencies and functions. When the House of Representatives was considering a climate change bill in 2009, the chair of the House Agriculture Committee made it clear he would kill the bill if it allocated responsibility for determining whether farmers would receive credit for "tilling and conservation practices that keep carbon dioxide stored in the soil" to the EPA, but would allow it to proceed if responsibility for the same task resided in the Agriculture Department.[78] The choice of location had real significance; "environmentalists and the bill's main sponsors feared that the Agriculture Department might use lax standards, which would blow a hole through the nationwide cap on carbon dioxide emissions."[79] When President Franklin Roosevelt's reorganization committee proposed to consolidate all federal loan programs under the Treasury Department, FDR vetoed the suggestion, observing "that won't work. If they put them in the Treasury, not one of them will ever make a loan to anybody for any purpose. There are too many glass-eyed bankers in the Treasury."[80] More recently, privacy advocates have expressed skepticism about the Obama Administration's Internet privacy proposals because the Commerce Department is taking the lead, instead of a more pro-consumer agency, like the FTC.[81]

As these examples illustrate, decisions about *where* to place certain responsibilities are simultaneously decisions about *who* will resolve certain disputes, and, in turn, *what* the outcome is likely to be.

Once regulatory authority has been allocated in the first instance, Congressional committees are extremely reluctant to cede authority. Like elsewhere, there are gains from expertise; individual members gain knowledge and experience with an agency's operations over a period of years, and proposals to transfer regulatory authority to an agency that is overseen by a different committee places that investment of intellectual capital at risk. In like fashion, a committee that is comfortable with the way a particular agency handles matters may be reluctant to allow others to take ownership of "their baby," fearing their successors may not share their priorities. Finally, individual members of Congress derive important electoral advantages from the committees on which they service, including access to campaign contributions from those who are affected by the activities of government agencies subject to the oversight of the committees. Oversight of a specific government agency creates a revenue stream that flows from the affected industry to the committee's members.

---

78 Derek Thompson, *The Collin Peterson Climate Change Compromise,* THE ATLANTIC, *available at* http://business.theatlantic.com/2009/06/the_collin_peterson_climate_change_compromise_1.php ("So it looks like the Waxman-Markey climate change bill will pass in the House this week: The sponsors hammered out an agreement last night with Collin Peterson, the chair of the Agriculture Committee. The main sticking point was over whether the EPA or the Department of Agriculture would administer a carbon offset program intended for farmers. Peterson got his way: The (more sympathetic) Department of Agriculture will do the work.").

79 Steven Mufson, *Vote Set on House Climate Bill,* WASH. POST, June 24, 2009, *available at* http://www.washingtonpost.com/wp-dyn/content/article/2009/06/23/AR2009062303456.html.

80 A.J. WANN, THE PRESIDENT AT CHIEF ADMINISTRATOR—A STUDY OF FRANKLIN D. ROOSEVELT 103-04 (PUBLIC AFFAIRS PRESS 1968). *See also* HAROLD SEIDMAN, POLITICS, POSITION AND POWER 88 (Oxford U. Press, 1970). For a similar observation about the Federal Housing Authority, *see* DENNIS D. RILEY & BRYAN E. BROPHY-BAERMANN, BUREAUCRACY AND THE POLICY-MAKING PROCESS 71 (2006) (noting that FHA was initially staffed by "real estate people and mortgage brokers," and the "values and prejudices" of those individuals resulted in a definition of agency success tied to "the number of loans made and the repayment record"— leading it to spend most of its resources on loan guarantees for newly constructed single family owner occupied homes—which resulted in the suburbs).

81 *See* Edward Wyatt, *White House, Consumers in Mind, Offers Online Privacy Guidance,* N.Y. TIMES, Feb. 23, 2012, at B1 ("'The real question is how much influence companies like Google, Microsoft, Yahoo and Facebook will have in their inevitable attempt to water down the rules that are implemented and render them essentially meaningless,' John M. Simpson, privacy project director for Consumer Watchdog, said in response to the administration's plan. 'A concern is that the administration's privacy effort is being run out of the Commerce Department.'").

Reorganization measures that alter an agency's powers can reduce or eliminate the revenue stream to a given committee. This dynamic makes it clear why Congress takes a keen interest in reorganization.[82]

Agency personnel are acutely conscious of these considerations, and they will dismiss out of hand organizational changes that create political difficulties. For example, NOAA resulted from a blue-ribbon commission set up by the Johnson Administration, which recommended the creation of an independent agency focused on the ocean and atmosphere, including bureaus drawn from various civilian departments plus the Coast Guard (which was then part of DOT).[83] After NOAA was created and placed in the Department of Commerce, a senior Commerce administrator contacted the Secretary of Transportation to discuss the possibility of transferring the Coast Guard, in keeping with the recommendations of the blue-ribbon commission. The Secretary of Transportation responded that he was supportive of the move, but in exchange he wanted the Maritime Administration to be transferred from Commerce to DOT. The senior administrator immediately responded "no deal," because he recognized that the swap would rob the Department of Commerce of the political support of the maritime industry, and would alienate a key congressman.[84]

The same considerations also help explain why the reorganization that yielded the Department of Homeland Security was so politically difficult. No committee was inclined to surrender oversight authority unless it got something of at least equal value in return. Even after the politics made reorganization inevitable, individual Congressional committees insisted on retaining regulatory oversight of "their" part of DHS.[85]

These dynamics tend to freeze in place existing allocations of policymaking power and to disable reform proposals that would move authority away from some government agencies and give it to others. In his State of the Union addresses in 2010 and 2011, President Barack Obama proposed to reorganize and simplify various elements of the federal government. This proposal seems certain to run afoul of the constraints discussed here, even in the most harmonious political environment.

In light of the political phenomena described here, it is tempting to simply acquiesce in the inevitability of the existing distribution of agency responsibility. But, major exogenous shocks (such as budget crises) can make substantial reorganizations politically possible (if not inevitable)—at which point the other six factors become more important in determining the allocation of res-

---

82 *See generally*, David C. King, Turf Wars: How Congressional Committees Claim Jurisdiction 2 (1997) ("For individual legislators, the payoffs for winning in turf wars include expanded power, greater prestige, opportunities to make a personal mark on important legislation, and improved services to voters.").

83 *See* http://www.tos.org/oceanography/issues/issue_archive/issue_pdfs/14_2/14.2_merrell_et_al.pdf.

84 Steven Eli Schanes, *Creating NOAA—The Coast Guard,* at http://schanes.wordpress.com/2008/05/24/creating-noaa-the-coast-guard/.

85 *See* Karen Tumulty & Ed O'Keefe, *The Government tends to resist reorganization,* Washington Post, Jan 28, 2011, at A1. ("After the Sept. 11, 2001, attacks, nearly two dozen agencies were melded into the new Department of Homeland Security, to better coordinate the government's resources for handling terrorism and other national emergencies. But the members of Congress overseeing those agencies were loath to give up any authority. That is why DHS gets marching orders from more than 100 congressional committees and subcommittees—a number that has grown in the past seven years, despite the 9/11 Commission's recommendation that those tangled lines of authority be consolidated.").

ponsibilities among the various bureaus, commissions, agencies, and departments that make up the United States government.

Finally, the simple fact there is an ongoing demand for reorganization, even in the absence of major exogenous shocks, means that these issues are constantly in play. No one ever permanently surrenders, and there is no final judgment rule enforced on the disputants.[86]

2. Which Criteria Matter Most?

What mattes most in our list of seven criteria? The problem is straightforward: as Judge Frank Easterbrook has noted, "Lists without metes, bounds, weights, or means of resolving conflicts do not identify necessary or sufficient conditions; they never prescribe concrete results."[87] We believe that three factors matter most in predicting the long-term success of any given agency design: political implications, coherence, and capacity/capability.

In our view, the most important factor is political support, or the lack thereof. An agency is doomed if it lacks a supportive constituency, or if the performance of its duties generates crippling political opposition.[88] More broadly, an agency will not be able to operate effectively if its structure raises serious doubts about its legitimacy or increases the vulnerability to political pressure that the performance of its duties will arouse.

The second most important factor is policy coherence. Greater coherence increases the likelihood the agency will define its aims more clearly, set priorities and design programs appropriately, and develop a well-recognized brand. Coherence makes it easier to recruit qualified staff and build the necessary capacity to implement whatever programs are prioritized. An agency with policy coherence is accordingly better able to establish its credibility with external audiences, including the legislators who will determine funding and otherwise oversee agency operations.

The third most important factor is the agency's capacity/capability to perform its assigned functions. A severe mismatch between the commitments in an agency's policy portfolio and its capacity and capability to deliver results is likely to result in highly visible failures, of which Congress is usually quite unforgiving. Agencies with an inadequate talent pool and frail resources are more likely to generate poorly conceived programs, and less likely to execute tasks effectively. The mismatch between commitments and capacities creates a grim set of options. An agency can engage

---

86 Cf. Wilson, *supra* note 6, at 299-300 ("Public policy making in Europe is like a prize-fight: two contenders, having earned the right to enter the ring, square off against each other for a prescribed number of rounds; when one fighter knocks the other one out, he is declared the winner and the fight is over. Policy-making in the United States is more like a barroom brawl: Anyone can join in, the combatants fight all comers and sometimes change sides, no referee is in charge, and the fights last not for a fixed number of rounds but indefinitely or until everybody drops from exhaustion. To repeat former Secretary of State George Shultz's remark, 'its never over.'").

87 Sears, Roebuck & Co. v. Commissioner, 972 F.2d 858, 863-64 (7th Cir. 1992).

88 *See, e.g.*, Norton Long, *Power and Administration*, 2 Public Administration Rev. 257 (1949) ("There is no more forlorn spectacle in the administrative world than an agency and a program possessed of statutory life, armed with executive orders sustained in the courts, yet stricken with paralysis and deprived of power, an object of contempt to its enemies and of despair to its friends. The lifeblood of administration is power.").

in policy triage, in the hope there will be no disasters in the ignored policy space and that no one cares enough about the tasks that are being ignored to make a fuss. Alternatively, an agency can try to cover all the assigned responsibilities with the predictable consequence of doing few (if any) of them well.

Of course, these factors are not fully independent: an agency is more likely to have the necessary resources (i.e., capability) if it has strong political supporters. An agency that slights or over-emphasizes a portion of its regulatory portfolio is skating on thin ice unless its political supporters are on board with that decision. (If those political supporters are voted out of office, the agency needs to quickly adapt, or there will be significant blow-back to subsequent initiatives, as the FTC learned to its dismay in the late 1970s.) Similarly, without policy coherence, an agency is less likely to attract and maintain political support in the first instance. Finally, there are further levels of complexity imbedded within some of the factors.[89]

Our typology raises other difficult questions. Are all of the factors scalable? Are any of them? Can one compensate for weakness on one factor with strength on another? Does one need a minimum quantum of all of the factors to get off the launching pad? And so on. These issues must await better data and require further research.

III. Application of Our Analysis to the FTC

We use the FTC as a case study because the Commission's experience provides an especially rich context in which to apply the criteria we have described above. Established in 1914, the FTC is the oldest and most closely studied independent regulatory commission in the federal government.[90] The FTC has inspired an immense body of scholarship and figured prominently in blue ribbon reports that examine the organization of government. No public regulatory body (much less an agency with roughly 1300 employees and a budget of under $300 million today) has elicited comparable scrutiny.

1. The FTC as a Multi-Purpose Agency

In the FTC's near-century of experience provides superb material to assess the wisdom of combining variations functions in a single government agency. Two closely-related characteristics of the

89 For example, we have identified capacity as a factor. Capacity is obviously affected by the allocated budget, but does it make a difference if the agency is funded with user fees v. dedicated taxes v. general appropriations? To what extent does the mix of funding among these choices reflect the impact of other factors—most importantly, political support?

90 The Interstate Commerce Commission, established in 1887, was the first independent federal regulatory agency. Its sole surviving component today is the Surface Transportation Board, whose chief function is to regulate tariffs and other terms of surface by railroads.

FTC's history make it an ideal test bed for our inquiry. The first is the breadth of the agency's charter. The FTC is a diversified policy conglomerate. It enforces the federal antitrust laws, performs economic research, publishes studies, and holds a broad consumer mandate that reaches advertising, non-bank financial services, marketing practices, product labeling, and privacy. Among other tasks, it is the agency that reviews mergers in the petroleum industry, enforces the Do-Not-Call telemarketing rule, defines energy labeling requirements for television sets, polices debt collection practices, reports on how media and entertainment companies disclose content unsuited for children, and prosecutes failures by companies to safeguard confidential data about their customers.

The second notable aspect of the Commission's history is the malleability of its policy-making portfolio. In 1914 Congress intended the Commission to focus on competition policy—to advance the development of antitrust legal norms through administrative adjudication, consultation with the federal courts and the Department of Justice, and through the publication of studies for Congress and other public bodies. The boundaries of the original remit have shifted dramatically over time. In some instances, the FTC absorbed new functions by accident.[91] The Commission became the nation's advertising and marketing practices regulator as an unintended consequence of its work to address complaints by firms that their rivals had gained an undue competitive advantage through dishonest sales tactics. In other instances the FTC obtained new duties because Congress deliberately added new functions by measures such as credit practices legislation enacted in the 1960s.

Additions of authority have been pronounced in periods, such as the early- to mid-1970s, when Congress enacted numerous extensions of the FTC's duties. The Commission's history features divestitures as well as acquisitions. In some cases, the Commission in effected incubated regulatory functions that Congress later chose to spin-off and assign to new, stand-alone regulatory institutions.[92] For example, this process led to the establishment of the Securities and Exchange Commission in the 1930s. These adjustments appear to have reflected a legislative judgment that the regulatory functions in question were so substantial that they warranted implementation by agencies dedicated to those activities alone. On other occasions Congress has divested or restricted FTC functions out of anger. Political backlash to FTC initiatives led Congress to enact curbs in the 1920s on the agency's authority involving agriculture and to adopt restrictions in 1980 upon the Commission's work concerning insurance and advertising directed toward children.[93]

2. The Evaluative Criteria Applied to the FTC

We organize our discussion around the seven factors identified in Part III. We consider to which the FTC's combination of functions is consistent with each criterion, and we use examples from FTC experience to illustrate our assessment.

---

91 *See supra* note 17 and accompanying text.

92 This history is recounted in Marc Winerman, *The FTC at Ninety: History Through Headlines*, 72 ANTITRUST L.J. 871, 880 n. 44 (2005).

93 On the limitations imposed in the 1920s and in 1980, *see* William E. Kovacic, *The Federal Trade Commission and Congressional Oversight of Antitrust Enforcement*, 17 TULSA L.J. 587, 623-25, 664-67 (1982).

2.1. Policy Coherence: Are the Functions Related and Consistent?

In principle, the combination of competition and consumer protection functions within the FTC is a coherent policy design. The two areas exhibit strong conceptual policy complementarities, and the agency's implementation of its competition and consumer protection powers achieves substantial policy consistency: in performing its responsibilities in both policy domains, the agency generally seeks to improve consumer well-being. As we discuss below, the interaction of the two policy areas can create tension, as each discipline can display a different view about how best to advance consumer interests. The attainment of the best policy outcome sometimes will require balancing between competing perspectives.

a. Relatedness: Significant Policy Complementarities

Competition policy and consumer protection policy have important complementarities. They share significant intellectual foundations in the economics of information and consumer behavior.[94] In general terms, antitrust seeks to improve performance on the supply side—to sustain the competitive pressures that drive firms to offer best possible array of goods and services. Antitrust agencies pursue this end by prosecuting private anticompetitive behavior (such as supplier cartels) and opposing public policies that restrict entry or expansion for the sake of protecting the interests of incumbent firms. Consumer protection seeks to improve the choice process on the demand-side. This principally involves programs to challenge deception and fraud, a consumer protection program helps ensure that sellers provide truthful information, which enables consumers to purchase goods or services that best satisfy their preferences. Transactions induced by deception and outright fraud do not satisfy the necessary conditions for making consumer sovereignty the force that determines what the economy will produce. A consumer protection also can enhance the quality of consumer decision making by ensuring that product and service disclosures, such as information required by legal mandates, are comprehensible to consumers.[95]

The complementarities between competition policy and consumer protection policy, as well as possibilities for substitution between them, here provide at least a theoretical basis for supposing that a competition agency with consumer protection responsibilities will realize synergies between the two fields and improve the quality of public policy. A unity of functions might put an agency in a better position to identify the source of market failures more accurately and proscribe superior cures that involve an optimal mix of regulatory strategies.[96] Many of the world's 120 competition agencies perform consumer protection functions, such as policing deceptive advertising.[97] We

94 *See* Timothy J. Muris, The Interface of Competition and Consumer Protection, Fordham Corp. Law Institute, 29th Annual Conference on International Antitrust Law and Policy (Oct. 31, 2002), at http://www.ftc.gov/speeches/muris/021031fordham.pdf.

95 James M. Lacko & Janis K. Pappalardo, Improving Consumer Mortgage Disclosures: An Empirical Assessment of Current and Prototype Disclosure Forms, Federal Trade Commission, Bureau of Economics (June 2007), at http://www.ftc.gov/os/2007/06/P025505MortgageDisclosureReport.pdf.

96 *See* Richard Craswell, *Tying Requirements in Competitive Markets: The Consumer Protection Issues*, 62 Boston University L. Rev. 661 (1982) (analyzing tying as a consumer protection problem).

97 *See supra* note 5 and accompanying text.

make no claim that the existing dual-function agencies ordinarily attain the theoretical synergies in practice, or that the combination of functions affords them superior insight into the causes of economic problems. In principle, the presence of strong policy complementarities indicates that the integration of these functions within a single agency has potential to improve policy making.

The presence of strong policy complementarities suggests a general principle that would apply in jurisdictions that do not choose to bundle complementary functions into the same agency. If policy complementarities are strong and policy responsibilities are assigned to single-function agencies, there should be close cooperation between the single-function agencies. In other words, if integration by ownership does not occur, close integration by inter-agency contract is desirable. Close cooperation by a single-function antitrust agency and a single-function consumer protection agency likely will yield better policy results than having the two institutions operate without regard to the other's activities.

b. Consistency: Common Consumer Orientation

As the discussion above suggests, competition and consumer protection share a common objective or promoting consumer well-being. This common objective imparts a substantial degree of consistency to policies adopted in the two domains. We can contrast this condition with other policies that might be considered to be related but not consistent. Antitrust law and trade restrictions can be considered to be complimentary to the extent that both regimes seek to prevent market distortions that arise when firms make certain sales below cost. The goals of the two regimes, however, are dissimilar. In antitrust law, the purpose of restrictions on predatory pricing is to preclude behavior that results in the exclusion of firms whose continued presence in the market would have driven suppliers to engage in activities (such as cost reduction and innovation) that serve consumer interests. An important aim of the anti-dumping regime, reflected in its operational standards, is the protection of domestic firms and the preservation of jobs they provide, even at the expense of purchasers of the products such firms manufacture.

Notwithstanding their complementarities, it also is possible to view competition policy and consumer protection policy as substitutes. As this simple example illustrates, competition can serve as a valuable form of consumer protection. We can imagine a hypothetical market in which the government can choose one of two approaches to encourage performance that best satisfies consumer preferences. One approach is to have a single firm serve the entire market, with the monopolist supplier being subject to comprehensive oversight with respect to pricing and quality. Even with extensive regulatory oversight, the monopolist may have relatively weak incentives to identify and satisfy consumer tastes, especially by introducing new products and services. A second approach is to encourage rivalry among suppliers to provide the best range of alternatives. The latter approach also involves greater reliance on market forces to counteract fraud and other forms of overreaching by suppliers. The pro-competition policy contemplated here includes efforts to preclude supplier collusion that would restrict the flow of truthful product information to consumers or would impede the work of expert intermediaries to give consumers advice about how to select among product options.

In a number of instances, the solution set for policy making will include a range of alternatives that include more or less relative emphasis on these two models. In most instances, the lawyers who practice in the fields of antitrust or consumer protection will be inclined to favor one model or the other, depending upon their training and experience. Specialists in one field rarely have extensive familiarity with the other. This form of specialization gives the two practice areas distinctive cultures, each with different preferences for the form of government intervention. Most antitrust lawyers are likely to have relatively greater confidence in the capacity of competition and related market-oriented processes to provide a desired level of consumer protection. By contrast, the consumer protection lawyer may less trusting of market processes and more inclined to perceive consumers as vulnerable and prone to supplier manipulation. This orientation will incline a consumer protection attorney to favor policies that more directly control business practices—for example, by setting greater limits upon the content of advertising. This orientation can be reinforced by an attorney's extensive experience in dealing with serious fraud. A heavy dose of cases involving products that are claimed to cure cancer, yield immense wealth, or secure lasting beauty can engender an underlying suspicion of the market system. Like an experienced homicide detective who fears that all of humankind is dangerously prone to violent crime, an experienced consumer protection attorney may come to think that most advertising is a form of falsehood.

These differences in culture and perspective between the two disciplines can be important for the operation of the regulatory process even within an agency that has both competition and consumer protection duties. The integration of perspectives to achieve the best policy result (for example, by designing an anti-fraud program that properly accounts for the role of advertising in promoting competition that serves consumer interests) will not occur automatically. Within the FTC, the Bureau of Economics is a major source of agency's policy integration. BE functions as an independent unit, and it supports the agency's competition and consumer protection groups. Among other contributions, BE has helped the agency account for the economics literature concerning the collection, analysis, and transmission of information and has highlighted its implications for the behavior of individual firms and groups of firms. This has improved the agency's understanding of how consumers make choices among the array of products and services available to them.[98] The FTC's experience shows that a dual function agency will need to take conscious steps to achieve effective integration and resolve tensions that can arise concerning the correct mix of regulatory measures.

c. Examples from FTC Experience

The FTC's experience with the health care, health-related advertising issues, and data protection provides illuminates the synergies and tensions that can arise between competition and consumer protection. In the 1970s, the Commission introduced pioneering programs to liberalize the provision of health care services and products.[99] Before the 1970s, regulatory policy at the federal and state levels tended to establish severe restrictions on advertising by physicians and strong limits on the ability of consumers to seek alternative suppliers for health care products such as eyeglasses.

To address these restrictions, the FTC used a mix of litigation, rulemaking, research, public consultations, and advocacy. The Commission initiated a series of cases that struck down absolute restric-

---

98 The literature on information economics provides the principal basis for the category of research now known as behavioral economics. *See* THE LAW AND ECONOMICS OF IRRATIONAL BEHAVIOR (Francesco Parisi & Vernon Smith eds., Stanford University Press 2005).

99 *See* William E. Kovacic, *Measuring What Matters: The Federal Trade Commission and Investments in Competition Policy Research and Development*, 72 ANTITRUST L.J. 861 (2005) (discussing development of FTC health care program).

tions on physician advertising and precluded medical societies from forbidding the revelation of truthful information. The agency also adopted a trade regulation rule (Eyeglasses I) that, among other measures, required optometrists to give a copy of eyewear prescriptions to their patients. The rule originated within the FTC's Bureau of Consumer Protection, and the agency's Bureau of Economics and Bureau of Competition played major roles in its design. Eyeglasses I fostered a dramatic increase in competition among eyewear manufacturers and retailers. Over the past decade, the FTC has used experience with the eyeglasses rule to implement legislation mandating steps to liberalize the sale of contact lenses. The agency also has filed an extensive series of comments with state legislatures to address existing or proposed adjustments to controls on the sale of health care services and products. To identify commercial trends and promote debate about its programs, the Commission also has held public consultations and published reports.

These elements of the FTC's health care program have built upon a generally effective collaboration among the agency's different disciplines. A major source of policy integration has been the Bureau of Economics, whose research and analysis have played a crucial role in assessing the asserted quality control justifications for the regulatory status quo. A second important force for integration has been the agency-wide Office of Policy Planning and the Policy Studies group of the Office of the General Counsel. Relatively few internal tensions have arisen in the formulation of this program, perhaps because the Commission ordinarily has been in the position of attacking fairly categorical competitive restraints that bear no plausible relationship to the quality control rationales that are said to justify limitations on advertising or marketing. Some of the agency's more recent initiatives, such as the contact lens matters, have involved practices with more subtle and complex quality control concerns. The Commission has analyzed these issues with care, a reflection of the Commission's awareness that a failure to account for legitimate quality control considerations could cause serious consumer injury and endanger the agency's entire program in this field.

An initiative with more mixed results and greater internal tension is the FTC's treatment of health-related advertising claims. For many years, public policy developed by the FTC and federal health agencies such as the Food and Drug Administration displayed an acute suspicion of food advertisements that attributed beneficial health effects to the consumption of a product. Federal policy tended to frown upon producer efforts to link product attributes to a reduction in the risk of disease. Research by the FTC's Bureau of Economics in the 1980s and 1990s called this approach into question. The FTC's economists raised the possibility that a more liberal approach would provide consumers with valuable nutritional information and promote product innovations (such as the introduction of higher fiber content into breakfast cereals) with generally positive health effects. The FTC has relied upon this line of research to loosen its own controls upon health claims and to advocate similar adjustments by the FDA.[100]

These initiatives have inspired considerable tension within the FTC and the larger policy making community. A task force consisting of the FTC, the FDA, the Department of Agriculture, and the Department of Health and Human Services recently released proposed guidelines for food advertising directed toward children. The guidelines are cast as voluntary measures, although the

100 *See* Pauline M. Ippolito, *What Can We Learn from Food Advertising Policy Over the Last 25 years?*, 12 George Mason L. Rev. 939 (2004).

agencies suggest that the industry's failure to embrace them or to take similar steps could result in additional government intervention. For the most part, the proposed guidelines reflect the longstanding tradition of suspicion that anchored public policy before the Bureau of Economics research of the 1980s and 1990s. A similar effort to toughen limits on nutritional advertising is evident in settlements that resolve recent FTC advertising cases. The Commission's settlements require producers to use more elaborate scientific testing to substantiate health-related claims. These measures reflect, at least implicitly, a doubtful view of the market-oriented prescriptions that came out of the Bureau of Economics studies of the 1980s and 1990s.

Issues related to data protection and information privacy provide another context in which debates have arisen about what mix of competition and consumer protection initiatives will best serve consumer interests. In December 2010 and March 2012, the FTC released reports with proposals that firms to strengthen data security safeguards and increase the ability of consumers to control the collection and use about their purchasing and searches on the internet.[101] The reports recommended consideration of a 'Do-Not-Track' mechanism that would enable a consumer to instruct firms not to maintain records of the consumer's online activity. The FTC's reports revealed little evident input from the Commission's competition or economics operating bureaus.

2.2. Credibility: Does the Combination Create a Recognizable and Respected Brand?

The FTC has strived to establish general recognition that it is the principal federal agency for safeguarding consumer interests. This is common element of branding by agencies with a dual competition and consumer protection mandate. The United Kingdom's Office of Fair Trading (OFT), which has largely the same remit as the FTC, states its purpose as "making markets work well for consumers."[102] This short and statement of purpose is one of many ways that similarly situated agencies identify themselves with the promotion of consumer well-being.

In this aim, the Commission appears to have been generally successful. Its public reputation and its stature within Congress largely derive from its consumer protection work, especially highly visible initiatives such as the Do Not Call program.[103] There is only modest awareness of the Commission's role as a competition policy institution, and perhaps still weaker understanding of how the agency's combination of functions informs its choice and execution of programs. Thus, the agency is largely associated with consumer protection issues. The breadth of the agency's mandate can create unwanted expectations that the agency is the appropriate solution for all difficult economic problems that affect consumers.

---

101 *See supra* note 20 and accompanying text.

102 This phrase appears on the OFT's website and on the agency's promotional materials. The OFT website is www.oft.gov.uk.

103 On the Do Not Call Rule and its political implications for the FTC, *see* Sidney M. Milkis, *The Federal Trade Commission and Consumer Protection: Regulatory Change and Administrative Pragmatism*, 72 Antitrust L.J. 911 (2005).

a. Branding a Policy Conglomerate

As a policy conglomerate, the FTC faces the same difficulties that confront many diversified enterprises: How does the entity create a brand that internal observers (agency managers and staff) and external constituencies (e.g., legislators, businesses, and consumers) recognize and respect? The FTC's purpose is not evident from its name. In the modern world, a "federal trade commission" evokes associations with agencies that scrutinize imports and penalize foreign firms that sell goods below cost in the United States. When FTC employees return from overseas travel and present their official passports to U.S. immigration officers, they are to be asked if they made progress in trade negotiations with foreign governments. Over the years, the FTC has used various phrases to identify its purpose. In general, most of the agency's branding activities have sought to identify the Commission with the promotion of consumer interests.[104] Most of this branding effort takes place in official reports and speeches by top agency leadership, particularly the FTC Chair.

Within the FTC, administrative and professional staff members appear to share a general sense of purpose. If asked to respond to a survey, most would say that the agency seeks to protect consumer well-being. At the same time, we doubt that many could explain how the two principle mandates of the agency combine to fulfill that purpose. In 2008, the FTC performed a self-study and conducted internal and external interviews to identify paths for improvement.[105] Agency staff members ordinarily define the agency's brand and purpose in terms of the projects of their own operating units. It is relatively unusual to find personnel in the Bureau of Competition or Bureau of Consumer Protection who could identify five major pending initiatives of the other Bureau.

This raises a basic question about agency organization: is a dual purpose competition and consumer protection agency more likely to reinforce awareness of its dual, complementary nature among its own personnel and increase external understanding of its character if it takes formal steps to integrate these functions internally. We know of a single agency—the OFT—that has undertaken internal organizational reforms to create integrated operating units (both policy offices and teams of case handlers) that combine the disciplines of competition and consumer protection. The OFT adopted these reforms within the past decade, and it is difficult to tell how this has affected internal and external perceptions of the agency's brand and purpose. It is clear that efforts by OFT leadership to emphasize the conceptual and organizational fusion of the two disciplines have made internal and external constituencies increasingly aware of the combination of functions.

In testimony and speeches, FTC leaders have emphasized the conceptual links between competition and consumer protection, but the Commission has not undertaken the ambitious internal restructuring carried out by the OFT. The FTC has relied on much looser forms of integration to achieve a synthesis of competition and consumer protection policy internally and enhance its external branding efforts. There is relatively little routine collaboration between the Bureau of Competition and Bureau of Consumer Protection. The agency relies mainly on the agency's commissioners, the Bureau of Economics, the Office of Policy Planning, and the General Counsel's office of policy stu-

104 The Commission underscores its connection to consumers in various documents, and promotional materials. *See, e.g.*, Federal Trade Commission, The FTC in 2008: A Force for Consumers and Competition (Mar. 2008) (annual report).

105 William E. Kovacic, The Federal Trade Commission at 100: Into Our 2nd Century (Jan. 2009), at http://www.ftc.gov/ftc.workshops/ftc100/docs/ftc100rpt.

dies to see that both perspectives inform the treatment of problems facing the agency. An attempt to create dual purpose operating groups from the existing Bureaus of Competition and Consumer Protection will be prohibitively expensive in the eyes of most FTC chairs. Internal resistance will be ferocious and durable—good reasons for a chair to use precious time (a tenure of three or four years) and energy on other matters. Yet there are milder alternatives worth exploring. These include greater reliance on inter-bureau task forces and a routine program of secondments that assign personnel from one unit to work in another.

The desire to create broad awareness of an agency as a pro-consumer agency can affect, and distort, the agency's allocation of resources. As noted above, consumer protection initiatives generally have the greatest impact on consumer perceptions. The Do Not Call registry, cases that return monetary redress to victims of fraud, and educational materials on ID theft are but some of the many FTC initiatives that provide services which consumers readily understand. Antitrust matters (particularly matters involving widely known providers of consumer goods and services) sometimes create broad public awareness. Nonetheless, the typical antitrust case (such as a challenge to a merger involving suppliers of inputs to the production of industrial goods) has less ability than the typical consumer protection case to raise public awareness of the agency. To this one can add the generally accurate proposition that what might be called routine consumer protection cases (e.g., a case against fraud) are less expensive to prepare than routine antitrust cases.

A dual purpose agency that sees a greater return to its reputation (and stronger approval by its legislature) may choose to invest more resources in consumer protection, even though the investment of the same resources in an antitrust case would contribute more to economic performance. The FTC now spends about 55 percent of its resources on consumer protection, and the balance on competition. As a rough matter, the greatest legislative pressures in recent years have demanded more attention to consumer protection matters involving financial services and privacy. Competition issues (notably, involving prices for petroleum products) receive significant congressional attention, as well, but the focus of concern has been on consumer protection matters. This also creates strong incentives for a dual-purpose agency to shift resources toward the consumer protection agenda. Thus, for dual-purpose agencies it is worth examining their distribution of resources over time to determine whether different responsibilities are receiving suitable emphasis.

b. Branding and the Assignment of Regulatory Tasks

The assignment and performance of regulatory tasks can either reinforce or undermine the creation of a strong and favorable consumer-oriented brand. The FTC's deepest impact on consumer perceptions has come through its consumer protection activities. Like the FTC, most dual-function agencies derive the highest levels of public recognition from interventions dealing with consumer goods and services. Competition matters generally do not diminish recognition of the agency's consumer orientation, but they rarely reinforce it. Compared to consumer protection, competition policy activity tends to have a neutral impact on the FTC brand.

The consumer protection portfolio is not always an unmixed blessing for branding purposes. Under a large umbrella of consumer protection, a dual purpose agency is likely to find specific duties that blur or damage its image. In a number of instances, the FTC has sought to off load responsibilities that undermined its brand. One of these deals with cigarettes. The FTC was the first federal agency to propose regulatory action on cigarettes after the issuance of the Surgeon General's report on the hazards of smoking in 1964.[106] The FTC proposed a trade regulation rule that would have required tobacco companies to place health warnings on cigarette packages. Congress eventually adopted legislation mandating such labeling, but it assigned responsibility for testing tar and nicotine levels in cigarettes to the FTC—even though the agency had no particular expertise in testing, or in assessing the health risks of different levels of tar and nicotine.

For roughly twenty years, the FTC dutifully ran a "smoking laboratory," using machines that measured the tar and nicotine content of cigarettes smoked using a specified method. In 1987, the FTC ceased conducting the tests after concluding that it had no comparative advantage in running a testing laboratory. The FTC outsourced the work to an independent testing laboratory under the agency's supervision.[107] This mitigated but did not solve the FTC's problems. Health researchers identified that testing regime—which continued to be called "the FTC method"—did not account for how smokers adjusted their behavior. Smokers offset the lower tar and nicotine levels by smoking more cigarettes and inhaling more deeply. Aware of the deficiencies of the testing regimen and the harm to the agency's image from being associated with the tests, the FTC asked Congress to assign all responsibility for the testing program and the reporting of results to one of the federal departments responsible for health and science.[108]

The FTC also has sought to wave off the addition of new functions that might blur its brand or so divert resources that the enhancement of well-recognized product lines suffers. One contentious issue during the debates over the Dodd-Frank Wall Street Reform and Consumer Protection Act was the treatment of credit transactions carried out in connection with the purchase of a motor vehicle. The automobile dealers fought vigorously, and successfully, to keep these transactions outside the supervision of the new Consumer Financial Protection Bureau. However, they did not escape new regulatory oversight completely. Congress insisted that the new financial services framework place motor vehicle transactions under the oversight of some federal agency. Scanning the landscape of possibilities, Congress gazed at the FTC.[109] Fearing that it would receive a major new mandate without a commensurate increase in funds to carry it out, the Commission argued against receiving the new authority. These pleas were unavailing, as was the request for more funds. This experience highlighted a broader phenomenon that occurs as Congress assigns new duties to an agency with some experience in the general policy domain: it seldom provides appropriations to carry out the new commands. The Commission has competence in credit practices matters going back to the 1960s. Adapting this expertise to address automobile sales is manageable in concept, but the resource demands of the new oversight role

106 Trade Regulation Rule for the Prevention of Unfair or Deceptive Advertising and Labeling of Cigarettes in Relation to the Health Hazards of Smoking, 29 Fed Reg. 8324 (1964). The FTC's cigarette rule was drafted by Richard Posner, then an attorney advisor at the FTC.

107 The independent testing laboratory was the Tobacco Institute Testing Laboratory. On the history of the FTC's involvement in testing cigarettes for tar, nicotine, and carbon monoxide, see Prepared Statement of the Federal Trade Commission on Cigarette Tar and Nicotine Testing Before the House Commerce Subcommittee on Transportation, Tourism, and Hazardous Materials, United States House of Representatives (May 7, 1987).

108 Prepared Statement of the Federal Trade Commission Concerning Tobacco Advertising Before the Committee on Commerce, Science, and Transportation, United States Senate (Nov. 13, 2007), at http://www.ftc.gov/os/testimony/PO64508tobacco.pdf.

109 The FTC's responsibilities for protecting consumers in the sale and leasing of automobiles are described at 78 Fed. Reg. 14014 (Mar. 15, 2011).

could be daunting. With no additional funding, the only way to pay for the new program is to withdraw support internally from the fulfillment of other legislative commands

i. Portfolio Adjustments, Branding, and Planning

The addition or subtraction of functions has important implications for the definition of the agency's aims and its branding activities. As functions expand or contract, the agency must focus on how the adjustments will influence perceptions inside and outside the agency about what it does.

The need for greater attention to planning, priority setting, and brand positioning is perhaps greatest when an agency gains functions, or when possibilities for addition emerge. Augmentations can greatly affect the allocation of resources and the mix of programs the agency pursues. Will an expansion of existing activity to encompass an emerging area of concern dramatically alter the agency's character?

Over the past decade, privacy and data protection have ascended as FTC priorities. As the FTC's privacy program (now overseen in BCP's Division of Privacy and Identify Protection) grows, several paths are possible. One is a significant redirection of resources that inevitably has the effect of reorienting the mix of policy outputs and skewing the overall allocation of funds more heavily toward the consumer protection side of the FTC's house. If the FTC moved from a 55/45 split between consumer protection and competition to something like a 65/35 or 70/30 distribution, would the wisdom of retaining a competition competence within the FTC, rather than moving the function entirely to the Antitrust Division of the Justice Department, come into question? Would the growth of the agency's privacy role give rise to suggestions that Congress spin the unit off as a stand-alone data protection body—a move that would put the U.S. national data protection system on the same institutional footing used by most other jurisdictions? To answer these and other questions, a multi-function agency must have a mechanism for considering how dramatic and more subtle changes in its authority affect its ability to define its brand clearly and coherently.

2.3. Capacity and Capability

As described earlier, capacity refers to the pool of knowledge and resources that the agency can bring to bear, and capability refers to the range of policy levers and quality of the resulting decisions.

Throughout its history, the FTC has struggled to see that the commitments entailed by its multifaceted mandate do not outrun its capacity to deliver good policy results. Through most of its history, the Commission has suffered from a tendency to initiate ambitious programs without adequate attention to the basic prerequisites of effective implementation. These flaws played a major part in placing the agency in peril in the late 1970s and early 1980s.[110] The agency's extraordinary combination of competition and consumer protection measures elicited harsh political backlash and enmeshed the Commission in destructive turmoil with Congress. Although some FTC initiatives

110 *See* Kovacic, *supra note* 93, at 664-71.

from this period (such as the Eyeglasses I rule and the beginnings of the antitrust health care program) succeeded splendidly, many litigation and rulemaking proceedings foundered in the courts.

The FTC's performance on this score has improved greatly over the past 30 years. The agency has learned the hard way to ask basic questions about each new undertaking: How much will it cost? Who will do it? How long will it take? What do we expect to accomplish? What are the doctrinal, political, and management risks? How will we know if it's working? The bruising experiences of the late 1970s and early 1980s inspired stronger attention to planning and program management. The matching of the FTC's commitments to capabilities remains a massive challenge for the institution.

a. Chronic Underfunding of Mandates

Agencies seldom will receive the resources needed to fulfill all the regulatory commands assigned to them. This is the case of the modern FTC. In many instances, such as the automobile credit sales provision of Dodd Frank, Congress assigns major new responsibilities without providing resources to carry them out. The legislative process that generates new substantive legislation is detached from the process that appropriates funds. Thus, Congress rarely considers the resource implications of requirements that the agency enforce new laws, issue new rules, or prepare reports.

Agencies respond to these imperatives in one of two ways, both of which undermine agency effectiveness. The first is to undertake programs that exceed the agency's ability to execute them effectively. The agency will be tempted to cut corners by weakening internal quality control measures, understaffing ambitious projects, or assigning difficult litigation or rulemaking tasks to relatively inexperienced personnel. Even though senior personnel may recognize how much resource constraints limit agency capacity, they may still acquiesce in Congressional demands for the initiation of new projects. A short-term political appointee may regard the initiation of a new measure as a credit-claiming event and may see the risk that an improvidently conceived project may fail as a cost that will be borne by future agency leaders and will not be attributed fully, or at all, to the appointee who originated it. Without an effective feedback mechanism that forces the incumbent appointee to internalize such costs, it is easy to begin such projects, even when they outrun the agency's capacity.

A second mechanism is to fund new projects adequately by a relatively silent form of triage. This consists of draining resources away from other programs ostensibly designed to implement congressionally imposed duties. To support new programs in areas such as privacy, data protection, and mortgage lending fraud, the FTC over time has quietly abandoned other programs that used to be mainstays of enforcement. To some extent this is done with at least the implicit approval of Congress. Through official budget requests and oversight hearings, Congress is at least generally aware of how the Commission is spending its money. It can detect that some areas of policy responsibility seem to be inactive. Congress can observe, for example, that the FTC has brought two Robinson-Patman Act price discrimination cases in the past 23 years.[111] This reliably indicates diminished attention to a statute whose enforcement in the 1960s yielded hundreds of cases. For the most part, the FTC has constructed or retooled major programs involving privacy, financial

111 William E. Kovacic, *The Modern Evolution of U.S. Competition Policy Enforcement Norm*, 71 Antitrust L.J. 377, 410-15 (discussing patterns of federal government enforcement of the Robinson-Patman Act).

services, mergers, horizontal restraints, and single firm conduct by severely reducing outlays for the enforcement of the Robinson-Patman Act and consumer protection statutes dealing with fur and textile labeling.

Even if one accepts the notion that Congress has acquiesced in this repositioning, there is still an unsettling lack of accountability and transparency in this pattern. Nominal legal commands remain in place, yet the agency walks away from them without the type of public deliberation and debate that arguably ought to precede an important redirection of policy. Quiet abandonment and repositioning allow Congress and the agency to maintain an outward commitment to statutes whose implementing programs are hollow due to a lack of resources. A more honest approach would be to consider repeal of unenforced laws or to confront the commitments vs. resources issue more directly in discussions about new legislation. The agency also knows that if, for some reason, a seemingly dormant and neglected policy area comes to life, legislators will chastise it for not sustaining an adequate presence in the area. It is not honorable to make policy by crossing one's fingers and hoping that certain contingencies do not come to pass.

b. The Sirens of Expansive Authority

The FTC's history features a painful tendency to over-promise and under-deliver. One important cause of the mismatch between promises and performance is the exaggerated sense of capacity that can come from the broad grants of authority that a multi-function agency often possesses. As the agency's powers expand, and Congress urges the agency to use new authority aggressively, the Commission's leadership and professional staff sometimes have perceived that the agency has the ability and the obligation to solve all economic problems that come to its attention. In the 1970s, Congress dramatically enhanced the scope and power of the FTC's powers.[112] In addition, Supreme Court decisions early in the decade interpreted the Commission's existing powers broadly. Some FTC officials have found the possibilities inherent in these developments to be enervating and willingly grasped new opportunities to exercise them. Others were more cautious, but they felt a duty to use the agency's elastic mandates to address various forms of business behavior, even though the behavior takes place at or beyond the boundary of the agency's statutes.

In either case, the zone of what the agency and its leadership perceive to be appropriate forms of and occasions for intervention will tend to expand as Congress adds regulatory tools to its portfolio. This is especially true if the agency's mandates tend to be far-reaching and relatively open-ended. This arguably is the case of the FTC, whose foundational statute permits the agency to condemn "unfair or deceptive acts or practices" and to proscribe "unfair methods of competition." Over time, agency staff has tended to read these statutes in increasingly expansive ways. For example, in the 1970s, the FTC undertook an exceptionally ambitious program of competition and consumer protection matters. Some initiatives produced successful outcomes, but many ambitious endeavors failed in ways that caused long-lived harm to the Commission's reputation and endangered various areas of the FTC's mandate.[113]

---

112 Kovacic, *supra note* 93, at 631-42 (discussing congressional expansion of FTC powers from 1970 to 1976).

113 This history is recounted in William E. Kovacic, *Congress and the Federal Trade Commission*, 57 ANTITRUST L.J. 517 (1989).

The presence of seemingly expansive authority also makes the Commission an attractive congressional choice to solve any urgent economic problem that may emerge. If gasoline prices increase sharply in the wake of a natural disaster, Congress is likely to turn to the FTC, whose charter enables it to attack "unfair methods of competition" and "unfair or deceptive acts or practices,"[114] and demand that the agency use these broad grants of authority to do something about the problem. Any jarring dislocation in the economy—a price surge in a one sector, or a supply shortage in another—becomes fair game for legislators to demand that the FTC bring its seeming open-ended powers to bear upon the problem.[115] In December 2007, Congress enacted legislation to prohibit the manipulation of petroleum markets and gave the FTC authority to promulgate rules to enforce the measure.[116] In 2009 the FTC adopted an implementing regulation that Congress will call for the agency to enforce vigorously whenever gasoline prices rise significantly.[117] This measure has little prospect of addressing the two factors that most account for the prices of petroleum products: the supply of crude oil and the consumption demand of American consumers and business.

c. Recruiting and Retaining Human Capital

Whether an agency performs one function or many, its performance depends on whether it has the human resources to accomplish its assigned tasks. The decision to add a new area of policy responsibility requires an internal assessment of whether the institution has the right skills to perform the function. The FTC's expansion of efforts involving data security and privacy has led to an increase in personnel with forensic skills in computer technology, mobile telephony, and internet operations. To support the work of these professionals, the agency also has made major investments in internal laboratories and other investigative resources to deal with online fraud. Likewise, the FTC's initiatives to work more actively at the intersection between antitrust law and patent law have led to the hiring of patent attorneys to serve in the Bureau of Competition.

The failure to maintain a good fit between program demands and personnel capabilities has crippled FTC programs on a number of occasions in the past. From 1970 through the middle of the decade, the Commission undertook an ambitious agenda of programs.[118] On the competition side, the FTC initiated a broad program to challenge monopolization and shared monopolization in industries such as breakfast cereal, bread, petroleum, photocopying, and pharmaceuticals. The FTC also began challenge, described above, to restrictions on advertising imposed by the American Medical Association. The agency also attacked distribution practices in the soft drink sector and sought to forbid the parallel, non-collusive adoption of certain pricing and marketing practices by competitors.

---

114 15 U.S.C. Section 45.

115 These measures are described in William E. Kovacic, *Standard Oil Co. v. United States* and Its Influence on the Conception of Competition Policy, 11 Competition Law Journal 89 (2012).

116 This authority was created in Title VIII of the Energy Independence and Security Act of 2007, 42 U.S.C. §§ 17301-17305.

117 Federal Trade Commission, Prohibitions on Market Manipulation: Final Rule, 74 Fed. Reg. 40686 (Aug. 12, 2009), codified at 16 Code of Federal Regulations 317.

118 Kovacic, *supra* note 93, at 643-51.

The agency's consumer protection work during the 1970s was no less ambitious and perhaps more expansive. The FTC initiated over fifteen rulemaking proceedings. Some of these measures sought to modify doctrines with universal application in the economy, such as the holder in due course rule. Others attempted to impose requirements governing the provision of specific types of goods or services, including funerals, used cars, vocational schools, eyeglasses, dietary supplements, hearing aids, and advertising directed toward children.

The FTC's economic research program also pursued far-reaching objectives in the 1970s. The agency established a line-of-business reporting program that compelled a large number of enterprises to provide detailed information about their sales and profits in specific product groups. The Commission also undertook high profile studies involving specific sectors, including the business of insurance.

This impressive list of projects pressed against the weakest joints of the Commission's human capital infrastructure. The agency paid little attention to the fit between these ambitious measures, many of which involved novel legal theories and complex facts, and the FTC's capacity to execute them skillfully. FTC leadership blithely added new bet-your-agency initiatives to Commission's agenda without a careful examination of the human capital needed to handle difficult matters successfully. Nor did the agency anticipate what kinds of talent the affected industries would muster in opposition. Many of the FTC's antitrust cases and consumer protection rulemakings sought powerful remedies to transform the structure and behavior of the sectors in question. With massive commercial interests at stake, companies hired the best of the defense bar and the economic consultancies to represent them. In too many instances, the FTC sent small and relatively inexperienced teams to face legions of highly capable opposing counsel.

2.4. Resilience: Is the Existing Assignment of Functions Adaptable and Sustainable?

The FTC's mix of competition and consumer protection has proven to be adaptable and resilient. As described earlier, the agency's portfolio has changed substantially over time. Sometimes through its own repositioning and sometimes with congressional approval, the agency has entered new policy terrain. In the jargon of computer technology, the Commission's powers have proven to be highly scalable. At the same time, the Commission has undergone important divestitures, most notably the securities regulation remit in the 1930s, consumer product safety in the 1970s, and some elements of financial services in 2010. Each divestiture principally involved a consumer protection mandate.

On several occasions, the FTC has confronted circumstances where the original Congressional allocation of regulatory oversight turns out to be non-adaptive. Consider broadband information services. These products did not exist (nor were they even imagined) when Congress created the Federal Communications Commission. Indeed, the FCC's statutory framework is premised on the belief that the lowest cost way to provide telecommunications services is to have a single firm in each geographic area, and subject that firm to comprehensive oversight by a specialist public utility body. Over the past thirty years, changes in technology have made it apparent that this model is neither inevitable nor optimal, and that competition in a variety of areas is both feasible and desirable. The development of the Internet and broadband information services have resulted in considerable dispute over whether the FCC has exclusive regulatory authority, or whether the FTC has a role to play.[119] Jurisdiction over privacy on the Internet has created similar difficulties, as noted previously.

The FTC's experience shows both the promise and peril of scalable allocations of regulatory authority. On numerous occasions, the federal courts have declared that the FTC's unfairness authority under section 5 of the FTC Act confers broad powers to reach a range of conduct not previously condemned by statute or judicial decisions.[120] This expansive authority gives the FTC the ability to address new commercial phenomena and create new norms of conduct. For example, the FTC's emergence as the principal federal enforcement body concerning data protection and privacy built upon the application of the Commission's unfairness authority, but no one was thinking about the Internet and online privacy in 1914, when Section 5 of the FTC Act was written.

The FTC's experience also demonstrates that the application of a highly scalable mandate can create three distinct traps. First, legislators and other external observers come to regard the agency as a solution for all problems that have an apparent connection to the expansive mandate. For example, substantial increases in the prices of certain commodities can be depicted as the result of "unfair" or overreaching behavior by the suppliers of those goods. Suppose that armed conflict in a major crude oil production region causes crude oil prices soar. This shock, in turn, forces gasoline prices upward. Gasoline prices increase because the cost of the principal input for making gasoline has risen, yet legislators may attribute the price changes to collusion or unconscionable conduct by petroleum industry refiners. The agency with the highly elastic mandate will be urged to take steps (e.g., attacking "price gouging") to push prices downward, yet any measures taken will not address the underlying cause and may retard market responses that eventually would cure the problem.

Second, an agency with a sweeping and adaptable mandate has every incentive to push the outer boundaries of its authority, to show it is fulfilling the goals set for it by Congress. Unless the agency binds itself to do otherwise, it will find it easy to expand its claimed authority without grounding its initiatives in a rigorous conceptual framework that specifies the logic for intervention and simultaneously delimits the outer boundaries of the agency's assertion of authority. Open-ended assertions of authority invite carelessness in the application of the agency's powers and blind it to the broader institutional and political implications of expansive forms of intervention. These lapses can trigger rebukes from reviewing courts and provoke severe political backlash.[121] Spiderman said it best: with great power comes great responsibility. Agencies engaged in hot pursuit of what they perceive to be evil-doers have a distinct tendency to ignore this point.

The third trap arises from the possibility for the agency to exploit opportunities for what might be called regulatory leveraging across its range of policy duties. This is evident in recent FTC mat-

---

119 Nat'l Cable & Telecomms. Ass'n v. Brand X Internet Servs., 545 U.S. 967 (2005) (broadband services deemed not to be telecommunications services within meaning of Telecommunications Act); *see also* William E. Kovacic, FTC Jurisdiction Over Broadband Services, Testimony Before the U.S. Senate Committee on the Judiciary (June 14, 2006) (FTC prepared statement stating that *Brand X* gives FTC jurisdiction over broadband services), *available at* http://www.ftc.gov/Os/2006/06/pd52103commissiontestimonybroadbandinternetaccessservices06142006Senate.pdf.

120 The formative analysis of this jurisprudence is Neil W. Averitt, *The Meaning of 'Unfair Methods of Competition' in Section 5 of the Federal Trade Commission Act*, 21 Boston College Law Review 227 (1980).

121 This history is recounted in William E. Kovacic & Marc Winerman, *Competition Policy and the Application of Section 5 of the Federal Trade Commission Act*, 76 Antitrust L.J. 929 (2010).

ters involving mainstays of the information services sector such as Google. In the development of the agency's privacy program, the Commission in recent years has expressed a keen interest in encouraging companies to adopt stronger data protection measures and to afford consumers more control over the use of information that companies collect about their preferences. Some of the targets of the FTC's privacy related interests (e.g., Google) have appeared before the FTC in the course of inquiries related to issues arising under the Commission's competition authority. Google, for example, underwent extensive FTC antitrust reviews concerning its acquisition of Doubleclick and Admob, respectively.

During the FTC's deliberations over Google's mergers, some Commission officials and staff advocated that the agency use the merger review process (where companies are obliged by law to notify the federal antitrust agencies in advance of certain mergers) to exact concessions from the merging parties concerning their privacy policies and data protection practices. The Commission resisted this impulse in the Doubleclick and Admob matters, but it subsequently carried out parallel competition and consumer protection inquiries in connection with Google's search practices. These matters point to a scenario that might unfold in the future. An agency with multiple functions might use its gatekeeping powers under one function to induce a company to make concessions with respect to issues arising under separate elements of the agency's policy portfolio. For example, the FTC might tell an information services firm that it will approve a merger (or accelerate approval of a merger) if the enterprise promises to make changes to its privacy practices—a matter normally implicating the FTC's consumer protection powers. In this way, a multipurpose agency might achieve policy outcomes that a single purpose agency might find more difficult to realize.

2.5. Internal Organizational Cohesion: Will the Combination Result in Synergies, Distrust, or Civil War?

The FTC features a substantial degree of insularity with its Bureaus of Competition and Consumer Protection. The relationship between these two groups is more one of rivalry or indifference rather than cooperation. Policy integration takes place mainly at the Commission level and through the work of the Bureau of Economics and the FTC's Office of Policy Planning. This means that, if the analytical synergies between the two disciplines are substantial, a less than ideal amount of combined consumer protection and competition analysis takes place at the case handling and middle management levels.

We have mentioned earlier that multi-purpose agencies typically create single-purpose operating units to carry out specific duties. These units, in turn, tend to compete with each other for attention and resources, including outlays for personnel, office space, and control over infrastructure assets such as the information technology network. This phenomenon can be observed at the FTC and a number of other agencies that combine competition and consumer protection duties. Intramural competition for prestige and resources can cause agency officials to spend substantial effort refereeing disputes among rival divisions. These are resources that otherwise would be applied to serving program needs.

Intramural rivalry also can have other costs. If the rationale for combining functions is to realize synergies between discrete areas of responsibility, the rivalry for prestige and resources can create internal tensions that defeat the realization of synergies in practice. Where individual operating units strive to create separate identities, personnel within those units may establish strong loyalties to their own units and define success by the achievements of their units. Projects that entail cooperation across operating units may be seen by group as relatively unimportant or simply contrary to each group's interests, even though greater collaboration across units would advance projects that serve the larger aims of the institution as a whole. Where its main operating units are assigned specific functions, a multi-purpose agency may find it difficult to mobilize resources across units unless it can create a "we're all in this together" ethos. Otherwise, top agency leadership may have to spend substantial effort refereeing disputes among rival divisions. These are resources that otherwise would be applied to serve program needs.

That said, some dynamic tension across units can be helpful. As noted previously, at the FTC, the formulation of consumer protection policy (including financial services) has been informed by the analysis and research of the agency's Bureau of Economics (BE). In general terms, BE serves as a voice for the value of competition, for the inclusion of market-oriented strategies in the mix of regulatory tools, and for the awareness of costs associated with specific regulatory choices. BE also performs empirical research that has yielded major insights into how consumers perceive disclosures provided in financial services instruments. In all matters, BE makes an independent recommendation to the Commission about the desirability of specific cases, rules, or other proposed initiatives. BE has emphasized that excessively stringent regulatory controls can (a) overlook strategies that harness market processes to achieve social policy goals, and (b) suppress forms of competition that themselves can yield significant benefits to consumers.

The institutional arrangements through which the Bureau of Economics makes an independent recommendation to the board helps prod the board to pay attention to regulatory costs and to the role of competition and market-based responses in protecting consumer interests. The FTC's Bureau of Economics (and, to a lesser extent, the FTC's Bureau of Competition) help ensure the FTC takes account of the economic costs and benefits of law enforcement and rulemaking proposals from the Bureau of Consumer Protection—and the knowledge that their proposals will be scrutinized in this fashion forces the FTC's Bureau of Consumer Protection to explicitly take account of these matters in making its recommendations in the first instance.[122]

Consider a concrete example. In 2007, Michael Sallinger, the head of the FTC's Bureau of Economics, spoke at a conference jointly sponsored by the FTC and the National Association of Attorneys General to discuss policy toward the gasoline industry, including the enforcement of price gouging laws. His narrative underscores the value of economic analysis as a discipline upon the FTC's decision-making process:

> After hurricane Wilma, a man in Miami with a flatbed truck drove it to North Carolina—several hundred miles away—and purchased a set of portable generators, paying roughly $300 for some and $500 for others. He drove the truck back to Miami and sold the generators for approximately double what he had paid for them. The state sued him for price gouging.

122 Luke Froeb et al., *The Economics of Organizing Economists* (Vanderbilt Law and Economics Research Paper No. 08-18), July 2008, *available at* http://ssrn.com/abstract=1155237.

As a matter of economics, this suit was seriously misguided policy. The initiative shown by this truck owner helped alleviate the shortage of electricity. We do not need to give him an award for his initiative. The market did that, or at least it would have if he had not had to pay a fine to the state. But we certainly should not be penalizing him. The next time a disaster strikes Miami, perhaps the truck owner will try to think of ways to help ease a shortage and simply decline to profit from it. Perhaps. But that's not where I would put my money. More likely, he will just stay put; and those people who would have voluntarily purchased whatever supplies he chose to provide will simply go without. I am confident that professional economists would agree with my assessment of this case.

But not everyone in the workshop did. As the discussion of the episode unfolded, it was clear that there was a divide in the room between the people who work on antitrust for the states and those who work on consumer protection. The consumer protection people in the room generally approved of the case and of price gouging laws more generally. It was that discussion that made me realize how valuable economics is to the consumer protection mission of the FTC. I cannot imagine people from our Bureau of Consumer Protection arguing for such a case; and I cannot help thinking that it is the result of the ongoing dialog between lawyers and economists at the Commission about what sorts of consumer protection cases make economic sense that the cases we bring do make economic sense.[123]

2.6. Collateral Effects upon the Regulatory Ecosystem

As noted earlier, Congress frequently assigns regulatory responsibility for a specific sector or practice to more than one federal agency. The FTC's expansive competition and consumer protection responsibilities overlap with or share boundaries the duties of numerous other federal agencies, as well as a host of state public bodies. The FTC's very formation in 1914 and the agency's subsequent movement into other policy domains, some by legislative fiat and others through the exercise of the FTC's discretion, have affected the larger regulatory ecosystem. To a large degree, the FTC coexists peacefully with its public agency counterparts. At the same time, the existing distribution of authority complicates the execution of routine regulatory tasks.

a. Inter-Agency Coordination

The agency devotes substantial resources to inter-government coordination. The need in many instances to collaborate with other public institutions delays the implementation of new initiatives. In a wide range of areas, the FTC cannot act unilaterally. Adjustments in the oversight of advertising involving food and health claims require close consultation with the Food and Drug Administration. The implementation of new legislative mandates involving market manipulation of petroleum products demands collaboration with the Commodity Futures Trading Commission, which pressed the FTC to narrow as much as possible the scope of its market manipulation rule. The drafting by

123 Michael A. Salinger, Economics Supporting the Twin Missions of the FTC (Apr. 20, 2007) at http://www.ftc.gov/speeches/salinger/070420breakfast.pdf.

the Department of Health and Human Services of the new rule on Accountable Care Organizations took place through an often contentious collaboration among the FTC, DOJ, and HHS. Dodd Frank mandates coordination between the CFPB and the FTC over the future allocation of enforcement tasks related to non-bank financial institutions. The fact of shared responsibility and common mandates means that few collaborative exercises in setting rules or bringing cases proceed expeditiously.

i. New Entry in an Existing Regulatory Arena: The Case of Antitrust

The FTC's establishment in 1914 placed the FTC into a policy domain already occupied by two other institutions. First, the Clayton and FTC Acts ended the Justice Department's position of exclusivity in the federal government's enforcement of the antitrust laws. In particular, the Clayton Act gave DOJ and FTC concurrent authority to enforce its provisions and did not specify a decision making rule to determine which agency would handle specific matters. The FTC Act moved the FTC into the adjudication of federal antitrust matters, a realm that had been the exclusive responsibility of the federal judiciary.

Neither of these incursions into the existing ecosystem pleased the incumbents. In its first decades, the FTC suffered many debilitating defeats in the federal courts. Some setbacks stemmed from serious weaknesses in the FTC's process. The Commission's early custom was to issue decisions without elaboration of their legal reasoning and to present the rationale for decisions only in briefs before the courts. This habit did the agency no favors when it came time to argue that it deserved deference before the appellate courts. Yet appellate decisions of this period also reveal a hostility that cannot be explained solely by the Commission's poor opinion-writing. The courts did not welcome the introduction of a new adjudication institution—to some degree, a rival—with open arms.

Nor was the Department of Justice pleased with the arrival of a new body with whom it would henceforth share decision making tasks. From early days until the present, the most frequent point of friction has been the allocation of files where both agencies have competence to review a matter. At times in the 1920s, the two agencies each opened a file to deal with the same conduct. The agencies devised informal methods of consultation to above duplicative parallel inquiries and embodied these understandings in a formal instrument in the late 1940s. The agreement established the process by which one agency would "clear" matters to the other.

Since the late 1940s, this liaison arrangement (commonly called "clearance") has provided the means by which the agencies avoid conflicts in the exercise of their concurrent power under the Clayton Act.[124] A 2002 press release describes how this process has worked (and not worked)

124 James C. Grimaldi, *Enron Case Attracts Lawyers Like a Flame Attracts Moths, More than You Can Shake A Stick At*, WASHINGTON POST, Jan. 28, 2002, at E2 ("There are a handful of industries in which both the FTC and Justice Department have expertise. So when a hot merger comes up, and the staff of each agency wants a piece of it, the assistant attorney general for antitrust and the FTC chairman have to sort it out. This had been done in an ancient ritual that included a series of athletic events such as arm wrestling, mud wrestling, greased-pig wrestling and a bull-riding competition, and an essay contest. Okay, we're making that up. Well, most of it. The agencies really *do* write essays explaining why they are best to review the mergers."). *See also* Lauren Kearney Peay, *The Cautionary Tale of the Failed 2002 FTC/DOJ Merger Clearance Accord,* 60 VANDERBILT L. REV. 1307 (2008).

over time, with agencies handling particular cases based primarily on their previous expertise in a particular industry:

> [B]ecause the FTC had experience with automobiles, it conducted investigations in that industry; similarly, DOJ investigated steel matters. . . .
>
> In recent years, the process has become more contentious as the convergence of industries has blurred bright lines between industry boundaries. For example, because the DOJ historically has investigated electricity, while the FTC has investigated all other energy matters, convergence mergers between electricity and natural gas companies have led to contentious disputes regarding which agency should investigate. Moreover, although the FTC predominantly has investigated computer hardware and the DOJ has investigated computer software, matters involving both have become increasingly common, resulting in clearance disputes.
>
> In the 1980s, there were only about 10 disputes per year. Since then, the average has exceeded 80. These disputes result in significant delays. Delays averaging three weeks occurred in 24 percent of the matters on which clearance was sought from the beginning of FY 2000 through January 28, 2002. . . . During this time, neither agency could investigate potentially serious allegations of illegal behavior.[125]

As this passage suggests, most matters are cleared quickly and unobtrusively. Some are highly contentious. The contested matters, though few in number, imbue the DOJ/FTC relationship with an undercurrent of suspicion and distrust that undermines the effectiveness of the relationship. The element of tension has become more acute with the ascent of the FTC in the modern era to a position of peer status with the DOJ. From 1914 through the 1960s, DOJ was clearly the preeminent U.S. antitrust body. Through a slow and at times uneven process of improvement, the FTC over the past twenty years has matched DOJ in prestige. This transformation has increased the stakes of clearance disputes as each agency seeks to claim policy terrain that will increase its visibility and accomplishments.

The FTC's dual identify as a competition and consumer protection agency promises to be a source of instability in the agency's relationship with DOJ. As noted above, consumer protection and competition law have important conceptual complementarities. In principle, the unification of supply and demand side perspectives can yield a better understanding of specific commercial phenomena, a better diagnosis of apparent problems, and the design of a more effective solution. In recent years, the FTC has made a point of issuing complaints that invoke an amalgam of competition and consumer protection theories of harm. The FTC's settlement in 2010 of claims of improper

125 *See* http://www.ftc.gov/opa/2002/04/clearanceoverview.shtm. *See also* Grimaldi, *supra* note 124 at E2 ("The 'discussions' would last more than two weeks sometimes, and that's almost half the 30 days in which investigators must decide whether to launch a more detailed review, called a "second request" for documents. Delays of more than 15 days occurred 32 times in 2000."). The clearance process also created other problems not mentioned in the press release. Resolution of clearance disputes was supposed to be based on the comparative expertise of each agency—but the agencies controlled whether or not they initiated cases in each area—and both knew that the first agency to bring a case in a new area would be more likely to get all cases arising out of that area into perpetuity. The clearance process thus encouraged "gun-jumping" by the agencies—each seeking to be the first-mover, irrespective of the relative strength of the case(s) in question.

single firm conduct by Intel relied upon competition and consumer protection theories of liability, and FTC officials have emphasized the hybrid nature of this resolution.[126] Earlier FTC decisions, such as the settlement in Negotiated Data Solutions (N-Data), also featured a mix of competition and consumer protection rationales.[127] Most recently, the FTC initiated parallel competition and consumer protection inquiries involving Google's practices in the market for internet-based search.

DOJ might view the FTC's application of hybrid competition/consumer protection theories with suspicion. DOJ might see the FTC's recent practice as a strategic move to establish a superior basis to claim clearance. The FTC might be preparing to assert that individual matters pose a mix of competition and consumer protection issues and therefore should be analyzed by an agency with jurisdiction over both domains. Let us assume that the FTC's move is not a strategic ploy to claim more policy terrain. Suppose, instead, that the FTC's work reflects the view that the application of the two disciplines can product better policy outcomes in some cases. Three solutions are possible in these situations. One is to allocate such files to the FTC because the FTC's mandate encompasses both competencies. The second solution is to give the file to the DOJ on the condition that the two agencies cooperate closely to permit the FTC to contribute its consumer protection expertise to DOJ's analysis. The third is for DOJ to hire officials with consumer protection backgrounds to work on its cases.

There is another way in which the FTC's application of a fusion of competition and consumer protection perspectives could upset the existing order of federal antitrust enforcement. That is the possibility for regulatory leveraging described above. The FTC could be tempted to use its competition policy mandate to obtain policy concessions that relate mainly to consumer protection. In the guise of doing a competition policy analysis, the FTC might inform the firm that it will allow the transaction to proceed if the firm makes commitments with respect to other policy commands (e.g., data protection) within the Commission's policy portfolio at a protection regime. For example, regulatory leveraging could enable the FTC to realize privacy policy objectives that might not be obtainable directly through the prosecution of a consumer protection case or the promulgation of a consumer protection rule.

There is a constraint on the FTC's ability to engage in this type of leveraging. If it became apparent that the FTC was using merger review to advance a consumer protection agenda, the existing framework of merger analysis (which does not incorporate consumer protection considerations) would be called into question. Success with such an approach would depend on the FTC's ability to depict the consumer protection issues as elements of a more sophisticated form of competition analysis.

Whether its duties encompass only competition law or competition law plus other functions, an agency rarely has exclusive power to shape policy within the policy domains assigned to it. Single-purpose and multi-purpose agencies often share responsibility for a given field of oversight with still another government agency or agencies. By the conscious design of a legislature or by accident, a multiplicity of regulatory decision makers for the same policy area tends to emerge over time. In the field of competition and consumer protection policy, for example, it is common for the

126 *In re* Intel Corp., D. 9341 (FTC Oct. 29, 2010) (decision and order), at http://www.ftc.gov/os/adpro/d9341/101102inteldo.pdf.

127 *In re* Negotiated Data Solutions LLC, C-4234 (FTC Sept. 22, 2008) (decision and order), at http://www.ftc.gov/os/caselist/0510094/080923ndsd0.pdf.

competition agency to share policy making responsibility with sectoral regulators that have concurrent or sequential power to review mergers or allegations of abusive behavior by dominant firms.

2.7. Political Implications

The dual-role nature of the FTC presents the agency with political benefits and disadvantages. The principle benefit, mentioned above, is the possibility of cross subsidization that improves the effectiveness of the FTC competition program. Consumer protection measures such as the Do Not Call registry have created substantial policy capital surpluses for the Commission, and these can be spent effectively to initiate difficult new matters or to resist political pressure to engage in programs that the agency believes to be improvident.

There are disadvantages in the existing distribution of power, although these may be rooted mainly in the FTC's inherently close relationship to Congress. The FTC's ties to Congress introduce severe rigidities into the agency's ability to allocate tasks to other agencies with whom it shares policy responsibilities. In 2002, the Agencies sought to implement a permanent structural solution to the clearance problem by explicitly allocating exclusive responsibility for particular sectors of the economy to either the FTC or the DOJ.[128] Among other features, the agreement would have dedicated the telecommunications and media sectors to DOJ while reserving electric power, health care, and aerospace to the FTC.[129] Although the proposal attracted bipartisan support and was hailed by antitrust practitioners, business groups, and former FTC and DOJ personnel, it was ultimately sunk by the vehement opposition of Senator Ernest Hollings, who argued that mergers among media corporations should be reviewed by the FTC. Senator Hollings, as chairman of the Commerce Committee, had oversight authority over the FTC, but not over the DOJ (which fell within the jurisdiction of the Senate Judiciary Committee). Hollings had one other important pressure point to exploit. He chaired the Senate Appropriations Subcommittee that oversees the funding of both the Justice Department and the FTC, and he threatened to reduce the budgets of both agencies unless the clearance agreement was abrogated.

Senator Hollings and his staff feared that adoption of the FTC and DOJ's clearance agreement would have largely eliminated the flow of campaign contributions from telecommunication and media corporations to members of the Senate Commerce Committee, and he apparently concluded that any new campaign contributions from electric power, health care, and aerospace firms would not be enough to make up the deficit.[130]

In the 1970s, FTC management failed to foresee the political consequences of programs that applied the agencies expansive powers in a broad manner. The FTC did not anticipate the political feedback generated by matters that affected significant economic interests. The Commission's competition, consumer protection, and economic research programs cut an astonishingly broad swath through American commerce. Not only did the Commission take on well-known giants of

128 *See* http://www.ftc.gov/opa/2002/02/clearance/ftcdojagree.pdf.

129 *Id.*

130 This episode is described in William E. Kovacic, *Antitrust in High-Tech Industries: Improving the Federal Antitrust Joint Venture*, 19 George Mason L. Rev. 1097, 1111-12 (2012).

U.S. industry and, in many cases, threaten them with remedies such as divestiture and compulsory trademark licensing, it also attacked sectors that provided the backbone of small and medium-sized enterprise across the country. This dynamic set in motion powerful lobbying campaigns before Congress, resulting in strong legislative backlash. In its selection of measures, the FTC was inattentive to the political risk associated with each new initiative and to the aggregate political significance of its sweeping portfolio of programs.

Expansive grants of authority may also serve the electoral needs of individual legislators.[131] Once Congress has delegated an ambitious range of regulatory tasks to an agency, individual legislators or committees will predictably urge the regulatory agency to use its powers aggressively. Firms affected by the agency's activities will predictably complain to the Congress, especially to oversight committees whose members are recipients of contributions supplied by the regulated industry. Individual members or committees will predictably demand that the agency temper its intervention. One can accomplish some of the same objectives by introducing a bill to regulate the industry, but using a middleman leaves fewer fingerprints. Such strategies need not be deployed very often; affected firms will make campaign contributions even if there is not a live controversy, to ensure they will have access to members when they need it—meaning that service on an oversight committee is accompanied by an annuity from the affected firms.

IV. Divide or Conquer?

If a particular competition policy conglomerate is not "working," then there are at least two different ways of solving that problem: one can divide (separating the conglomerate into distinct entities, each of which has a sole area of policy responsibility), or conquer (turn responsibility for the conglomerate over to new management, drawn from a different part of the government.)[132] Part III contains multiple examples of such initiatives. Examples of division include the decision by Congress in 1947 to establish the Air Force as a separate body by divesting functions previously performed by the U.S. Army and its Air Corps, the spinning off in the 1974 of the National Transportation Safety Board from the Department of Transportation, and the repositioning of the Nuclear Regulatory Commission as a distinct institution removed from its former home within the Atomic Energy Commission. Prominent illustrations of conquest include the absorption of numerous border protection institutions (such as the U.S. Coast Guard) into the Department of Homeland Security, the amalgamation of various financial services regulatory functions into the Consumer Protection Financial Bureau, and the removal of the Fish and Wildlife Service from the Departments of Agriculture and its relocation inside the Department of the Interior.

Experience with competition agencies also features examples of division and conquest. A major example of division occurred in the 1930s, when the FTC incubated the securities regulatory functions eventually transferred to the new Securities and Exchange Commission. Conquest

---

131 Fred McChesney, *Rent Extraction and Rent Creation in the Economic Theory of Regulation,* 16 J. Legal Studies 101 (1987).

132 We do not view the addition of additional divisions to the competition policy conglomerate as an example of "conquer," since it will not solve the underlying problem.

episodes include the assimilation in 2011 by Ireland's Competition Authority of the country's consumer protection agency. A complex variation that exhibits elements of both is the pending restructuring of the United Kingdom's competition policy system. The existing Office of Fair Trading and the Competition Commission will be reconstituted as a new Competition and Markets Authority, with many of the OFT's consumer protection functions divested to other government bodies.

	Divide	**Conquer**
Competition Agencies	SEC spin-off from FTC Consumer protection spin-off from OFT	Absorption by Ireland Competition Agency of consumer protection
Other Agencies	US Army Air Corps recreated as US Air Force NTSB spun off from DOT	DHS absorption of border protection agencies CFPB absorption of financial services bodies

How should we decide between these two possibilities? Space precludes a full answer, but a campaign speech by then-Candidate (and later) President Franklin Delano Roosevelt suggests a framework for thinking about the decision, and for answering which agency (among the many that are available) should do the conquering.

> There are four different kinds of bears in the United States, and, of course, all these bears come under the jurisdiction of one Government department or another. I think it is the brown bear that comes under the jurisdiction of the Department of the Interior, and I think the black bear comes under the Department of Agriculture; and the Alaska bear comes under the Department of Commerce; and jurisdiction over the grizzly bear is held by the Department of War. That has been going on from time immemorial in Washington. Each bear—the care of the bear and everything else about the bear-falls under a different department, depending on the genus of the bear. And I am told confidentially that sometimes there is a most awful mixup, because sometimes a black bear falls in love with a brown bear, and then nobody knows under what department the puppies belong.[133]

Consider how each of the four listed "parent" agencies would behave in response to misconduct by their respective "bear-children" and "grand-bear-children." Those same characteristics are likely to inform the conquering agency's behavior if they are given responsibility for the competition agency.

133 Franklin Delano Roosevelt, Extemporaneous Campaign Address, Binghamton, N.Y., Oct. 17, 1928, *available at* 1 Public Papers and Addresses of Franklin D. Roosevelt 16 (1938).

V. Conclusion

Why should anyone care about the organization of the agency charged with implementing competition law? Professor Amy Zegart concisely answered the first question:

> Organization is never neutral. As any Washington taxi driver can point out, government organization has serious implications for policy outcomes. . . . When it comes to selecting, shaping, and implementing . . . policy, the devil often lies in the details of agency design.[134]

On the issue of whether the agency should be divided or conquered, not every problem in competition law and policy requires a "shoot first, shoot later, and then when everybody's dead try to ask a question or two" mindset.[135] If your competition agency behaves like that, it may be time for a change.

---

134 Amy B. Zegart, Flawed By Design: The Evolution of the CIA, JCS, and NSC I-II (1999).

135 Cf. Wild, Wild West (1999) ("Mr. West, not every situation requires your patented approach of shoot first, shoot later, shoot some more and then when everybody's dead try to ask a question or two.") *available at* http://www.imdb.com/title/tt0120891/quotes.

China's Competition Law in the Global Competition*

Xiaoye WANG

wangxy88@aliyun.com

Professor, Hunan University and Chinese Academy of Social Sciences
Consultant Expert, Chinese Antimonopoly Commission

In 2004, I had the honor of writing the preface to the Chinese version of David's book *Law and Competition in Twentieth Century Europe*. Once again, I am thrilled to be asked to write a preface to the Chinese version of David's new book, *Global Competition: Law, Markets and Globalization*, and to be given the opportunity to express my congratulations and share some of my own thoughts on this book.

It appears that two principal observations motivated David to research and write his new book. The first observation is the fact that global competition law issues are increasingly relevant to the economies of many countries around the world. A second and related observation is that, despite increasingly fierce global competition, competition law and competition law enforcement remain very much a country-specific issue, and there is no single unified competition law regime. Therefore, David believes that the analysis of global competition law issues may be relevant not only for the specific issue of competition law, but also for broader issues of global economic governance.[1] One of the most important points in David's book is that, due to the lack of a unified or standardized competition law regime, the competition laws of the world's major economies, in particular the United States' antitrust laws and the European Union's competition laws, have emerged as the norms that govern global competition, in part due to their extraterritorial application. However, as China and other emerging countries play increasingly important economic and political roles in global competition, their competition laws will gradually have a greater impact and influence on global competition. Further, the extraterritorial application of competition laws of various jurisdictions will inevitably create unavoidable conflicts of law and conflicts of jurisdiction. Such conflicts reduce legal certainty and predictability for multinational companies and increase their operating

* This short article was based on the author's presentation titled *Interplay between National and Transnational Dynamics-from the Perspective of China's AML* that was addressed at the Global Competition Law Conference hosted by the IIT Chicago-Kent College of Law on October 28, 2011, and the Preface to the Chinese version of the book titled GLOBAL COMPETITION: LAW, MARKETS AND GLOBALIZATION by DAVID J. GERBER. This translation "全球竞争：法律、市场和全球化" was published by China Legal Publishing House in April 2012. The author expresses her thanks to Professors David Gerber and Sungjoon Cho for their kind invitation to attend this Conference.

1 *See* DAVID J. GERBER, GLOBAL COMPETITION: LAW, MARKETS AND GLOBALIZATION 345 (Oxford University Press 2010).

costs and business risks. Therefore, David believes that there should be an effective legal regime for global competition that is aimed at promoting global economic and political development.[2]

I agree with David's views. In 2002 and 2003, in my role as the Head of the Advisory Group on Trade and Competition Policy Issues in the Doha Development Round to China's Ministry of Commerce (MOFCOM), I gave serious consideration to the issues related to competition policy under economic globalization.[3] My view was that the Chinese Government should adopt a positive attitude in its multilateral negotiations regarding competition policy under the World Trade Organization (WTO) framework. Such a global competition policy would help curb the adverse effects of transnational anticompetitive restraints in the Chinese market, help Chinese businesses enter global markets, be conducive to the development and improvement of Chinese competition law, and help the establishment of independent Chinese competition law enforcement agencies. Further, China had in fact fully accepted the core principles of the WTO competition policy, including non-discrimination, transparency, and procedural fairness.

However, I do not believe that the establishment of a unified global competition policy under the WTO framework is a realistic goal. As David has emphasized in his book, global competition is not just an economic process—political, social, cultural, and other factors must also be considered. This means that even if a unified global competition policy were successfully negotiated and established via the WTO framework, its effectiveness as a legal weapon to protect global competition will be limited. In part this difficulty arises because the line between private and public restraints on competition is often unclear, and it is often very hard to curb public restraints on competition using a competition law that is directed at regulating private restraints. One such example is the North American Free Trade Agreement (NAFTA). Even though this free trade agreement established a competition policy, it was unable to resolve the dispute between United Parcel Service and the Government of Canada, in which the United Parcel Service accused the Government of Canada of adopting anticompetitive restraints.[4] Further, transnational private restraints, to a certain extent, reflect more general political, economic, cultural, and legal issues and differences that exist amongst countries. Therefore, it is unrealistic to expect that a global competition policy can resolve the problems of anticompetitive restraints that arise from global competition.

On the other hand, the European Union's competition law represents the successful establishment and implementation of a multilateral agreement on competition law and policy. The success of EU competition law lies not only in the establishment of a powerful competition regulator, the European Commission, but more importantly in the successful integration of the European economy and the key role that competition law has had in that regard; competition law is considered to be the cornerstone of the European internal market. Further, with the Lisbon Treaty coming into effect at the end of 2009, the European Union has also become more politically integrated. Obviously, the European Union's experience cannot apply on a global scale. Countries have different levels of economic development and political, social, cultural, and legal structures. In particular, in many

2 *Id. supra,* at title page.

3 *See* Wang Xiaoye & Tao Zhenghua, *WTO Competition Policy and Its Influence in China,* Soc. Sci. in China, Spring 2004, at 43.

4 United Parcel Service of America, Inc. v. Government of Canada, An Arbitration under Chapter 11 of the North American Free Trade Agreement, *available at* http://www.state.gov/s/l/c3749.htm (last visited Jan. 8, 2013).

developing countries, industrial policy often takes priority over competition policy. For these reasons, it is difficult to envision a unified global competition policy in the foreseeable future. In such circumstances, even though the use of extraterritorial jurisdiction is not a good way to deal with transnational anticompetitive conduct, at present there is no better alternative. Here, I agree with David's view that, "[w]ithout political support for competition as a process, it is difficult to generate support for laws and institutions to protect that process."[5]

David is also concerned with the interaction between domestic competition law and cross-border economic activities, in particular the impact of Chinese competition law on the global economy and global competition. I fondly remember our lengthy Wednesday afternoon conversations during my time as a visiting Fulbright scholar at the IIT Chicago-Kent College of Law in 2005 and 2006. We agreed that transnational and global competition had greatly impacted China's competition law and its development. China began its economic reform process in the late 1970s. Even though the motivation for embarking on economic reform came from within China, undoubtedly China was also affected by the international community, especially the economic reforms undertaken by the former Soviet Union and the Eastern European countries. The formulation and adoption of China's Anti-Monopoly Law (AML) is also the product of international cooperation, as it draws upon the experience of developed market economies—in particular Germany, the United States, and the European Union—and many foreign competition law experts were directly involved in its drafting. In May 2005, the State Council Legislative Affairs Office invited more than ten of the world's leading antitrust experts, such as Professor Jürgen Basedow of the Max Planck Institute for Comparative and International Private Law and Professor Josef Drexl of the Max Planck Institute for Intellectual Property and Competition Law, to participate in discussions on the draft AML. I remember that the draft at that time regarded refusal to grant access to a network as conduct amounting to abuse of dominant position. The draft provision provided that:

> In the case that an undertaking is unable to compete with the undertakings with a dominant market position without the access to a network or other infrastructure owned by those dominant undertakings in relevant market, the undertakings in dominant position shall not refuse to grant access to the network or other infrastructure to other undertakings at reasonable prices. However, the undertaking in a dominant position may be exempted if it can establish that it is impossible or unreasonable to grant access to the network or other infrastructure to other undertakings on account of technology, security or other justifiable reason.[6]

As a result of these discussions with foreign antitrust experts, this provision was eventually removed from the draft AML.

Even today, transnational dynamics influence the AML to a certain extent. In 2003, the MOFCOM and the European Commission signed Minutes of Meetings related to the consensus that was reached regarding the establishment of a competition policy dialogue between the two parties. This was the first document signed by China with a foreign party regarding the establishment of a com-

---

5 *See* Gerber, *supra note 1,* at 337.

6 Article 22 of Draft of Anti-Monopoly Law of the People's Republic of China on April 8, 2005. This draft was not published.

petition policy dialogue. Its purpose was to improve both sides' understandings of competition policy, competition law, and related matters. More recently, in July 2011, the agencies responsible for the enforcement of the AML—the National Development and Reform Commission (NDRC), the MOFCOM, and the State Administration for Industry and Commerce (SAIC)—entered into a Memorandum of Understanding with their U.S. counterparts. The purpose of the Memorandum of Understanding is to promote cooperation between Chinese and U.S. competition enforcement agencies by keeping each informed of significant competition policy developments and enforcement activities, exchanging experiences on competition law enforcement where appropriate, and exchanging views on multilateral competition law and policy.[7] This mechanism contributes to improving and strengthening the relationship between the agencies and could potentially lead to joint antitrust enforcement in the future. In September 2011, the SAIC held the 2nd BRICS International Competition Conference in Beijing. Representatives from 42 countries and regions participated in the conference. The Chinese Government's cooperation with the international community in the field of competition law demonstrates that the formulation and implementation of China's competition law has been influenced by transnational and global competition and other countries' experiences, in particular that of the United States and the European Union.

There is no doubt that the formulation and adoption of the AML have also affected the development of the global economy and global politics. This impact is especially apparent and reflected in Article 2 of the AML, which provides that the AML "is applicable to monopoly conduct outside the territory of the People's Republic of China that eliminates or has a restrictive effect on competition in the domestic market of the People's Republic of China." The AML has been in effect for more than three years. The MOFCOM has reviewed about 400 cases of M&A, many of which related to foreign markets. For example, the Panasonic/Sanyo case represents a significant development relating to the extraterritorial application of the AML. Before this case, the MOFCOM's condition for the clearance of an offshore transaction focused only on the parties' assets or interests within China. In this case, the MOFCOM expanded its remedies to the parties' overseas assets by requiring that the parties divest businesses located in Japan and that Panasonic reduce its ownership and waive board representation and voting rights in an offshore entity located outside China.[8] The MOFCOM has become one of world's most important and influential competition regulators due to the rapid development of the Chinese economy and the extraterritorial application of the AML.

Since the adoption and effectiveness of the AML, international scholars have expressed concerns that the Chinese Government will use the AML as a protectionist measure and enforce the AML only against foreign companies. A welcome development has been the announcement by the Price Supervision and Anti-Monopoly Bureau of the NDRC on 9 November 2011 that it had initiated an anti-monopoly investigation into China Telecom and China Unicom. This case is being closely monitored, as it is the first time that China has launched an anti-monopoly investigation into large state-owned enterprises. As the deputy director of the Price Supervision and Anti-Monopoly Bureau of the NDRC said, if the allegation of price discrimination based on abuse of dominant position

---

7 *See* the Report "China's anti-monopoly authorities signed an MOU on anti-monopoly cooperation with their U.S. counterparts" on July 27, 2011. Chinese version *available at* http://www.gov.cn/gzdt/2011-07/27/content_1914969.htm.

8 Panasonic v. Sanyo, [2009] Order No.53 of the Ministry of Commerce, October 30, 2009. Chinese version *available at* http://fldj.mofcom.gov.cn/aarticle/ztxx/200910/20091006593175.html.

proves to be true, the two companies may be liable for a fine of 1% to 10% of their revenue of the previous year, which could amount to hundreds of millions to billions of Chinese Yuan. I applaud the NDRC's investigation, as it demonstrates that the AML will be enforced against state-owned enterprises and will not be solely enforced against foreign companies. This investigation also shows that the enforcement of the AML is progressively maturing and that the enforcement agencies' knowledge and awareness of the competitive dynamics in markets is growing and that they are increasingly giving priority to consumer welfare; thus the enforcement of the AML is becoming increasingly effective.

In October 2011, I accepted David's invitation to attend the Chicago-Kent Global Competition Law Conference. At that conference, I pointed out that whilst competition law might easily be transplanted from one country into another, the values and conceptions inherent in the law cannot be so easily rooted in the latter. In light of the various problems in the current Chinese legal regime, the enforcement of the AML also faces a variety of serious challenges. However, as global competition encompasses not only economic competition but competition amongst various types of governance regimes, including legal regime competition, and because the type of competition protected and promoted by the AML can bring consumers the lowest prices, highest quality, and greatest material advancement, I believe that the enforcement of the AML will see a better tomorrow. Enforcement efforts to date show that there is some convergence of the AML with the competition laws of the United States and the European Union. For example, in its China Telecom and China Unicom investigation, the NDRC considered whether the companies had engaged in margin squeezing in the broadband network market because the broadband wholesale price was much higher than the broadband retail price, which resulted in many internet service providers being forced from the market. More generally, many countries' competition laws have converged due to the adoption of a market system. Market economies must be able to use market mechanisms and competition as the basic way to allocate resources, and the duty of competition law is to protect market competition and not consider the ownership or nationality of the companies under investigation.

David believes that China's increasing role in the global economy is likely to challenge and perhaps modify the long-standing leading role that U.S. antitrust law has held in providing the international standard for competition law, but it is unclear whether and to what extent China will seek to replace it.[9] While I do not know whether China is able to challenge or change the United States' leading position in competition law, I hope that, at the very least, China can, through the enforcement of competition law and the ensuing benefits, encourage the emergence of a Steve Jobs or more.

9 *See* GERBER, *supra note 1, at 236.*

Réflexions sur la convergence des droits de la concurrence

Laurence IDOT*

laurence.idot@sfr.fr

Professeur, Université Paris II Panthéon Assas - Collège européen de Paris

Dans les années 70/80, les études comparatives en droit de la concurrence[1] se limitaient souvent à un examen du droit antitrust américain et du droit communautaire de la concurrence, avec parfois de timides références au droit national d'un État industrialisé. Il n'y avait aucune recherche d'ensemble sur le développement des droits de la concurrence en Europe. Le premier ouvrage de David Gerber[2] a heureusement comblé cette lacune en proposant une approche historique et globale dépassant la seule présentation technique des textes. Les données ont depuis considérablement changé. En 2012, le champ de la comparaison peut désormais couvrir les cinq continents. La consultation du site de *l'International Competition Network* est à cet égard éclairante: plus de 100 législations existent désormais dans le monde, dont les trois quarts ont été adoptées ces vingt dernières années, l'élément le plus marquant ayant été l'introduction en 2007 d'un droit de la concurrence en Chine.[3] Prenant acte de cette évolution, David a naturellement poursuivi sa réflexion en nous proposant son deuxième ouvrage, dont le titre est significatif, *Global Competition*.[4] Après avoir exposé l'évolution des deux grands systèmes américain et européen, sans oublier les droits des nouveaux entrants,[5] l'auteur s'interroge sur le projet d'un droit de la concurrence transnational, ce qui le conduit à

---

* L'auteur s'exprime à titre purement personnel. Ce texte a pour origine la communication "A French View on the convergence of antitrust laws" présentée lors de "The Global Competition Law Conference" organisée par le Chicago-Kent College of Law le 28 octobre 2011 en l'honneur de D. Gerber, dans le cadre de la session "National and Transnational Dynamics: The Interplay."

1 Le droit de la concurrence sera compris dans l'acception étroite, qui prévaut dans les différentes organisations internationales, comme regroupant l'ensemble des règles qui visent à préserver l'existence de la concurrence entre les entreprises sur les marchés.

2 David J. Gerber, Law and Competition in Twentieth Century Europe (Oxford University Press 1998).

3 François Souty, *Chine: La loi anti-monopole du 30 août 2007*, Concurrences n° 4-2007, n° 14266, pp. 158-164. À ce jour, les autorités chinoises ne sont pas membres de l'ICN.

4 David J. Gerber, Global Competition. Law, Markets and Globalization (Oxford Univeristy Press 2010). V. à propos de cet ouvrage, l'interview de D. Gerber, in *Concurrences* n° 4-2010, pp. 7-12, et le compte-rendu de V. Couronne, *Concurrences* n° 2012, p. 215.

5 Global Competition Law, préc., part II, pp. 121-272.

consacrer un chapitre aux phénomènes de convergence, dont il reconnaît l'existence tout en en soulignant les limites.[6]

Les propos qui vont suivre seront plus modestes et strictement juridiques. Partant du constat reconnu par tous de l'existence en droit de la concurrence de deux grands modèles (le modèle américain et le modèle européen), de la généralisation des phénomènes de rapprochement, l'objet de la présente étude est uniquement de porter un regard général sur la convergence des droits de la concurrence en corrigeant certaines conclusions opérées au début des années 80, qui ont parfois toujours cours en France, mais qui ne correspondent plus à la réalité du début de ce siècle.

Les données sont naturellement différentes suivant la zone géographique par rapport à laquelle on raisonne. En Europe, il existe une idée commune selon laquelle les droits nationaux des États membres sont alignés sur le droit de l'Union; l'on assisterait à une "communautarisation" du droit de la concurrence. Ce dernier étant lui-même fortement marqué, ne serait-ce qu'historiquement, par le droit antitrust américain, dans une perspective plus globale, il y aurait un phénomène "d'américanisation" du droit de la concurrence.

Ces deux idées reçues sont partiellement fausses. La réalité est beaucoup plus complexe. Au sein de l'Union européenne, la convergence n'obéit plus uniquement à un modèle vertical descendant (I) tandis que, dans une perspective globale, le modèle américain n'est plus le modèle dominant (II).

I. La convergence des droits de la concurrence au sein de l'Union européenne

La "communautarisation" éventuelle ne concerne que les branches du droit de la concurrence communes à la fois à l'ordre juridique de l'Union européenne et aux ordres juridiques nationaux, soit le droit des pratiques anticoncurrentielles et le contrôle des concentrations, qui constituent le noyau dur commun à toutes les législations modernes. De plus, même au sein de ce dernier, une distinction doit être opérée entre ces deux composantes, non seulement pour des raisons historiques et techniques, mais surtout du fait d'une organisation différente des relations entre droit de l'Union et droit nationaux. Alors que, pour le contrôle des concentrations, le système de "guichet unique" au cœur du premier règlement n° 4064/89 a été maintenu dans le règlement n° 139/2004,[7] le règlement

6 *Idem,* part III, pp. 273-293.

7 Règlement (CE) n° 139/2004 du Conseil du 20 janvier 2004 relatif au contrôle des concentrations entre entreprises, JOUE n° L. 24, 29 janv. 2004, art. 1. Le "guichet unique" est toutefois atténué du fait de la généralisation des mécanismes de renvoi. V. not., Dominique Berlin, *Contrôle des concentrations*, in Commentaire Megret, *Droit de l'Union européenne—Droit communautaire de la concurrence*, Bruxelles, Presses de l'ULB, 2009.

n° 1/2003 a finalement confirmé à l'article 3 un système d'application parallèle limitée pour le droit des pratiques anticoncurrentielles et affirmé la règle dite de convergence.[8]

Compte tenu de ces rapports organisés sur des bases opposées (application alternative vs/application cumulative), la convergence devrait être plus forte en droit des pratiques anticoncurrentielles qu'en matière de contrôle des concentrations. De manière *a priori* paradoxale, le résultat est inversé. La convergence est plus grande en contrôle des concentrations (1.) qu'en antitrust (2.).

1. Une forte convergence en matière de contrôle des concentrations

Que l'on raisonne sur le principe même et la structure du contrôle (1.1.) ou sur ses modalités (1.2.), le contrôle des concentrations de l'Union européenne est un modèle pour les contrôles nationaux, qui existent désormais dans tous les États membres.[9]

1.1. Un consensus sur le principe et la structure du contrôle

Dans les États industrialisés qui ont introduit dès les années 50/60 un droit de la concurrence, la nécessité d'un contrôle spécifique des concentrations a longtemps été débattue et, à ce titre, cette composante, jugée désormais indispensable à tout droit de la concurrence moderne, est apparue comme un droit de deuxième génération.[10]

En 1989, lors de l'adoption du règlement n° 4064/89, des contrôles spécifiques des concentrations n'existaient que dans trois grands États membres, l'Allemagne,[11] le Royaume-Uni,[12] la France.[13] En pratique, le contrôle n'était effectif qu'en Allemagne qui avait mis en place un contrôle *ex ante*, le Royaume-Uni et la France ayant opté pour des contrôles dits mixtes avec un système de notification facultative.

L'entrée en vigueur du règlement a eu un premier effet. Dans les États membres où le contrôle existait sans être pratiqué, le contrôle est devenu effectif. L'exemple français est à cet égard intéressant. À partir des années 92/93, les entreprises, qui avaient pris l'habitude de notifier leurs opérations à la Commission, ont commencé, pour des raisons de sécurité juridique, à notifier les concentrations internes au Ministre de l'économie alors compétent en ce domaine. De leur côté, les États membres

8 V. not., Laurence Idot, Droit communautaire de la concurrence. Le nouveau système de mise en œuvre des articles 81 et 82 CE (Bruxelles, Bruylant 2004).

9 Le Luxembourg fait toutefois exception.

10 V. sur ce point, Louis Vogel, Droit de la concurrence et concentration économique (Paris, Economica 1988).

11 Le contrôle a été introduit en 1973 (art. 23, GWB), alors que le GWB a été adopté en 1957.

12 Le contrôle a été introduit par le *Monopolies and Merger Act* de 1965 alors que le *Monopolies and Restrictive Practices Act* fut adopté en 1948, puis remplacé par le *Restrictive Practices Act* en 1956.

13 Loi du 19 juillet 1977.

qui n'avaient pas dans leur arsenal juridique de contrôle des concentrations[14] s'en sont progressivement dotés si bien qu'à la fin des années 90, ces contrôles s'étaient généralisés.

Le succès du contrôle communautaire a eu un deuxième effet. Les contrôles nationaux se sont alignés sur ce dernier, soit immédiatement lorsqu'ils étaient nouveaux, soit progressivement. Là encore, l'exemple français est topique. Une fois devenu effectif, le contrôle mixte, peu touché par l'ordonnance du 1er décembre 1986,[15] a été profondément remanié par la loi sur les nouvelles régulations économiques du 15 mai 2001,[16] qui l'a transformé en un pur contrôle *ex ante*. La réforme de 2001 était toutefois incomplète dans la mesure où le contrôle était toujours exercé par le Ministre de l'économie, la France étant le dernier État membre de l'Union dans lequel le contrôle des concentrations n'était pas opéré par une autorité de concurrence indépendante. Cet anachronisme a disparu avec l'adoption de la loi du 4 août 2008 qui a transféré le contrôle des concentrations à la nouvelle Autorité de la concurrence.[17] À ce jour, seul le Royaume-Uni, qui a maintenu un contrôle mixte, fait figure d'exception.

De plus, au-delà du consensus sur la nécessité d'un contrôle assuré par une autorité indépendante au regard d'objectifs de nature concurrentielle,[18] la convergence sur les modalités du contrôle ne fait que s'intensifier.

1.2. Un rapprochement certain des modalités du contrôle

En-dehors du niveau des seuils nécessairement différents, les contrôles nationaux des concentrations sont très proches du règlement n° 139/2004, qu'il s'agisse de la notion de concentration, des méthodes d'évaluation et des tests d'appréciation, ou encore du recours à la technique des engagements pour lever les problèmes de concurrence qui pourraient découler des opérations.

Le droit français fournit à nouveau un exemple. Dans les Lignes directrices sur le contrôle des concentrations de 2009,[19] sur toutes les grandes questions, l'Autorité française n'hésite pas à s'appuyer sur la jurisprudence de la Cour de Justice et la pratique décisionnelle de la Commission. Même le législateur français renvoie sur certains points techniques, comme les modalités de calcul des chiffres d'affaires pour la vérification des seuils, directement à un article du règlement du Conseil.[20]

---

14 Peuvent être cités les exemples des Pays-Bas ou de la Finlande, qui, pour des opérations posant problème, ont été obligés de faire jouer le renvoi ascendant de l'article 22, § 3 du règlement n° 4064/89, pour que la Commission exerce un contrôle.

15 V. not., Louis Vogel, *op. cit.*, n° 374 et s. et les références citées.

16 V. not., Laurence Idot, *La réforme du droit français des concentrations*, *JCP éd. E*, *Cah. dr. ent.*, 2001, n° 4.

17 V. la présentation de la réforme sur le site de l'Autorité de la concurrence, www.autoritedelaconcurrence.fr.

18 Sur l'intervention éventuelle soit des ministres en droit national, soit des États en droit de l'Union, v. *infra* notes 97 et 98.

19 2 mars 2009. Disponibles sur le site de l'Autorité de la concurrence. Elles remplacent les précédentes lignes directrices adoptées par le ministre de l'économie en 2005 et revues en 2007. Une procédure de révision devrait être lancée à la fin de l'année 2012 pour intégrer la pratique décisionnelle de l'Autorité.

20 C. com., art. L. 430-2-V qui renvoie à l'article 5 du règlement n° 139/2004.

Le processus connaît toutefois des limites.

Certaines règles propres peuvent toujours être justifiées eu égard aux particularités de chaque État membres. Tel est le cas en France des seuils spécifiques de contrôle mis en place pour l'appréhension des concentrations dans le secteur de la grande distribution ou dans les départements d'outre mer.[21]

Plus intéressant à relever est le fait que des solutions adoptées en droit de l'Union peuvent trouver leur origine dans les droits nationaux. Ainsi, par exemple, alors que le premier règlement avait une conception restrictive des entreprises communes dites concentratives au regard des solutions françaises ou britanniques, ces dernières l'ont emporté et ont entrainé un élargissement de l'applicabilité du règlement à toutes les entreprises communes structurelles lors de la première réforme de 1997.[22] De même, lors de la discussion intervenue en 2003 sur la pertinence du test d'appréciation, qui a opposé les partisans du critère de la position dominante à ceux de la diminution sensible de la concurrence,[23] c'est en partie la solution française qui a été retenue pour la rédaction du nouveau test de l'article 2 du règlement n° 139/2004.

Lorsque des différences persistent et qu'une solution nationale paraît plus appropriée, les autorités nationales n'hésitent pas à peser de tout leur poids pour appeler une réforme et un alignement de la solution du droit de l'Union. L'on assiste à l'heure actuelle à une discussion de cet ordre sur le traitement à réserver aux participations minoritaires qui ne confèrent pas le contrôle d'une société, dans laquelle les autorités allemandes et autrichiennes défendent la supériorité de leur système.[24]

En définitive, malgré le système de guichet unique qui laisse au droit national toute latitude pour se développer et en dépit de l'absence de réseau officiel entre les autorités,[25] la convergence des contrôles des concentrations au sein de l'Union européenne est très élevée. Le phénomène est aisé à expliquer. Il s'agit d'abord d'une branche du droit nouvelle dans laquelle les États membres n'avaient pas d'histoire, ensuite de la composante du droit de la concurrence dans laquelle l'analyse économique et le rôle des économistes sont les plus importants. Le contrôle est par ailleurs de type administratif et ne laisse aucune place, en dehors du contrôle juridictionnel des décisions adoptées, au juge de droit commun. Dans ce contexte, les autorités de concurrence n'ont aucune difficulté à travailler ensemble pour trouver les solutions les plus efficaces. Les données sont plus complexes en matière de pratiques anticoncurrentielles.

---

21 C. com., art. L. 430-2-II et III.

22 Règlement n° 1310/97 du Conseil du 30 juin 1997 modifiant le règlement n° 4064/89. La nouvelle solution a donné satisfaction et a été conservée lors de la réforme de 2004.

23 Le débat était résumé dans la formule PDC vs SLC. Le "compromis espagnol" retient comme critère l'entrave significative à la concurrence, notamment du fait de la création ou du renforcement d'une position dominante (comp. art. L. 430-6 c. com.: atteinte à la concurrence, notamment par création ou renforcement d'une position dominante). La reprise du test n'est que partielle car le test français prévoit dans un deuxième temps la prise en compte de la contribution de l'opération au progrès économique. Cela étant, en pratique, comme le confirme la comparaison des Lignes directrices communautaires et françaises, l'alignement est total, du fait du recours éventuel à la théorie des efficacités.

24 V. not., *varii actores* Tendances, *Participations minoritaires et concentrations*, Concurrences n° 1-2012, www.concurrences.com.

25 Le principe de liaison constante entre la Commission et les Autorités Nationales de Concurrence (ANC) est rappelé dans le règlement. De plus, les ANC ont adopté des *Best Practices* sur le traitement des concentrations transfrontalières le 8 novembre 2011 (v. *Europe*, décembre 2011, focus 67).

2. Une convergence progressive en matière de pratiques anticoncurrentielles

Dans le domaine de l'antitrust (articles 101 et 102 TFUE), il faut tout d'abord tenir compte du poids de l'histoire et de la situation très différente suivant les États.[26] Dans les anciens États membres, à l'exception de l'Italie, des législations, au demeurant ineffectives, préexistaient au droit communautaire. L'Allemagne était un cas particulier, l'adoption de la GWB ayant coïncidé avec celle du traité de Rome. Les situations se sont diversifiées avec les élargissements successifs, mais l'exemple français, caractérisé au départ par une absence de "culture de concurrence," demeure représentatif du cas le plus répandu

À cela s'ajoute l'évolution du droit de l'Union lui-même. La situation a, en effet, radicalement changé à compter du 1er mai 2004, date d'entrée en vigueur du règlement n° 1/2003. Cela étant, ce règlement n'a fait que mettre en lumière une distinction qu'il fallait déjà faire antérieurement, entre les règles de fond (2.1.) et les règles de mise en œuvre (2.2.).

2.1. Un rapprochement certain des règles de fond

Une comparaison des 27 législations nationales au regard des articles 101 et 102 TFUE étant exclue, nous nous limiterons à deux séries d'observations générales. Certes, la convergence est une réalité indéniable qui a changé de nature ces dernières années, mais quelques idées fausses circulent encore sur le phénomène.

L'avancée de la convergence

La convergence existait déjà avant 2004, de manière apparemment paradoxale dans les États membres dans lesquels le droit de la concurrence (au sens de droit antitrust) ne faisait pas partie de la culture juridique. En raison de la supériorité technique du droit communautaire, l'on a assisté, en effet, à un alignement progressif des textes et à une intégration dans le droit national des solutions dégagées par la Cour de Justice.

Ainsi, en France, si l'interdiction des ententes préexistait au traité, c'est sur le modèle communautaire qu'a été introduite en 1963 l'interdiction des abus de position dominante. De même, sans attendre l'ordonnance du 1er décembre 1986, l'ancienne Commission de la concurrence avait adopté la notion de pratiques concertées en s'appuyant sur l'arrêt de la Cour dans l'affaire des matières colorantes, tandis qu'à partir des années 80, la chambre criminelle de la Cour de cassation avait accepté d'appliquer l'interdiction des ententes, initialement conçue pour les seules ententes hori-

26 Pour un regard extérieur sur la situation en Europe avant le règlement n° 1/2003 avec de nombreuses références historiques, v. le premier ouvrage de D. Gerber, préc.

zontales, aux relations verticales. L'adoption de l'ordonnance du 1er décembre 1986 n'a fait que conforter cette tendance et ce rapprochement progressif.[27]

Des évolutions similaires pourraient être relevées dans les États membres voisins, notamment en Belgique et aux Pays-Bas, ou encore en Espagne, au Portugal ou en Grèce.[28] L'on se bornera à donner l'exemple de l'Italie. La loi italienne sur la concurrence, adoptée tardivement en 1990, reprend, s'agissant des règles de fond, le contenu des articles 101 et 102 TFUE.[29]

Cette convergence était choisie. Certes, la Cour de Justice avait affirmé dès l'arrêt *Walt Wilhem*[30] le principe de primauté du droit communautaire. Toutefois, aucune obligation d'appliquer les interdictions des articles 101, § 1, et 102 TFUE ne pesait sur les autorités nationales de concurrence (ANC) et, en 1997, une étude menée par la Commission avait montré que seules 8 des 15 ANC étaient à l'époque habilitées par leur État à le faire.[31] Pour les autorités, qui avaient ce pouvoir, comme les autorités françaises ou allemandes, les applications effectives étaient rares. En France, elles étaient de 2 à 4 par an en moyenne.[32]

En d'autres termes, l'ancien système permettait aux États membres d'affirmer la spécificité de leur droit national. C'était un choix politique adopté, par exemple, pour des raisons au demeurant différentes, par l'Allemagne, ou par le Royaume-Uni. Même dans les pays où le droit communautaire était *a priori* suivi comme modèle, les législateurs pouvaient continuer à affirmer des spécificités. En droit français, en-dehors du maintien d'un titre IV sur les pratiques restrictives, l'on peut citer l'introduction de l'interdiction en 1986 des abus de dépendance économique[33] puis, en 1996, des prix abusivement bas,[34] ou plus significatif, en 2001, une modification de l'article L. 420-4 c. com. sur les exemptions pour mentionner au titre du progrès économique "la création ou le maintien d'emplois . . . ."[35]

L'article 3 du règlement n° 1/2003 a radicalement modifié les données. La convergence est désormais, sinon imposée, du moins vivement encouragée. L'article 3, § 1 oblige toutes les ANC et juridictions nationales à appliquer les articles 101 et 102 TFUE lorsque les pratiques sont susceptibles

27 V. en particulier, les nombreuses études intervenues lors de l'adoption de l'ordonnance. Pour une bibliographie, v. not. Louis Vogel, *Traité de droit des affaires* T. 1. Du droit commercial au droit économique, (Ripert et RoblotParis, LGDJ, 19ème éd., 2010, p. 838

28 V. dans les rapports annuels de la Commission européenne sur la politique de concurrence ainsi que dans les rapports du Comité "Politique de concurrence" de l'OCDE la présentation des principales évolutions législatives dans les États membres.

29 Loi n° 287 du 10 octobre 1990, art. 2 et 3.

30 CJCE, 14 février 1969, aff. 14/68, Rec., p. 1.

31 Cette étude avait conduit à l'adoption par la Commission de la Communication du 15 octobre 1997, relative à la coopération entre la Commission et les autorités de concurrence des États membres pour le traitement d'affaires relevant des articles 81 et 82 du traité CE (97/C 313/03), JOCE, n° C 313 du 15 oct. 1997. En droit français, v. art. 56 bis de l'ordonnance du 1er décembre 1986, adopté en 1992, devenu art. L. 470-6 c. com.

32 V. not., les rapports annuels du Conseil de la concurrence; *adde*, J.-B. Blaise, L. Idot, chron. "Concurrence", *RTDeur.*, à partir de 1995.

33 C. com., art. L. 420-2.

34 C. com., art. L. 420-5.

35 C. com., art. L. 420-4-I.2°.

d'affecter le commerce entre États membres. Le changement a été plus radical pour les ANC que pour les juridictions. Ainsi, par exemple, en France, plus de la moitié des affaires traitées par le Conseil puis l'Autorité relèvent désormais du droit de l'Union.[36] Il n'y a plus d'échappatoire . . . De plus, l'article 3, § 2 pose la règle dite de convergence, qui doit être totale pour les ententes, les États membres étant seulement autorisés à conserver des règles plus strictes en matière de pratiques unilatérales, soit pour les pratiques abusives.[37]

Les conséquences d'un tel système ont été immédiates. Pratiquement tous les États membres ont été obligés de revoir leur législation pour l'adapter au nouveau système,[38] en particulier les États membres qui avaient un droit national assez différent de l'article 101, § 1 TFUE en matière d'ententes et faisaient encore une distinction entre les ententes horizontales et les ententes verticales comme le droit allemand.[39] Toujours en matière d'ententes, le passage pour l'application de l'article 101, § 3 TFUE d'un système dit d'autorisation préalable à un système dit d'exception légale a conduit les États membres qui imposaient la notification des ententes à abandonner ce système,[40] la dualité de règles devenant impossible à gérer.[41] Paradoxalement, la France qui était la seule à connaître avant la réforme un système d'exception légale s'est retrouvée en pleine conformité avec le droit de l'Union et a pu se contenter de procéder à des ajustements techniques mineurs de ses textes.[42]

Une deuxième phase a désormais débuté. Les grandes réformes législatives sur les règles de fond sont intervenues. Les difficultés se posent maintenant lors de l'application des règles, car si les droits nationaux sont globalement le reflet des articles 101 et 102 TFUE, des différences peuvent naturellement subsister sur des points plus techniques, soit par choix politique, soit de manière plus prosaïque, parce que le copier/coller a été mal opéré . . . .

Un intéressant exemple est fourni par la théorie du seuil de sensibilité en matière d'ententes qui a été introduite en mars 2004 comme règle de procédure en droit français alors qu'il s'agit d'un

---

36 V. les statistiques précises dans les différents rapports annuels du Conseil puis de l'Autorité.

37 V. not., Le nouveau système de mise en œuvre des articles 81 et 82 CE, préc.

38 V. not., les informations données par la Commission européenne dans le rapport annuel sur la politique de concurrence, 2005 (part. III, COMP-2006-01560-01-07-FR). Postérieurement, v. ECN Working Group on Cooperation Issues, *Results of the questionnaire on the reform of Member States (MS) national competition laws after EC Regulation No. 1/2003* (2008). *Adde*, égal., le n° spécial de l'ECN Brief, 2010, *A Look Inside the ECN: Its members and its Work* (ec.europa.eu/competition/ecn/brief/05_2010/brief_special.pdf), qui permet d'avoir un accès à une version en langue anglaise des lois en vigueur à la fin de l'année 2010.

39 Une grande réforme du droit allemand est intervenue en 2005, suivie de modifications plus mineures en 2009.

40 V. par ex., en-dehors du cas allemand, les réformes opérées en Autriche (2005), Belgique (2006), Bulgarie (2008), Chypre (2008), République tchèque (2004), Grèce (2005), Hongrie (2009), Irlande (2006), Lettonie (2004), Lithuanie (2009), Malte (2004), Pologne (2007), Espagne (2007). Le Luxembourg a par ailleurs été conduit à adopter une loi sur la concurrence en 2004.

41 La Roumanie (réforme du 6 août 2010) et la Grèce (loi du 15 avril 2011) sont les derniers États à avoir abandonné le système de notification.

42 Ordonnance n° 2004-1173 du 4 novembre 2004 portant adaptation de certaines dispositions du code de commerce au droit communautaire de la concurrence. De même, les modifications ont été en général mineures dans les nouveaux États membres.

élément de qualification de l'entente en droit de l'Union.[43] Dans une affaire *Expédia*, la chambre commerciale de la Cour de cassation a posé une question préjudicielle à la Cour de Justice sur ce point.[44] Un tel exemple conduit à s'interroger sur la réalité de la convergence.

La réalité de la convergence

Deux éléments sont trop souvent négligés et certaines idées erronées doivent être rectifiées pour avoir une vision plus exacte de l'état de la convergence en droit des pratiques anticoncurrentielles.

En premier lieu, la convergence ne joue pas seulement dans le sens habituel vertical descendant. Elle joue et se développe de plus en plus dans le sens ascendant. Une telle inversion s'explique par le rôle prédominant que jouent désormais les ANC dans l'application des articles 101 et 102 TFUE au sein du *Réseau européen de concurrence*. La disparition du système de notification obligatoire des ententes pour le bénéfice de l'article 101 § 3 TFUE a totalement modifié le rôle de la Commission, qui a recentré son action sur la lutte contre les cartels. En-dehors de ce domaine où elle est effectivement la mieux placée pour appréhender les cartels internationaux qui persistent, ses interventions dans les affaires individuelles sont limitées. Au quotidien, ce sont les ANC qui traitent des problèmes, y compris des nouvelles problématiques. Fortes de cette expérience, elles peuvent ensuite faire valoir leur point de vue lors de l'adoption des textes à portée générale.[45]

Dans ce paysage nouveau, grâce en partie à son système procédural, l'Autorité française bénéficie d'une pratique diversifiée et occupe la première place au sein du Réseau.[46] Ce n'est donc pas un hasard si elle a joué un rôle important lors de l'adoption des "Orientations" de la Commission sur l'article 102 TFUE en 2009.[47] Bien plus, lors de la révision des règlements d'exemption sur les accords verticaux, ses positions ont été déterminantes, puisqu'elle était pratiquement la seule autorité à pouvoir s'appuyer sur une pratique importante,[48] la seule à avoir été confrontée à la problématique nouvelle de la rencontre entre distribution sélective et vente par Internet, illustrée par la célèbre affaire *Pierre Fabre*.[49]

En d'autres termes, en droit des pratiques anticoncurrentielles, il est totalement erroné de percevoir le droit de l'Union comme un droit imposé par la Commission européenne. C'est un droit construit en commun par la Commission et les ANC. Pour en prendre conscience, il faut non seulement travailler sur le texte final, le produit fini, mais examiner également en amont son origine et les conditions de son élaboration.

---

43 V. *La qualification de la restriction de concurrence*, in La modernisation du droit de la concurrence, sous la dir. de Guy Canivet (Paris, LGDJ 2006), p. 86-107.

44 Cass. com., 10 mai 2011, *Société Expédia*, *Europe*, juillet 2011, comm. 260, et *RDC,* 2011-4, pp. 1208-1214. Aff. C-226/11, et les concl. de l'avocat général Kokott du 6 sept. 2012.

45 V. not., pour une analyse du phénomène, Ch. Lemaire, "Premier bilan de l'application du règlement n° 1/2003", in AFEC, *2008: une année charnière en droit de la concurrence ? LPA* n° 251, 17 déc. 2008, pp. 38-48; Laurence Idot, *Regards sur le règlement n° 1/2003*, 205-218 Études à la mémoire de F.-C. Jeantet (Paris, LexisNexis 2010).

46 V. les statistiques sur le fonctionnement du Réseau sur le site de la Commission européenne, DG concurrence.

47 Orientations sur les priorités retenues par la Commission pour l'application de l'article 82 du traité CE aux pratiques d'éviction abusives des entreprises dominantes, JOUE, n° C. 45, 24 février 2009.

48 Sur ce point, *La pratique de l'Autorité française concurrence en matière de relations verticales*, Revista Concorrencia e Regulaçao, 2010-4, pp. 139-168.

49 CJUE, 13 octobre 2011, *Pierre Fabre*, aff. C-439/09.

En deuxième lieu, il est vrai que convergence ne veut pas dire harmonisation et le problème se pose de savoir si l'on doit aller plus loin. À la suite du rapport de 2009 sur les cinq premières années d'application du règlement n° 1/2003,[50] la Commission s'est interrogée sur l'opportunité de mettre fin à "l'exception" prévue à l'article 3, § 2 du règlement n° 1/2003 pour les pratiques unilatérales. Si l'on imposait une telle convergence en ce domaine, l'on serait obligé en France de supprimer l'interdiction des abus de dépendance économique et celle des prix abusivement bas. Cela étant, il n'est pas certain qu'empêcher les États membres de conserver dans leur arsenal juridique des dispositions inutiles ou mal placées soit le vrai problème, même si l'on y gagnerait en termes de cohérence et de lisibilité.

La véritable difficulté est liée à l'étendue du principe d'autonomie institutionnelle et procédurale. La particularité du système européen tient au fait que les mêmes règles de fond sont appliquées dans un cadre institutionnel et procédural variable suivant les États membres. En effet, si toutes les ANC et juridictions nationales appliquent désormais les articles 101 et 102 TFUE,[51] elles le font en suivant les principes de leur système institutionnel et leurs règles procédurales nationales.[52] L'on est par conséquence en présence de 28 à ce jour (27 + la Commission) systèmes différents de mise en œuvre, ce qui soulève deux séries de problèmes.

L'on se heurte d'abord à un problème classique de qualification.[53] Une répartition doit être opérée entre les questions de fond, qui relèvent de l'interprétation des articles 101 et 102 TFUE telle que donnée par la Cour de Justice, et les problèmes de procédure traités au regard des solutions du droit national. L'hypothèse n'est pas d'école et les enjeux parfois importants. En France, un premier exemple est fourni par les conditions d'octroi des mesures provisoires lorsque la pratique relève de l'article 101 TFUE. Alors que la cour d'appel de Paris avait opté pour la qualification règle de fond, l'arrêt a été cassé par la chambre commerciale de la Cour de cassation au nom de l'autonomie procédurale.[54] Une autre question très débattue par les entreprises est celle de la responsabilité des sociétés mères du fait des agissements de leurs filiales. L'Autorité de la concurrence, suivie par la Cour d'appel de Paris, considère qu'il s'agit d'une question de fond liée à l'interprétation de la notion d'entreprise et s'est alignée sur la jurisprudence de la Cour de Justice. Il semblerait qu'en Allemagne une solution différente soit actuellement défendue. Il appartiendra à la Cour de Justice de trancher ce conflit de qualifications.[55]

À supposer que le problème relève de la qualification "règle de procédure," surgit une seconde difficulté. Il faut alors déterminer si la diversité des solutions est tolérable ou s'il faut aller plus loin dans la convergence des règles.

---

50 Communication de la Commission au Parlement européen et au Conseil, Rapport sur le fonctionnement du règlement n° 1/2003 (COM (2009) 206 final, 29 avril 2009).

51 Avec l'adoption du règlement n° 1/2003, la Commission a perdu la seule compétence exclusive dont elle disposait pour les exemptions individuelles de l'article 101, § 3 TFUE. Les ANC et juridictions nationales peuvent également appliquer l'article 106 TFUE, du moins les §§ 1 et 2, reconnus d'effet direct.

52 V. pour une étude récente, les travaux de la 2ème table ronde, *Procedural Autonomy: Is it time for convergence in Europe?*, New Frontiers of Antitrust, 10 fév. 2012, CONCURRENCES n° 2-2012, avec les interventions de Guy Canivet, Eric Barbier de la Serre, Henk Don et Laurence Idot.

53 Laurence Idot, *Les leçons du droit international privé*, in table ronde préc.

54 Cass. com., 14 déc. 2004, *Pharmalab*, pourvoi n° 02-17012.

55 Sur tous ces points et la jurisprudence citée, v. *Les leçons du droit international privé*, préc.

2.2. Un rapprochement progressif des règles de mise en œuvre

Au moment de l'adoption du règlement n° 1/2003 et de la mise en place du *Réseau européen de concurrence*, la question a été débattue de savoir s'il fallait procéder à une harmonisation des règles de procédure et de sanctions, ou laisser jouer le principe d'autonomie institutionnelle et procédurale avec ses limites habituelles que sont le principe d'équivalence et d'effectivité.[56] Sous réserve des quelques règles nécessaires au fonctionnement du Réseau introduites dans le règlement n° 1/2003, il avait été décidé de ne pas aller plus loin.

Huit ans plus tard, une deuxième phase a débuté et la question se pose de savoir si ce patchwork procédural est encore tolérable. Pour prendre position, il est nécessaire d'introduire la distinction fondamentale en droit des pratiques anticoncurrentielles entre le *public enforcement* et le *private enforcement*.

En matière de public enforcement

Pour des raisons historiques évidentes, les systèmes institutionnels demeurent variés, même si un modèle européen d'autorité de concurrence est en train de se dessiner peu à peu.[57] Deux évolutions sont intervenues.

Dans les années 90, pour beaucoup d'États membres, le débat a d'abord porté sur le transfert des pouvoirs détenus par l'administration économique à une autorité indépendante.[58] On s'est orienté vers le modèle d'une autorité administrative indépendante unique, dont le *Bundeskartellamt*, puis plus tard l'*Autorità Garante della Concorrenza e del Mercato* (AGCM) ont été les exemples phares. Cette évolution s'est faite progressivement et, là encore, l'exemple français est topique.[59]

Les données sont aujourd'hui différentes. L'organisation doit respecter les règles de l'article 6 CEDH, dont les prescriptions, bien qu'intégrées de longue date dans l'ordre juridique de l'Union européenne paraissent renforcées depuis le Traité de Lisbonne et la proclamation de la Charte. Il n'y a pas de règle universelle et les solutions sont variées, que l'on organise la séparation des fonctions au sein d'une autorité unique,[60] ou que l'on confie le pouvoir d'infliger les sanctions de nature pénale à un juge, qui est souvent un juge spécialisé,[61] mais peut être le juge de droit commun.[62]

---

56 V. en particulier les débats, 7th European Competition Law Annual. Constructing the Network of EU Authorities, (Claus Dieter Ehlermann et Isabel Atanasiu editors, Oxford, Hart Publishing 2004).

57 Pour une présentation à jour à la fin de l'année 2010, v. ECN Brief, Special Issue, 2010, *A Look Inside the ECN: Its members and its Work*. Pour une réflexion sur l'évolution des modèles, Fabien Zivy, *Quel schéma institutionnel pour la régulation de la concurrence ?*, Concurrences n° 4-2007, n° 14479, pp. 50-63.

58 V. sur ce point, toutes les études faites sur le développement des autorités administratives indépendantes dans les États continentaux, sur les QANGOS au Royaume-Uni.

59 Les évolutions ont été similaires dans les États membres voisins du Benelux, les États méditerranéens (Espagne, Portugal, Grèce), ainsi que dans les PECO.

60 C'est la solution retenue en France, la séparation entre les services d'instruction sous la responsabilité du Rapporteur Général et le Collège qui adopte les décisions ayant été renforcée par la loi du 4 août 2008. Une séparation identique existe au sein des autorités des États membres voisins qui ont procédé à un regroupement ces derniers mois (B, E, Lux.).

61 Une telle solution a les faveurs des pays nordiques (Danemark, Suède, Finlande) et de l'Autriche.

62 C'est le choix fait par l'Irlande, mais également par l'Estonie, sous réserve que l'Office de protection de la concurrence dispose d'un pouvoir d'injonction, que n'a pas l'office irlandais qui n'a qu'un rôle de détection et de poursuites.

La liberté de l'État membre dans le choix de son modèle institutionnel est dès lors doublement encadrée, non seulement par les traditionnelles limites au principe d'autonomie institutionnelle et procédurale (équivalence et effectivité), mais également par les exigences des droits fondamentaux. La jurisprudence récente montre que les contraintes pèsent davantage sur l'autorité qui intervient en première instance que sur le système de contrôle juridictionnel. La Cour de Justice a donné une lecture restrictive de l'article 5 du règlement n° 1/2003 quant aux types de décisions que l'autorité pouvait adopter,[63] alors qu'elle confortait par ailleurs son statut procédural devant la cour de contrôle.[64] De son côté, la Cour européenne des droits de l'Homme a validé en septembre 2011 l'étendue du contrôle juridictionnel opéré.[65]

C'est toutefois sur le déroulement des procédures stricto sensu que la convergence peut être observée le plus nettement. Le contrôle des pratiques anticoncurrentielles étant de nature quasi-répressive, on retrouve toujours les trois grandes étapes (enquête, instruction, décision) d'une procédure pénale classique. De plus, les mêmes exigences liées à l'application de l'article 6 CEDH constituent un fonds commun à l'ensemble des États membres. Le travail en réseau, le benchmarking permanent que cela implique au travers des échanges de vues et des rencontres entre les autorités à tous les niveaux, ont permis un indéniable rapprochement des législations nationales.[66]

Les résultats les plus spectaculaires ont d'abord été obtenus dans les domaines nouveaux, comme celui des procédures dites négociées. Cela s'est traduit par l'introduction et la généralisation des procédures d'engagements,[67] puis de clémence, plus récemment des procédures dites de transaction.[68] Dans le cas particulier des procédures de clémence, plus difficiles à organiser, un travail de rapprochement des textes, souvent de *soft law*, a été opéré par les autorités elles-mêmes, qui a abouti à un programme modèle sur lequel les programmes nationaux ont été volontairement alignés.[69]

---

63 CJUE (Gde ch.), 3 mai 2011, *Télé 2 Polska*, aff. C-375/09, *Concurrences* n° 3-2011, pp. 173-177, note C. L., *Europe* 2011, comm. 258, obs. L. Idot, *RLDC* 2011, n° 28, n° 1870, obs. E. B.S., *RTDeur.* 2011.841, note J-B.B.

64 CJUE (Gde ch.), 7 déc. 2010, *VEBIC*, aff. C-439/08; v. not., *Concurrences* n° 1-2011, pp. 179-181, note A. M., *Europe* 2011, comm. 71, obs. L. Idot, *JDI* 2011 pp. 553-556, note C. Prieto, *RTDeur.* 2011.418.

65 CEDH, 27 sept. 2011, *Menarini Diagnostics*, CONCURRENCES N° 4-2011, n° 40019, obs. P. Cardonnel, p. 166.

66 V. sur ce point, "La mise en réseau des autorités de régulation," *RDP* 2008-3, pp. 787-821.

67 La procédure, purement informelle avant le règlement n° 1/2003 en droit communautaire, a été formalisée à l'article 9 pour la Commission. Difficilement concevable dans le système français de l'ordonnance du 1er décembre 1986, elle a été introduite, comme mesure d'adaptation de l'article 5 du règlement n° 1/2003, par l'ordonnance (préc.) du 4 novembre 2004 (C. com., art. L. 464-2-I, al. 1). V. le communiqué de procédure de l'Autorité du 2 mars 2009 et sur la pratique décisionnelle, le site de l'Autorité, sous la rubrique "procédures négociées/engagements."

68 La procédure de transaction (en anglais *settlement*) a été introduite dans la procédure de la Commission par le règlement n° 662/2008 du 30 juin 2008 (JOUE, n° L 171, 1er juill. 2008; *adde,* la communication qui explicite la procédure, JOUE, n° C 167, 2 juill. 2008). Elle est assez différente de la procédure dite de non contestation des griefs introduite en droit français par loi NRE du 15 mai 2001 (C. com., art. L-464-2-III), qui vient de donner lieu à un communiqué de procédure de l'Autorité du 10 février 2012.

69 Introduite par une communication du 18 juillet 1996 en droit communautaire, la procédure a été reprise en droit français par la loi NRE (C. com., art. L-464-2-IV). Pour une étude récente sur la situation dans l'Union européenne, v. *Les procédures de clémence en droit de la concurrence* in LA CLÉMENCE ET LE DROIT (sous la dir. de J-M. Jude) (Paris, Economica 2011), et les références indiquées.

Une nouvelle phase débute maintenant en ce sens que le travail de rapprochement porte sur les procédures traditionnelles. Tel est le cas des procédures d'enquête où le développement de l'informatique a modifié les données. Un groupe de travail sur les enquêtes dites informatiques a été constitué au sein du Réseau. Parallèlement, les autorités travaillent également sur la convergence des sanctions pécuniaires infligées aux entreprises.[70] Cela s'est traduit par la multiplication ces derniers mois de lignes directrices sur ce sujet particulièrement sensible.

C'est là au demeurant un point commun révélateur d'un autre aspect de la convergence. Cette dernière ne concerne pas seulement le contenu de la règle, mais sa nature même. Dans le cadre déterminé par le législateur, les ANC développement via la *soft law* de nouveaux outils, qui deviennent pour les entreprises et leurs conseils, des outils quotidiens.[71] Il s'agit là assurément d'une évolution difficilement concevable dans le cadre du private enforcement.

En matière de private enforcement

Les données sont totalement différentes pour de multiples raisons. C'est tout d'abord un domaine où du fait de l'incomplétude du droit de l'Union, il y a un renvoi total aux droits nationaux qu'il s'agisse du principe même des sanctions civiles, ce que recouvre mieux la notion anglaise de remedies, de leurs conditions, du cadre juridictionnel et procédural dans lequel elles peuvent être sollicitées. Le *private enforcement* fait appel aux principes les plus classiques du droit des obligations (droit des contrats, droit de la responsabilité civile) mis en œuvre devant les juridictions de droit commun. Le poids de l'histoire est omniprésent et le droit des pratiques anticoncurrentielles n'est alors pas dans une situation différente de celles d'autres branches du droit de création récente, comme par exemple, le droit de l'environnement.

Si la première conséquence civile qu'est la nullité de l'acte juridique, support d'une pratique anticoncurrentielle, n'a guère retenu l'attention des autorités de concurrence,[72] tel n'est pas le cas de-

70 Groupe de travail ECA sur les sanctions, *Les sanctions pécuniaires des entreprises en droit de la concurrence Principes pour une convergence*, disponible notamment sur le site de l'Autorité, avec un communiqué de presse du 7 octobre 2008.

71 Sur ce phénomène qui n'a fait que s'intensifier depuis l'étude, *À propos de l'internationalisation du droit. L'exemple de la soft law en droit de la concurrence*, in VERS UN NOUVEL ÉQUILIBRE ENTRE LES ORDRES JURIDIQUES. MÉLANGES EN L'HONNEUR DE H. GAUDEMET-TALLON (Paris, Dalloz 2008).

72 En revanche, de nombreux travaux doctrinaux lui ont été consacrés (en-dehors des développements qui figurent dans tous les traités, par ex., MICHEL WAELBROECK, DROIT DE LA COMMUNAUTÉ EUROPÉENNE. COMMENTAIRE MEGRET, VOL. CONCURRENCE (Bruxelles, ULB 1997) v. not., Emanuelle Claudel, *Ententes anticoncurrentielles et droit des contrats*, thèse, Paris X, 1994; pour une synthèse, CL. LUCAS DE LEYSSAC ET G. PARLÉANI, L'ATTEINTE À LA CONCURRENCE, CAUSE DE NULLITÉ DU CONTRAT, LE CONTRAT AU DÉBUT DU XXIÈME SIÈCLE. MÉLANGES J. GHESTIN (LGDJ 2001), p. 601; L'empiètement du droit de la concurrence sur le droit des contrats, débat, *Revue des Contrats* 2004, n° 3, p. 882 et s., avec les interventions de, C. Prieto, M. Chagny, M. Behar-Touchais, L. Idot). Les données sont établies. Le principe de la nullité est affirmé par les textes (art. 101, § 2 TFUE, art. L 420-3 c. com.) et les grandes lignes du régime ont été posées par la Cour de Justice, en particulier quant à l'étendue de la nullité.

puis quelques années des actions en réparation. Désireuse de favoriser cette sanction civile,[73] la Commission a commandité plusieurs études sur les différents droits des États membres, qui ont révélé des divergences plus importantes qu'on aurait pu le penser, aussi bien sur les conditions de fond de l'action en réparation que sur le cadre procédural.[74]

À ce jour, les interventions de la Cour de Justice ont été limitées. Initialement interrogée sur le statut procédural des articles 101 et 102 TFUE et la question du relevé d'office devant le juge de droit commun,[75] la Cour avait fait jouer assez largement le principe d'autonomie procédurale.[76] Quelques années plus tard, elle s'est montrée plus exigeante pour confirmer le droit des victimes de pratiques anticoncurrentielles à réparation et écarter les règles procédurales qui auraient pu conduire à sa remise en cause au nom du principe d'effectivité dans les fameux arrêts *Courage*[77] et *Manfredi*.[78] En revanche, en 2011 dans l'arrêt *Pfleiderer*,[79] saisie de la question actuellement sensible de l'accès au dossier des autorités de concurrence dans le cadre des actions en réparation consécutives, dites

---

73 Commission européenne, Livre vert sur les actions en dommages et intérêts pour infraction aux règles communautaires sur les ententes et les abus de position dominante, COM (2005) 672 final, Livre blanc sur les actions en dommages et intérêts pour infraction aux règles communautaires sur les ententes et les abus de position dominante, COM (2008) 165 final, 2 avril 2008. De très nombreux travaux ont accompagné ou suivi la publication de ces documents. En France, parmi les travaux collectifs, v. not., *Les sanctions judiciaires des pratiques anticoncurrentielles,* Colloque Université Paris I, 29 avril 2004, *Petites affiches* 20 janvier 2005, n° 14; *La réparation du préjudice causé par une pratique anticoncurrentielle en France et à l'étranger: bilan et perspectives*, Cycle "*Droit et économie de la concurrence*" de la Cour de cassation, 17 octobre 2005, disponible DVD droit *in situ* et sur le site de la Cour de cassation; "*Les actions civiles à l'encontre des pratiques anticoncurrentielles,*" Atelier de la concurrence de la DGCCRF, 4 octobre 2006; colloque du Mans, décembre 2006, *Les sanctions civiles des pratiques anticoncurrentielles: Compléments ou substituts des sanctions du droit de la concurrence* ? Concurrences, n° 2-2007, p. 90.

74 Rapport dit Ashurst, *Study on the conditions of claims for damages in case of infringement of EC competition rules,* 2004. CEPS, Making antitrust damages actions more effective in the EU: welfare impact and potential scenarios, 2007. Toutes les études sont disponibles sur le site de la DG concurrence. V. égal., dans une perspective comparative et strictement juridique, "*Les contentieux de droit privé (actions en réparation) dans le domaine des pratiques anticoncurrentielles devraient-ils être encouragés et, si tel est le cas, à travers quelles mesures concrètes ?*", Congrès de la Ligue internationale de droit de la concurrence, Amsterdam, 5-8 octobre 2006, travaux disponibles, www.lidc.org.

75 CJCE, 14 déc. 1995, *Van Schijndel*, aff. C-430 et 431/93, Rec., p. I-4705, *Europe,* 1996, comm. 57, obs. D. Simon et A. Rigaux, *JDI* 1996-2, p. 468, obs. D. Simon; *adde*, G. Canivet J.-G. Huglo, *L'obligation pour le juge judiciaire national d'appliquer d'office le droit communautaire au regard des arrêts Jeroen Van Schijndel et Peterbroeck,* Europe 1996, chron. 4 ;CJCE, 1er juin 1999, *Eco* Swiss, aff. C-126/97, Rec., p. I-3055, *Europe* 1999, comm. 302, *Rev. Arb.* 1999.641, note L. Idot, *JDI* 2000, pp. 299-307, note S. Peruzzetto et pp. 504-506, note C. Prieto.

76 Cela contraste avec son attitude en matière de contrôle des aides d'État, où le principe d'effectivité semble l'emporter, v. par ex., sur la question de l'accès aux preuves dans le contexte du droit français, CJCE, 7 septembre 2006, *Laboratoire Boiron*, aff. C-526/04, Rec., p. I-7529, *Europe* nov. 2006, comm. n° 324.

77 CJCE, 20 septembre 2001, *Courage Ltd* c/ *B. Crehan*, aff. C-453/99, *Rec*. p. I-6297. Parmi les commentaires en français, *Europe* nov. 2001, comm. n° 330; *Contrats conc. consom.* janv. 2002, n° 14, obs. S. Poillot- Peruzzetto; *RDC* 2003, p. 71, obs. J.-S. Bergé., *JCP éd. ent*. 2002, p. 1-6, note S. Ramet.

78 CJCE, 13 juillet 2006, *Vincenzo Manfredi*, aff. C-295/04 à C-298/04, *Rec*. p. I-6619; Europe oct. 2006, comm. n° 295; Concurrences n° 4-2006, chron. Procédures, p. 118, obs. F.Z, RLDC 2006, n° 9, n° 650, note P. Iannuccelli, et n° 659, note M. Chagny, *JDI* 2007, pp. 671-674, note C. Prieto.

79 CJUE (Gde ch.), 14 juin 2011, *Pfleiderer AG*, aff. C-360/09, Concurrences n° 3-2011, pp. 177-178, note A. L., Europe 2011, comm. n° 308, RLDC 2011, n° 29, n°1937, note E. Barbier de la Serre et S. Quilès, *RTDeur.* 2011-4, chron. "Concurrence", p. 844, note J-B. B.

"follow on" et ne voulant pas choisir entre des objectifs contradictoires et également importants pour la politique de concurrence, la Cour de Justice a laissé les juges nationaux libres de trancher, ce qui conduit naturellement à des solutions variées.[80]

Dans d'autres situations, les juridictions de droit commun ignorent purement et simplement la contrainte qui pourrait résulter de l'application au fond d'une règle du droit de l'Union du fait du principe d'effectivité. Peut être mentionnée à cet égard l'attitude de la deuxième chambre civile de la Cour de cassation qui a donné une interprétation étroite de l'action en représentation conjointe ruinant les efforts de l'association *UFC Que Choisir* pour obtenir réparation des préjudices subis par les consommateurs dans l'affaire de la téléphonie mobile.[81] Au demeurant, la question des recours collectifs est l'une de celles sur lesquelles les divergences de solution sont les plus fortes et les obstacles politiques les plus nombreux.[82]

Si l'on veut éviter le *forum shopping*, situation rendue possible compte tenu des multiples options ouvertes en matière de compétence internationale par le règlement n° 44/2001 dit "Bruxelles I"[83] qui commence à se développer en matière d'actions en réparation, une intervention du "législateur européen" est nécessaire.[84] La Commission en est parfaitement consciente et des travaux sont en cours. Un premier avant projet a avorté en 2009 en raison des oppositions de certains États membres, dont la France, sur la question des recours collectifs et l'on attend toujours une proposition de directive. Dans cette perspective, l'arrêt *Pfleiderer* a pu être interprété comme un appel du juge à l'intervention du législateur.

Plusieurs points devraient être traités. S'agissant de l'établissement de la faute, l'on s'oriente vers la reconnaissance de l'autorité de chose décidée d'une décision devenue définitive de l'autorité de concurrence, solution déjà adoptée au moins en Allemagne. Un document d'orientation devrait également être adopté pour aider les juges dans la quantification du préjudice,[85] la question de fond étant par ailleurs celle de la réparation du préjudice indirect, ou dans la terminologie du droit de la concurrence, la *passing on defense*. Restent deux questions sensibles : l'accès aux preuves, dont le dossier de l'autorité n'est qu'un élément, et, en amont, les actions collectives.[86]

---

80 On dispose à ce jour de jurisprudence en Allemagne, en France, en Italie, au Royaume-Uni. V. sur le site www.concurrences.com.

81 Cass. civ. 1ère, 26 mai 2011, pourvoi n° 10-15676, Concurrences n° 3-2011, p. 190.

82 Pour la position de l'autorité de concurrence française, Cons. conc., Avis du 21 septembre 2006 relatif à l'introduction de l'action de groupe en matière de pratiques anticoncurrentielles., dont les conclusions demeurent fondées. Pour une étude d'ensemble dans une perspective comparative, Silvia Pietrini, L'action collective en droit des pratiques anticoncurrentielles. Perspective nationale, européenne et internationale, Thèse (Paris X Nanterre, 2010, coll. Concurrences, Larcier, Bruxelles, 2012).

83 Règlement n° 44/2001 du Conseil du 22 décembre 2000 concernant la compétence judiciaire, la reconnaissance et l'exécution des décisions en matière civile et commerciale, *JOCE* n° L. 12 du 16 janvier 2001.

84 Sur cet aspect, v. déjà, les travaux du colloque du Mans, décembre 2006, préc. Pour une étude plus complète, International Antitrust Litigation. Conflicts of Laws and Coordination (Oxford, J. Basedow, S. Francq, L. Idot, co-ed., Hart Publishing 2012).

85 La Commission a lancé au cours de l'été 2011 une consultation publique sur un "Projet de document d'orientation— La quantification du préjudice dans les actions en dommages et intérêts fondées sur des infractions à l'article 101 ou 102."

86 La Commission a décidé d'avoir une approche globale et a lancé en février 2011, *Staff Working Document*, "Towards a Coherent European Approach to Collective Redress" (SEC (2011)173 final). V. "Cohérence européenne des recours collectifs—Réponse à la consultation publique de la Commission européenne" sous la direction de C. Prieto, vol. II, TEE, sept. 2011.

Plusieurs conclusions peuvent être tirées de l'expérience européenne. En-dehors du constat prévisible que la convergence est plus forte dans les domaines techniques propres au droit de la concurrence, le travail en réseau a profondément modifié les données. Il convient de se demander si les résultats sont identiques lorsque, dépassant le cadre de l'Union européenne, l'on examine la convergence dans un contexte global.

II. La convergence des droits de la concurrence dans un contexte global

Compte tenu de l'ampleur du sujet, qui a donné lieu récemment à plusieurs études importantes,[87] l'on se bornera à quelques réflexions d'ordre général. Comme il a été rappelé, les données ont radicalement changé au cours de ces quinze dernières années.

Dans les années 70/80, le droit de la concurrence semblait être le monopole des États dits industrialisés, lesquels débattaient des questions communes au sein d'une organisation qui leur était propre, l'OCDE, dont le Comité sur la politique de concurrence continue à jouer un rôle très actif. Dans les relations avec les pays émergents, encore appelés en voie de développement, le droit de la concurrence ne faisait l'objet que d'une assistance technique via la CNUCED.[88]

La fin du millénaire a été marquée par la globalisation de l'économie que l'on connaît. En droit de la concurrence, deux conséquences principales en ont résulté: d'une part, pratiquement tous les États se sont dotés d'un droit de la concurrence, d'autre part, cela a relancé le débat sur la nécessité de penser le droit de la concurrence dans un contexte global.

Sur ces deux points, la situation en 2012 n'est pas celle à laquelle l'on aurait pu initialement s'attendre. Si la généralisation des droits de la concurrence s'est faite sur la base de modèles, le modèle qui s'est imposé n'est pas le modèle américain (1.). Alors que l'Organisation mondiale du Commerce apparaissait initialement comme l'enceinte naturelle pour penser un droit de la concurrence au niveau mondial, les tentatives d'instauration d'un cadre commun amorcées en 1996 ont échoué

---

87 V. not., GLOBAL COMPETITION: LAW, MARKETS AND GLOBALIZATION, préc.; l'ouvrage collectif, paru pour le Xème anniversaire de l'ICN en 2011, THE INTERNATIONAL COMPETITION NETWORK AT TEN. ORIGINS, ACCOMPLISHMENTS AND ASPIRATIONS (Paul Lugard ed., Cambridge, Intersentia 2011).

88 Sur les travaux des différentes organisations internationales en droit de la concurrence à la fin des années 80, en particulier, ceux de l'OCDE et de la CNUCED, v. notre thèse, *Le contrôle des pratiques restrictives de concurrence dans les échanges internationaux,* Paris II, 1981, sp. 2ème partie, titre I. Pour un bilan plus récent des travaux de l'OCDE et de la CNUCED, v. NATHALIE JALABERT-DOURY, *Les instruments de coopération plurilatéraux et multilatéraux de soft law élaborés par l'OCDE*, PHILIPPE BRUSICK, *La Cnuced: le code des Nations Unies sur la concurrence*, in MONDIALISATION ET DROIT DE LA CONCURRENCE, colloque de Dijon (sous la dir. de W. Abdelgawad), travaux du Credimi, Paris, Litec, 2007.

et les travaux ont été abandonnés après le cycle de Doha.[89] En revanche, et de manière spontanée, les autorités de concurrence dans le monde se sont regroupées en octobre 2001 au sein d'un réseau informel, l'*International Competition Network,*[90] enceinte inédite dont la finalité est précisément la recherche de la convergence (2.).

1. L'existence de modèles

En droit de la concurrence, il existe à l'heure actuelle deux principaux modèles qu'expliquent naturellement la puissance économique du groupe représenté et l'histoire: un modèle américain, un modèle européen. S'il n'est pas possible de nier le rôle joué par le droit antitrust américain dans la conception et le développement du droit européen,[91] les données sont actuellement autres. L'on assiste à un phénomène à double détente: le modèle européen l'emporte indéniablement vis à vis des pays émergents (1.1.), même s'il reste naturellement influencé par le modèle américain (1.2.).

1.1. La domination du modèle européen

À une époque où les droits de la concurrence se généralisent dans le monde, les États ou organisations régionales qui souhaitent se doter d'un tel outil se tournent naturellement vers les deux systèmes dominants. Or, contrairement à ce que l'on pourrait penser, le modèle européen l'emporte,[92] comme le montre l'étude des dernières législations adoptées dans les pays émergents, en particulier, les BRIC,[93] comme le Brésil, la Chine, l'Inde. D'autres exemples pourraient être trouvés dans les lois notamment d'États du sud-est asiatique.[94]

---

89 Pierre Arhel, *La tentative d'élaboration d'un accord multilatéral ou plurilatéral: les leçons tirées des travaux du groupe de travail de l'OMC en matière de concurrence* in Mondialisation et droit de la concurrence, préc. De nombreuses thèses, surtout de publicistes, ont été consacrées à ces développements. V. not., Nicolas Ligneul, L'élaboration d'un droit international de la concurrence entre les entreprises (Bruxelles, Bruylant 2001); Habib Kazzi, Le contrôle des pratiques anticoncurrentielles et des concentrations entre entreprises dans une économie mondialisée. Contribution à l'étude de l'application internationale du droit économique (PUAM 2008); Ali Cenk Keskin, Pour un nouveau droit international de la concurrence (Paris, l'Harmattan 2010).

90 Sur les origines, le développement, les caractéristiques de l'ICN, v. en particulier, Merit E. Janow et James F. Rill, *The Origins of the ICN*, François Souty, *From the Hallos of Geneva to the Shores of the Low Countries: The Origins of the International Competition Network*, Hugh M. Hollman et William E. Kovacic, *The International Competition Network: its Past, Current and Future Role*, in The International Competition Network at Ten, préc., respectivement p. 21, 39 et 51.

91 V. not., D. Gerber, *Law and Competition in Twentieth Century Europe*, préc.

92 V. égal. le constat fait par une américaine, E. Fox, lors de l'*European Competition Forum* du 2 février 2012, (disponible sur le site de la Commission, DG conc.) dans la 3ème table ronde sur "le modèle européen".

93 Sur la loi chinoise de 2007, v. F. Souty, préc.; sur la loi brésilienne, Ricardo Ingles de Souza, *Brazilian competition law: Fifteen years of developments*, Concurrences n° 1-2010, p. 210, n° 30049 et, en dernier lieu, sur la réforme de 2011, Elizabeth Farina et Fabiana Tito, *Brazilian Competition Defense: New Year, New Law*, Concurrences n° 1-2012, n° 41412, www.concurrences.com; sur la loi indienne de 2007, Farhad Sorajbee et *alii*, *Indian Competition Law: Entry into force of the 2007 reform*, Concurrences n° 3-2009, n° 26543, www.concurrences.com.

94 Tel est le cas pour les pays de l'ASEAN. V. not., la loi de l'État de Singapour (Competition Act de 2004) mais également la loi du Viet-Nam (3 déc. 2004).

Plusieurs caractéristiques du modèle européen expliquent cette suprématie de prime abord surprenante.

i) Les premières raisons sont d'ordre institutionnel. Les différences sont profondes entre les systèmes américain et européen. Le système américain est judiciaire. Les juridictions des États-Unis exercent au final le pouvoir de décision tant en antitrust qu'en contrôle des concentrations, et, même s'il existe des agences, comme la *Federal Trade Commission*, elles ne possèdent pas les caractéristiques des autorités de concurrence européennes, dont l'indépendance par rapport au pouvoir exécutif est le trait majeur. À l'inverse, le modèle européen est principalement de type administratif, qu'il s'agisse de la Commission ou des Autorités Nationales de Concurrence, souvent conçues sur le modèle des AAI.

Ce modèle dit administratif, au cœur du système européen, qui s'accompagne d'une distinction claire entre le *public enforcement* et le *private enforcement*, est plus adapté aux pays émergents, dans lesquels le système judiciaire est encore souvent fragile et pas nécessairement familiarisé avec la matière économique. S'il y une volonté politique en ce sens, la mise en place d'une autorité administrative indépendante pour la mise en œuvre des règles permet de nommer des personnes compétentes et d'assurer la séparation vis-à-vis du pouvoir politique, souhaitée par les organisations internationales. Dans tous les États récemment dotés de droits de la concurrence, des autorités, aux les noms variés (conseils, commissions), mais aux pouvoirs comparables, ont été mises en place.

À cette première donnée, s'ajoute une seconde raison institutionnelle. Dans les continents, où des organisations régionales d'intégration économique ont été mises en place,[95] de manière paradoxale, l'expérience des relations entre Union européenne et États membres en droit de la concurrence est plus opérationnelle que le modèle fédéral américain. Les américains nous envient le *Réseau européen de concurrence*, car les relations entre les structures fédérales et les structures étatiques sont pratiquement inexistantes en droit antitrust,[96] comme l'ont illustré notamment les épisodes américains de l'affaire *Microsoft*.

ii) D'autres explications concernent le fond du droit. Sur le plan substantiel, le modèle européen, qui ne fait pas de la concurrence un objectif en soi, dominé par des objectifs d'efficacité économique à court ou moyen terme, permet plus facilement d'intégrer d'autres considérations d'intérêt général dans la décision. Pour les ententes, cela découle du mécanisme d'exemption de l'article 101, § 3 TFUE. Pour le contrôle des concentrations, il existe, tant en droit de l'Union européenne,[97] que dans les droits nationaux,[98] des mécanismes, qui permettent aux autorités politiques d'avoir le dernier mot, du moins si des intérêts légitimes sont en cause. De tels dispositifs sont plus adaptés aux systèmes des pays émergents.

---

95 V. pour l'Afrique, Mor Bakhoum, L'articulation du droit communautaire et des droits nationaux de la concurrence dans l'Union Économique et Monétaire Ouest Africaine (UEMOA) (Bruxelles, Bruylant, Collection munichoise du droit de la concurrence européen et international, vol. 13, 2007).

96 Pour une présentation du système américain, Barry Hawk et Jeffrey Beyer, *Lessons to be drawn from the Infra-National Network of Competition Authorities in the U.S.: The National Association of Attorneys General (NAAG) as a Case Study*, in European Competition Law Annual 2002: Constructing the EU Network of Competition Authorities, préc., p. 97-117.

97 V. règlement n° 139/2004, préc., art. 21, § 4. *Adde*, Nicolas Petit, *Non-competition concerns under the ECMR—An overview*, Concurrences n° 4-2008, p. 182.

98 V. en droit français, art. L. 430-7 c. com.; *adde*, Frédéric de Bure et Ianis Girgenson, *Le pouvoir d'intervention du ministre de l'Économie en matière de contrôle des concentrations*, Rev. Lamy de la conc. n° 18, janv./mars 2009, p. 9, n° 1265; en droit allemand, Josef Drexl, *L'expérience allemande du contrôle des concentrations*, Rev. Lamy de la conc. n° 18, janv./mars 2009, p. 144, n° 1323.

Il en est de même d'une autre différence qui touche au champ d'application du droit de la concurrence, lequel est beaucoup plus large en Europe, en raison de différences avec le droit antitrust américain sur trois points fondamentaux. En premier lieu, le droit de la concurrence s'applique à toutes les activités économiques et il n'y a aucune exception. En deuxième lieu, le droit de l'Union appréhende non seulement les comportements des entreprises publiques et celles dotées de droits exclusifs, mais dispose d'outils qui lui permettent de contrôler les interventions étatiques.[99] En troisième lieu, le droit commun de la concurrence est intégralement applicable aux secteurs régulés, même s'il existe par ailleurs une régulation sectorielle qui accompagne une ouverture à la concurrence.[100]

Là encore, pour des États dans lesquels le secteur public est encore souvent important et où les industries de réseaux (télécommunications, énergie, . . .) jouent un rôle déterminant dans l'économie, l'expérience européenne est particulièrement utile.

Cela étant, cette supériorité du modèle européen concerne, il est vrai, plus le cadre général que le contenu de la règle et, sur ce dernier point, le modèle américain retrouve son emprise.

1.2. La persistance du modèle américain

Dès que dépassant le système législatif dans son ensemble, l'on regarde les applications concrètes des règles, le modèle américain redevient dominant. Les solutions adoptées outre-Atlantique et en particulier les évolutions jurisprudentielles sont examinées avec une particulière attention, non seulement en Europe, mais dans le reste du monde.[101] Outre les raisons historiques, géopolitiques, la force du modèle américain tient essentiellement au soubassement économique de l'analyse, ainsi qu'à la diffusion de véritables doctrines relayées par des groupes d'intérêts puissants et bien organisés.

La prédominance du modèle américain suppose toutefois que l'analyse économique soit déterminante dans le jugement porté sur la pratique ou l'opération. L'exportation des méthodes et des théories dominantes peut alors intervenir.

Le contrôle des concentrations fournit un bon exemple. Les méthodes d'analyse, notamment pour

---

99 En-dehors du contrôle des aides d'État (art. 107 et 108 TFUE), toute réglementation nationale peut être contrôlée au regard des articles 101 et 102 TFUE si elle conduit à des pratiques anticoncurrentielles. Telle est la conséquence de la jurisprudence dite *Leclerc* de 1985, qui a été systématisée à partir des arrêts *Meng/Ohra/Reiff* du 27 novembre 1993 pour l'article 101 TFUE, puis étendue à l'article 102 TFUE (V. not., "Nouvelle invasion ou confirmation du domaine d'application du droit de la concurrence. À propos de quelques développements récents", *Europe* janv. 1996). Cette jurisprudence a été reprise en France par le Conseil d'État dès l'arrêt FFSA du 8 novembre 1996 (antérieur d'un an à l'arrêt Million et Marais qui a étendu la solution au droit français de la concurrence) et permet au juge administratif de contrôler les textes réglementaires et plus généralement tous les actes administratifs au regard des règles de concurrence.

100 Comp., aux États-Unis, la solution qui découle de l'arrêt *Trinko* du 13 janvier 2004 (Cour Suprême des États Unis, *Verizon Communications Inc*. v/ *Trinko LLP*, 540 US 398 (2004)).

101 V. not., H. Kazzi, préc., n° 773 et s.

délimiter les marchés, conçues aux États-Unis, comme le SNIPP test, ont été généralisées.[102] S'agissant de l'appréciation de l'opération, le test américain dit du SLC *(substantial lessening of competition)* a finalement été repris en droit de l'Union lors de la réforme de [103] de même que les économistes ont réussi à introduire la théorie des *efficiencies* en Europe.[104]

Comme il n'y a pratiquement pas de contentieux en contrôle des concentrations, la circulation des idées se fait essentiellement entre les économistes, qu'il s'agisse des autorités de concurrence, ou des conseils des entreprises.

En matière de pratiques anticoncurrentielles, les données sont plus complexes. Non seulement, le consensus sur le caractère nocif de la pratique peut faire défaut, mais de plus, au-delà des autorités de concurrence, les cours de contrôle sont souvent appelées à vérifier la légalité des décisions. Au cours de la période récente, l'on dispose d'au moins deux exemples qui illustrent une résistance nette des institutions européennes, prises dans leur ensemble, vis à vis des solutions adoptées aux États-Unis. En matière de pratiques unilatérales, le juge communautaire a maintenu une lecture de l'article TFUE plus offensive vis-à-vis des entreprises en très forte position dominante comme *Microsoft*,[105] même si la Commission s'est montrée favorable à l'introduction d'une analyse des effets concrets des pratiques. En matière de relations verticales, les récents débats sur le *resale price maintenance* (RPM) ont montré qu'une évolution jurisprudentielle jugée majeure de la Cour suprême aux États Unis n'était pas nécessairement reprise ensuite au sein de l'Union européenne.[106] Le dernier règlement n° a confirmé que l'interdiction des prix imposés était en Europe une restriction caractérisée.[107] De plus, en rappelant que toute restriction de concurrence, y compris une restriction par l'objet, pouvait prétendre à une exemption, si les entreprises rapportaient la preuve des conditions requises,[108] la Commission a rappelé l'originalité de la structure de l'article TFUE, comparé à la section du *Sherman Act*.

En revanche, s'il y a un consensus sur le caractère nocif d'une pratique, le modèle américain peut s'exporter relativement aisément. L'exemple des cartels internationaux est à cet égard topique. La lutte contre ces pratiques anticoncurrentielles, jugées particulièrement nocives, fait désormais l'una-

102 V. la reprise du SNIPP test dans la communication (97/C 372/03) de la Commission sur la définition du marché en cause aux fins du droit communautaire de la concurrence (*JOCE* C 372, p. 3) et dans les Lignes directrices (préc.) de l'Autorité de la concurrence.

103 V. tous les débats qui ont précédé l'adoption du règlement n° 139/2004 (préc.). V. la "traduction" de l'article 2 du règlement dans les deux communications de la Commission (préc.) sur l'appréciation des concentrations horizontales et non horizontales. *Adde*, H. Kazzi, préc., n° 824 et s.; VALLET VIALLARD, LE CRITÈRE D'APPRÉCIATION SUBSTANTIELLE DES CONCENTRATIONS (Paris, Dalloz, Nouvelle bib. des thèses, 2007).

104 H. Kazzi, préc., n° 838 et s.

105 TPICE, 17 septembre 2007, *Microsoft c/ Commission*, T- 201/04, Rec., II, p. 1491. Pour une comparaison avec les solutions adoptées aux États-Unis sur ces premiers épisodes, C. Prieto, "Mondialisation et abus de position dominante. Étude à partir des affaires Microsoft", in *Mondialisation et droit de la concurrence*, préc., p. 383. Les données ont évolué depuis.

106 Cour Suprême des États-Unis, *Leegin Creative Leather Products* v/ *PSKS*, 551 US 877 (2007).

107 Règlement n° 330/2010, préc., art. 4, sous a).

108 Commission, Lignes directrices sur l'appréciation des restrictions verticales, *JOUE* C 130, p. 1.

nimité. Les autorités américaines ont convaincu leurs homologues au sein de l'OCDE,[109] puis de l'ICN,[110] dont cela reste l'un des chantiers prioritaires.

Pour organiser de manière plus efficace cette lutte, ils ont exporté leur outil de détection, les programmes de clémence,[111] et l'on réfléchit maintenant à la sanction optimale, ce qui impose de dépasser les amendes, dont les montants atteignent des sommes de plus en plus élevées, en incluant les sanctions pénales[112] et les sanctions civiles.

Cela étant, même des outils procéduraux spécifiques au droit de la concurrence, comme les programmes de clémence, doivent en toute hypothèse être adaptés dans le contexte particulier des procédures administratives européennes. Ainsi, alors qu'aux États-Unis, un programme de clémence permet à son bénéficiaire d'échapper aux poursuites, en Europe, l'entreprise ne pourra au mieux bénéficier que d'une immunité d'amende.[113] Des remarques du même ordre pourraient être faites sur les *consent decrees* qui ont inspiré les procédures d'engagements en Europe.[114]

Ces adaptations au contexte institutionnel et procédural européen sont naturellement plus faciles à réaliser dans le cadre du *public enforcement*. Dès que l'on touche le *private enforcement*, les obstacles se multiplient.[115] La convergence ne peut avoir qu'un domaine matériel limité. Elle est désormais recherchée au sein d'un réseau informel, l'ICN.

---

109 V. l'adoption de la recommandation concernant une action efficace contre les ententes injustifiables, 25 mars 1998 (C (98) 35 final).

110 V. les différents travaux en matière d'ententes injustifiables sur le site de l'ICN. *Adde,* not., Mathieu Cardon, *Le réseau international de la concurrence: une question de foi?*, in Mondialisation et droit de la concurrence, préc., p. 187, sp. p. 211.

111 V. not., Jean-Chritophe Roda, La clémence en droit de la concurrence. Étude comparative des droits américain et européen (Aix Marseille, PUAM 2008).

112 Wouter Wils, The Optimal Enforcement of EC Antitrust Law (Wolter Kluwer 2001); Emmanuel Combe, *Quelle sanction contre les cartels? Une perspective économique*, Rev. int. dr. eco. 2006, p. 9 et s.

113 Sur cette différence fondamentale trop souvent passée sous silence, Laurence Idot, *Les procédures de clémence en droit de la concurrence*, in La clémence et le droit, (J.-M. Jude dir.) (Paris, Economica 2011), p. 109-134, sp. n° 3.

114 V. *supra,* note 67.

115 V. *supra,* n° 30 et s.

2. L'existence d'un réseau informel

Le succès de l'*International Competition Network* est sans doute l'une des évolutions les plus marquantes de la dernière décennie. Lorsqu'il a été créé officiellement le octobre [116] l'avenir de ce réseau informel n'était nullement garanti. Outre qu'il était vu avec méfiance par les européens en raison de ses origines "américaines,"[117] il devait trouver sa place au sein des organisations internationales qui débattaient depuis de longues années des questions de concurrence dans un cadre institutionnel bien rodé, comme l'OCDE,[118] la CNUCED, et plus encore l'OMC.[119] Le droit de la concurrence ayant finalement disparu de l'agenda de l'OMC,[120] l'ICN s'est retrouvé au cœur des phénomènes de convergence.

L'ICN se définit lui-même comme un réseau informel d'autorités de concurrence qui discute des questions de politique et de mise en œuvre du droit de la concurrence d'intérêt commun et émet des propositions pour une convergence sur les questions de procédure et de fond.[121] Sa structure originale () a permis des résultats que l'on ne pouvait envisager au moment de son lancement ().

2.1. Une structure originale

La grande originalité de l'ICN tient au fait que c'est un réseau informel des autorités de concurrence. L'objectif des créateurs a été d'éviter le "brick and mortar" et par conséquent la lourdeur qui caractérise les organisations internationales classiques.

---

116 En septembre 2010, les recommandations de l'ICPAC (v. ci-dessous) en faveur d'une *Global Competition Initiative* reçurent le soutien officiel des responsables des autorités américaines et européennes (J. Klein pour le DOJ et M. Monti, alors commissaire en charge des questions de concurrence), soutien qui fut réitéré des deux côtés lors de la conférence annuelle de Fordham. À la suite de ces prises de position, l'International Bar Association réunit une quarantaine de représentants d'autorités de concurrence et de praticiens expérimentés à Ditchley Park en février 2001 pour discuter de la faisabilité d'un tel réseau global. Les résultats furent positifs, ce qui permit de franchir l'étape suivante. Le lancement officiel intervint le 25 octobre 2001.

117 L'idée de créer un réseau d'autorités a été formulée par l'ICPAC, soit *l'International Competition Policy Advisory Committee,* mis en place par l'US Department of Justice en 1997 pour réfléchir sur les conséquences de la globalisation en droit antitrust, dans son rapport final déposé en février 2000. V. le rappel de l'historique sur le site www.internationalcompetitionnetwork.org. *Adde,* M. E. Janow et J. F. Rill, "The Origins of the ICN"; comp. François Souty, *From the Halls of Geneva to the Shores of the Low Countries: The Origins of the International Competition Network*, in The International Competition Network at Ten, préc., respectivement p. 21, 39.

118 Frédéric Jenny, *The International Competition Network and the OECD Competition Committee: Differences, Similarities and Complementarities, in* The International Competition Network at Ten, préc., p. 93. Parallèlement, l'OCDE a créé un Global Competition Forum, ouvert aux non membres de l'OCDE.

119 H V. Hugh M. Hollman & William E. Kovacic, *The International Competition Network: Its Past, Current and Future Role*, préc., p. 51-92, sp. p. 61 et s.

120 V. François Souty, préc., not. sur les raisons de l'échec, Eleanor M. Fox, *"Linked-In: Antitrust and the Virtues of a Virtual Network*, in The International Competition Network at Ten, préc., p. 105.

121 Tel est l'objectif affiché sur le site de www.internationalcompetitionnetwork.org: "The International Competition Network (ICN) is a project-oriented, consensus-based, informal network of antitrust agencies that addresses antitrust enforcement and policy issues of common interest and formulates proposals for procedural and substantive convergence through a results-oriented agenda and structure."

Sont membres, non des États, mais des autorités de concurrence. À l'origine [122] elles sont désormais plus de réparties sur les cinq continents[123] rattachées à États et organisations régionales d'intégration économique. À ce jour, les autorités chinoises sont les seules absentes notoires.

L'adhésion à l'ICN est une initiative de la seule autorité et non de l'État dont elle dépend. Pour les autorités de petits pays, ou les jeunes autorités, la participation à l'ICN présente de nombreux avantages. Indépendamment de l'assistance technique qu'elles peuvent en retirer, elle leur permet d'affirmer une certaine indépendance vis à vis des instances politiques de leur État et d'acquérir une reconnaissance de leurs compétences.[124]

Une autre originalité de l'ICN tient au fait qu'indépendamment des officiels qui représentent leur autorité, participent également à la partie scientifique des travaux les NGA, soit les *Non Governmental Advisors*, qui sont désignés par une autorité en raison de leurs compétences dans la matière.[125] Il peut s'agir d'universitaires, de praticiens . . . .[126]

Il n'y a aucune structure, aucune localisation physique. Le fonctionnement est de même informel.

---

122 Australie, Canada, Union européenne, France, Germany, Israël, Italie, Japon, Corée, Mexique, Afrique du Sud, Royaume-Uni, États-Unis et Zambie.

123 Ce chiffre est important car plusieurs autorités d'un même État peuvent participer à l'ICN. Ainsi, par exemple, en France, sont membres l'Autorité de la concurrence, mais également la DGCCRF, aux États-Unis, la FTC et le DOJ . . . Au 1er mai 2012, en Europe : étaient représentés les 27 États membres de l'Union européenne, les 3 États membres de l'AELE (Suisse, Norvège, Islande), aux quels il faut ajouter Jersey et les Iles Féroé, 7 États des Balkans (Albanie, Bosnie-Herzégovine, Croatie, Kosovo, Monténégro, Macédoine, Serbie). Sont rattachés également à l'Europe, la Russie et trois anciennes républiques (Biélorussie, Moldavie, Ukraine), ainsi que la Turquie, soit un total de 44. Pour l'Amérique du Nord et centrale, sont représentés 10 États: USA, Canada, Mexique, mais également le Groenland, le Honduras, le Costa Rica, Panama, San Salvador, la Jamaïque et la Barbade; pour l'Amérique du Sud, 6 États: Argentine, Brésil, Colombie Chili, Pérou, Venezuela. Pour l'Asie, on relève 3 États au proche Orient (Israël, Jordanie, Yémen) 6 anciennes républiques d'URSS (Arménie, Azerbaïdjan, Kazasthan, Kirghizstan, Ouzbékistan, Tadjikistan) ainsi que 13 autres pays (Pakistan, Inde, Sri Lanka, Malaisie, Singapour, Thaïlande, Vietnam, Philippines, Indonésie, Taiwan, Corée, Japon et Mongolie). Pour l'Afrique: 3 États d'Afrique du Nord (Tunisie, Maroc, Egypte), 2 de l'Océan Indien (Maurice et les Seychelles), 8 États du Sud et de l'Est (Afrique du Sud, Swaziland, Namibie, Botswana, Zimbabwe, Zambie, Tanzanie, Kenya). L'Afrique de l'Ouest subsaharienne est sous représentée, puisque ne sont membres que les autorités du Sénégal et de la Gambie. Cela s'explique essentiellement pour des raisons linguistiques. Pour l'Océanie, sont représentés 4 États (l'Australie et la Nouvelle-Zélande, mais également, les îles Fidji et la Papouasie Nouvelle Guinée). L'on arrive ainsi à un total de 101 États, auxquels il faut ajouter les autorités d'organisations régionales d'intégration économique: la Commission pour l'Union européenne, l'Autorité de Surveillance de l'EFTA, mais également les autorités du CARICOM et du COMESA.

124 V. sur ce point, les témoignages de Mariana Tavares, *The ICN-One of the Many International Priorities. A Portuguese Perspective*, Dan Sjöblom and Monica Widegren, *ICN Membership: Opportunies and Challenge for a Competition Authority, in* The International Competition Network at Ten, préc., respectivement p. 333 et p. 349.

125 Dave Anderson, *Reflections on the ICN and its NGAs: Advocacy and Implementation*, Calvin S. Goldman, Robert E. Kwinter and Navin Joneja, *A Perspective on the Role and Contribution of NGAs at the ICN, in* The International Competition Network at Ten, préc., respectivement p. 277 et p. 383.

126 L'auteur a été NGA pour la DGCCRF de 2002 à 2007 et, à ce titre, a présenté une étude sur l'articulation du droit de la concurrence/régulation sectorielle en 2005 à la conférence annuelle de Bonn. Le groupe de travail sur ce thème a depuis lors pris fin.

Le réseau est dirigé par un *steering group*, un groupe de direction, composé de dix huit membres qui représentent les autorités, quinze élus pour un mandat de deux ans, trois membres d'office représentant les autorités qui accueilleront les grandes conférences annuelles.

L'essentiel des réflexions a lieu au sein des groupes de travail constitués sur des thèmes définis par le *steering group*. Les membres échangent par des voies diverses, avant de présenter les résultats lors de séminaires spécialisés et surtout lors de la grande conférence annuelle. Les thèmes peuvent évoluer, mais depuis l'origine, les groupes de travail ont porté sur les cartels, les concentrations. La question des pratiques unilatérales n'a été introduite que plus récemment en À ces groupes qui travaillent sur le cœur de la matière, il faut ajouter les deux groupes consacrés respectivement à l'*advocacy,* soit le plaidoyer en faveur des politiques de concurrence, et l'efficacité des autorités de concurrence.

En définitive, l'ICN est avant tout un extraordinaire lieu d'échanges et de rencontres entre personnes de tous les horizons géographiques, mais qui partagent une préoccupation commune: appliquer le mieux possible les règles de concurrence et les améliorer. Son grand avantage est d'être la seule enceinte exclusivement consacrée aux politiques de concurrence, ce qui permet de débattre des questions, sans qu'elles soient liées à d'autres considérations.[127]

2.2. Des résultats inespérés

N'ayant aucune origine étatique, l'ICN n'a aucun pouvoir pour adopter des règles, fussent elles des recommandations, comme l'OCDE, ou des codes de conduite, comme la CNUCED. Il n'en demeure pas moins qu'elle est malgré tout à l'origine de textes. Il s'agit pour l'essentiel de bonnes pratiques, mais également de boîtes à outils, de guides. En l'absence de valeur contraignante, leur sort dépend uniquement de la manière dont les autorités de concurrence se les réapproprient ensuite.

L'objectif n'est nullement de parvenir à une harmonisation des solutions, mais d'obtenir un consensus sur des standards et des méthodes en droit substantiel, ainsi que sur les procédures et les méthodes de gestion d'une autorité de concurrence.[128]

Compte tenu de leur objet, les deux groupes sur l'advocacy et sur l'*agency effectiveness* travaillent d'une manière différente des trois autres. Par exemple, en matière d'*advocacy*, certaines autorités ont présenté à La Haye en les actions entreprises pour promouvoir leur politique et cela va du film publicitaire au tee-shirt . . . , certaines autorités se montrant très en pointe dans l'utilisation des techniques modernes de communication. Ces échanges permettent de constituer une boîte à outils (*toolkit*) à destination des autorités qui en ont besoin. Le groupe sur le travail des autorités est centré de son côté sur les questions de management et de prioritisation des tâches.[129]

---

127 V. en particulier, sur cet avantage par rapport aux organisations internationales classiques, PHILPH MARSDEN, *Acta No Verba: Keep 'Talking Shop', Don't Become Another Talking Shop*, in 135 THE INTERNATIONAL COMPETITION NETWORK AT TEN, préc.

128 V. Hugh M. Hollman & William E. Kovacic, *The International Competition Network: Its Past, Current and Future Role*, préc., p. 51, sp.,61.

129 V. en dernier lieu, l'*ICN Advocacy workshop*, organisé par l'Autorité de la concurrence à Paris les 26-27 oct. 2012.

Dans une perspective juridique, ce sont surtout les travaux des trois autres groupes qui doivent retenir l'attention. Ces derniers mènent en premier lieu un important travail d'identification des différentes règles sur un modèle commun, les *templates*,[130] qui peuvent dans un deuxième temps donner lieu à un ou plusieurs workbooks.[131] Ces documents généraux sont précédés de toute une série de rapports, qui portent soit sur des questions de droit substantiel, comme dans le groupe "pratiques unilatérales," les principales pratiques abusives,[132] soit plutôt sur des questions de mise en œuvre pour le contrôle des concentrations[133] et les cartels.

Pour ces deux groupes, l'une des tâches essentielles est, en effet, de faciliter l'appréhension des pratiques et opérations de dimension transnationale. Cela explique que les travaux se soient centrés sur la coordination des procédures: notification pour les concentrations, techniques d'investigation, transactions . . . pour les cartels. L'un des grands succès du groupe anti-cartels est l'élaboration d'un *Anti-Cartel Enforcement Manual*, qui contient des indications très concrètes sur les inspections, les programmes de clémence, les enquêtes informatiques . . . .

En fin de course, ces travaux fondés sur des échanges d'expérience peuvent aboutir à l'adoption de bonnes pratiques. Cela a été fait en en matière de cartels sur la base du manuel.[134] L'adoption de "pratiques recommandées" en matière de contrôle des concentrations est plus ancienne. Il y en a deux: l'une de sur les procédures de notification, l'autre de sur l'analyse au fond.[135] Deux "pratiques recommandées" ont également été proposées en matière de pratiques unilatérales.[136]

L'influence réelle de ces documents est naturellement très variable suivant l'autorité, le contenu . . . , mais elle ne saurait être niée. Les pratiques recommandées de sur la notification des concentrations ont été prises en compte lors de l'adoption du règlement n° 139/2004 et ont permis d'accepter la notification d'un projet, ce qui était exclu antérieurement.[137] Le Président de l'autorité néerlandaise

---

130 Sur la base d'un questionnaire commun, les autorités exposent les solutions retenues dans leur législation en donnant les références officielles. Ces *templates* existent dans les trois champs d'étude: concentrations, cartels, pratiques unilatérales.

131 Là encore, les trois domaines sont concernés, mais celui sur les pratiques unilatérales n'est pas encore achevé. Il ne comporte à ce jour que le chapitre sur le pouvoir de marché, l'objectif de 2012 étant d'ajouter deux chapitres portant respectivement sur les objectifs et l'analyse des prix prédateurs. En matière de concentrations, il y a deux ouvrages: le Merger Guidelines Workbook, le Investigative Techniques Handbook.

132 Par exemple, dans le groupe "pratiques unilatérales," on trouve toute une série de rapports sur les principales pratiques abusives: ventes liées, refus de fourniture, prix prédateurs, exclusivités, rabais et remises.

133 V. en particulier les rapports sur la définition du champ du contrôle (seuils, notion de concentration, informations requises lors de la notification), sur les questions de procédure (renonciation à la confidentialité) et des remèdes.

134 Compilation of "Good Practices" from the Anti-Cartel Enforcement Manual of the ICN Cartel Working Group.

135 ICN Recommended Practices for Merger Notification Procedures (2002); *ICN Recommended Practices for Merger Analysis* (2008). Ces documents sont à lire avec les *Guiding Principles For Merger Notification and Review*, qui donnent les principales définitions.

136 ICN-RIC Groupe de travail sur les comportements unilatéraux, Analyse d'une position dominante ou d'une puissance commerciale importante relativement à des comportements unilatéraux, Pratiques recommandées; Analyse des monopoles publics à la lumière des lois sur les comportements unilatéraux, Pratiques recommandées

137 V. égal., Maria Coppola & Cynthia Lagdameo, *Tacking Stock and Tacking Root: A Closer Look at Implementation of ICN Recommended Practices for Merger Notification & Review Procedures*, 297 The International Competition Network at Ten, préc.

indiquait, quant à lui, que le manuel sur les techniques d'investigation en matière de cartels était très utile sur le terrain.[138]

L'un des prochains chantiers de l'ICN est précisément de vérifier leur impact, tout en conservant les objectifs initiaux qui n'ont pas besoin d'être modifiés. L'ICN continuera à travailler sur la recherche de la convergence, ce qui inclut le concept d'"informed divergence." L'idée d'une *ICN Academy* a également été lancée pour approfondir les recherches. Les recherches sur la convergence des droits de la concurrence vont se poursuivre.

138 Pieter Kalbfleisch, *From Ditchley Park to the Hague—A Journey Worthwile*, Paul Lugard, *An Introduction*, in The International Competition Network at Ten, préc., respectivement p. 1 et p. 5.

Ten Things I (Really) Like about Gerber's *Global Competition*

Spencer WEBER WALLER

Swalle1@luc.edu

Professor and Director, Institute for Consumer Antitrust Studies, Loyola University Chicago, School of Law

I am indebted to David Gerber on two very different levels. Besides being a friend and mentor, his scholarship has been an inspiration and a major contribution to international competition policy. His earlier book *Law and Competition in Twentieth Century Europe: Protecting Prometheus* made a compelling case that there is a European competition law that stands apart from U.S. antitrust law and policy.[1] He documented how EU competition law and its national analogues share common roots going back to prior to World War II as a true pan-European body of law with indigenous roots and a common frame of reference.

Gerber now expands his field of inquiry to global competition policy in *Global Competition: Law, Markets and Globalization*. He analyzes the history and current state of national and international solutions to international competition law and sets forth a path forward where past efforts have failed. The key to understanding Gerber's arguments is to appreciate his view that the past efforts did not fail, or at least did not fail as to the substance of the idea that global markets require global solutions to prevent anticompetitive conduct on a global scale. He provides one of the best and most nuanced accounts of the attempts in the 20th century to develop international competition law and the forces outside of the competition arena that prevented its adoption. In this essay, I want to highlight a very personal "top ten" list of the features that make Gerber's *Global Competition* such a special and lasting contribution to the literature in the field.

I. Nuanced Use of History

One of the keys to appreciating *Global Competition* is its nuanced use of history. Gerber emphasizes the early international efforts to develop international controls for competition problems in international markets. He highlights the discontinuities in this history where internal and outside influences prohibited any linear progress in the field and how national sovereignty and unilateral extraterritoriality emerged more as default solutions than as conscious choices.

---

1 David J. Gerber, Twentieth Century Europe: Protecting Prometheus (Oxford University Press 2001).

He begins with the League of Nations conference in the 1920s on global cartels and the glimmering of a consensus that some conduct-based rules against cartel abuses were appropriate. These efforts were overwhelmed by forces outside the competition debate itself, such as the failure of the U.S. to ratify the League Charter, the advent of the Great Depression, the rise of the Axis powers, and the eventual collapse of the League itself.

Gerber tells a similar story of the emerging competition norms following World War II in the draft Havana Charter of the International Trade Organization. Here the heavily negotiated compromise provisions were undermined by the failure of the U.S. to ratify the Charter for other reasons and the almost immediate division of the world economy in the ensuing Cold War. He continues with a similarly sophisticated telling of the more familiar story of post-war U.S. jurisdictional unilateralism as a partial solution for the next fifty years and the promise (and limitations) of convergence as a strategy in more recent times following the collapse of the Soviet Union. It is fascinating to reflect on what might have emerged decades ago, but for these factors and the second best solutions that arose in their place.

II. Contributions to Comparative Law

Global Competition also succeeds as a work of general comparative law scholarship, even if one were not deeply immersed in competition law as a specialty. Gerber makes his argument with a deep knowledge of, and appreciation for, the proper understanding of the development of both EU and member state competition law. He is deeply versed in the civil law tradition and how it has influenced developments in the competition field. He avoids salesmanship or the notion that one system's laws are inherently superior to another. He is probably one of the very few U.S. scholars to be able to pull off this feat given his ability to do primary research in English, German, French, and Swedish and the ability to tie together the various strands of discourse in multiple legal systems.

Throughout *Global Competition* Gerber uses a much wider and more cosmopolitan lens than the often U.S.-centric approach to these issues. He is as interested in the EU and the rest of the world in figuring out the possibilities of the current and past approaches and his proposals for what he dubs a "commitment pathway" in lieu of continued sole reliance on soft harmonization and convergence. Gerber brings to bear important insights from extensive qualitative empiricism in the form of countless interviews with decision makers in multiple jurisdictions. He also makes important contributions to the continuing debate over the transferability of law from one jurisdiction to another and the differences between the law in action versus the law on the books.

III. Models and Lens

Throughout the book, Gerber uses a variety of models and lens to illustrate and support his thesis and arguments. Some of the effective examples include:

- Law versus administrative discretion in regulating competition and markets;
- The United States experience in evaluating and (mis)understanding the rest of the world;
- The notion of "elders" and "others" in the international competition law community;
- The notion of classical eras in evaluating the evolution of competition law and policy.

These different concepts appear throughout the book and help the reader understand how discourse and assumptions limit our ability to evaluate history and difference.

IV. The Role of Communities

Gerber also emphasizes the importance of epistemic communities for understanding the history, law, and politics of international competition law and policy. These communities can be professional (law, economics, competition enforcers, civil law judges, etc.). They can be either national or transnational. They can be based on expertise, language, or discourse. Regardless of their precise composition, such communities (or networks) play an increasing role in formulating and implementing international competition law principles.

V. Ideas Matter

Competition law is a field where ideas matter. Legal rules, procedures, and institutions change in response to the rise and fall of broader economic, political, historical, and social movements. Gerber weaves in many of the intellectual movements that have played in a key role in the successes and failure of our field.

Throughout the book, Gerber also focuses on the uneven nature of globalization. He explores the winners and losers of globalization, the consequences of this uneven distribution of benefits, the opposition that globalization has generated, and the effects on the development of competition norms.

VI. The Concept of Embeddedness

Gerber develops a very important notion of "embeddedness" in *Global Competition* and other parts of his scholarship. He reminds us of the need to understand concepts like the role of economics, not in the abstract but, in their institutional, cultural, historical, and social context. This insight has important implications for how competition law systems implement concepts borrowed from other areas of the law or other jurisdictions. For example, a more economic approach to competition law generally, or with respect to a particular issue, may be impossible unless competition agencies and tribunals have the practical ability to gather, interpret, present, apply, and review economic evidence with sophistication and accuracy.[2]

---

2 *See also* David J. Gerber, *Convergence in the Treatment of Dominant Firm Conduct: The United States, the European Union, and the Institutional Embeddedness of Economics*, 76 Antitrust L.J. 951 (2010).

VII. Depth, Breadth, and Cosmopolitan Vision

What is so remarkable is how *Global Competition* flows effortlessly across time and continents. It covers more than a century of developments involving large developed economies, transitional market economies, smaller economies, newer competition systems, lesser development countries, regional jurisdictions, and international organizations. The needs of the broader global community are never forgotten without losing sight of the primacy of national sovereignty as a default solution that has emerged for regulating global markets. Gerber shows great compassion and concern throughout for the poorer nations and citizens who have benefited little, if at all, from either the spread of globalization or competition law. He can both make large sweeping connections between competition, trade, and development law and then switch to focus in closely on the impact of a single event or scholar on the progress toward or away from international consensus on competition norms.[3]

VIII. Linking the National to the Global

One of the points that Gerber makes in a variety of contexts is that it is not always about the United States. So many of the early efforts at international competition law were truly international in scope and involved a rather minimal role for the United States, including the League of Nations and the Interparliamentary Union. Gerber also highlights the role played by other key legal systems in influencing other national and international developments.

Looking from the other end of the telescope, he details the influence of international systematic needs and their effects on national law. These include the spread of extraterritorial jurisdictional, extensive intergovernmental cooperation, the rapid deployment of leniency programs, and the growing importance of both public and private sector networks in competition law and enforcement.

IX. Pathways and Commitments

Above all, Gerber contests the inevitability of failure in formulating international principles of competition law as well as the notion that convergence will occur naturally or effectively. He

3 This ability to pull back and then swoop in reminds me of the science documentary "Powers of Ten." There, the filmmakers show two picnickers in a park "with the area of each frame one-tenth the size of the one before. Starting from a view of the entire known universe, the camera gradually zooms in until we are viewing the subatomic particles on a man's hand." *See* http://www.imdb.com/title/tt0078106/plotsummary.

identifies more clearly the external reasons for past failure such as the Great Depression and the rise of the Cold War almost immediately after the conclusion of World War II. He eschews broader institutions, sweeping agreements, or grand bargains linking competition law treaties to other area of international economic law.

In place of grandiose solutions, he proposes what he terms a "commitment pathway." He describes this approach as: The basic concept is that participants sketch a path towards agreed goals and establish obligations to support movement toward these goals. Elements of the pathway are expected to take on sharper form as states interact in moving along it. The strategy would establish shared commitments to create and maintain an effective regime for global competition. Commitments would be 'shared' in the sense that project's success would depend on the commitment of all participants to the project's goals.[4]

This approach drawn from the international relations literature call for four basic elements: 1) a set of objectives; 2) delineation of the types of steps that are expected to be taken toward the agreed goals; 3) an obligation to support these steps both domestically and internationally; and 4) an obligation to engage in regular and extensive feedback with other participants in moving toward the agreed goals.[5]

He argues that this is the best approach to seek a flexible solution evolving over time with sensitivity toward difference. Picture this approach as convergence with a destination (my words, not his).

As Gerber concedes, this sensible solution bears the risk that external events will once again derail the slow, but steady, progress that pathways and commitments suggest. However, events in the real world in both competition policy and other regulatory areas suggest this is possible. Outside competition policy, consider such diverse areas as banking, securities regulation, taxation, anti-corruption, environmental policy, and human rights for a sense of when such approaches appear to be working and when they do not.

I would suggest that in competition policy two developments provide support the possible success of this strategy. The first is the success of the first decade of the International Competition Network.[6] Second, the increased commitment to competition enforcement in Japan over the past twenty years, following the negotiation of the Strategic Impediments Initiative with United States, also suggests that a guided set of commitment can indeed bring progress and help tip other parts of international competition policy in this important direction.

---

4 David J. Gerber, Global Competition: Law, Markets and Globalization 295 (Oxford University Press 2010).

5 *Id.* at 304.

6 *See generally* The International Competition Network at Ten: Origins, Accomplishments and Aspirations (Paul Lugard ed., 2011).

X. Teaching Us (U.S.) about the Rest of the World and about Ourselves

David Gerber's work on this impressive volume is of course finished, but his work as a scholar continues. He has helped us understand the history, law, and culture of competition in other jurisdictions. In so doing, he has helped us learn more about the nature of competition law in the United States and the limitations of merely exporting our complex history, doctrine, procedures, institutions, and culture to other contexts. He has also taught us the immense need to harness the power of competition and competition law to improve the real world lives and opportunities of people around the world. Now the real work begins to implement that vision.

From Unilateral Jurisdictionalism to Commitment Pathways: A Roadmap for International Competition Law

André FIEBIG

andre.fiebig@bakermckenzie.com

Partner, Baker & McKenzie LLP, Chicago, Illinois
Adjunct Professor, Northwestern University School of Law

"In order to be effective, a global competition law strategy will have to adapt to the new context in which it will operate. This will require rethinking competition law in ways that synergistically intertwine national and transnational institutions, objectives and dynamics."—Global Competition: Law, Markets and Globalization at 339.

I would like to congratulate Professor Gerber on a stimulating and comprehensive book which not only describes competition law from a comparative perspective, but uses this comparative analysis to propose a possible solution to bring global competition law into line with globalization. There are many proposals which have been discussed over the years to deal with the conflicts and inefficiencies caused by the extraterritorial application of domestic competition laws to global markets, but in my view one needs to examine the issue from a comparative perspective in order to advance a realistic solution. I would also like to thank Professor Cho, Professor Gerber and the organizers of the Global Competition Law Conference for inviting me to say a few words.

I. The Commitment Pathway Approach to International Competition Law

The starting point of Global Competition: Law, Markets and Globalization is the assertion that globalization has altered the economic and political context in which the current competition law system operates. The reduced significance of territorial boundaries and distances has created truly global markets. At the same time, competition law has failed to keep up with these changes. The current system of applying national competition law to global markets—what Gerber refers to as "unilateral jurisdictionalism"—is inadequate in dealing with these new realities. It results in conflicts at the inter-state level and inefficiencies at the firm level.

Unilateral jurisdictionalism is based on what has arguably become an international customary rule of law: objective territoriality. The Lotus case decided by the Permanent Court of Justice almost a century ago implicitly approved the application of domestic law to conduct occurring outside the borders of the state whose law was being applied.[1] The U.S. relied on this principle in applying the Sherman Act extraterritorially.[2] As Global Competition: Law, Markets and Globalization documents, this, of course, created much consternation among our trading partners: "Many perceived the U.S. claims as a threat to the jurisdictional framework that had been constructed by the interactions and understandings of states over centuries." (at 66). However, once these trading partners became serious about the application of their own competition laws, they too were confronted with the challenge of prohibiting conduct occurring outside their borders but which had an anti-competitive effect within their borders. The Europeans finally conceded to the necessity of the extraterritorial application of competition law in the Woodpulp case.[3] In that case, the European Court of Justice affirmed the application of European competition law to conduct occurring outside what was then the European Economic Communities based on the theory that the conduct was "implemented" in the EEC. The implementation test is now a standard doctrine in EU competition law.

Although markets have globalized, competition law has not. This is a widely-known fact, and some would say deficit. We are forced to address restrictions on competition on global markets by applying national law extraterritorially. This sovereignty-based system, according to Professor Gerber, is inadequate to address global competition: "Factors such as reduced transportation costs, increased mobility of assets, and faster communication make markets more global, but they also facilitate restraints on competition, and this can foreclose or at least impede the application of domestic laws. This paradox inheres in the tension between the sovereignty-based system, on the one hand, and the political and economic changes we know as globalization, on the other. Globalization creates pressures in the jurisdictional regime that it is not well equipped to handle." (at 89). This "scissors paradox," as Gerber calls it, results in an undermining of deterrence, increased political conflict and risk, uncertainty, inconsistency and compliance costs (at 93-94). These are themes which have been echoed by other participants at this conference.[4]

Gerber recognizes that the various responses proposed so far have proven successful or have been ineffective or too ambitious. "Horizontal approaches," as Professor Fox would call them,[5] are not sufficiently comprehensive because the focus on mitigating the costs of the sovereignty-based system rather than addressing the underlying problem. Convergence, for example, which was favored by the U.S. and is the method employed by the International Competition Network, is inadequate because it lacks sufficient contours and the agreement which Gerber deems necessary. An international antitrust code within the context of the WTO ran into resistance from both

---

1 The S.S. Lotus Case P.C.I.J. Ser. A, No. 10, at 4 (1927).

2 United States v. Alcoa, 148 F.2d 416 (2d Cir. 1945).

3 Cases 89/85, 114/85, 116-117/85, 125-129/85, A. Ahlström Osakeyhtiö v. Commission, 1988 E.C.R. 5193 (1988).

4 Eleanor M. Fox, *Can We Solve the Antitrust Problems of Globalization and Extraterritoriality and Cooperation?*, 48 Antitrust Bull. 355 (2003).

5 Eleanor M. Fox, *International Antitrust and the Doha Dome*, 43 Va. J. Int'l L. 911 (2003).

the U.S. and a group of developing countries. While Professor Gerber does not totally preclude the possibility of a solution within the context of the WTO, he sees a distinct danger that the discussion will be disadvantageously caught up in the trade debate.

The answer, according to Gerber, is a commitment pathway approach. In Professor Fox's dichotomy,[6] this would place him squarely in the internationalists' camp. Under this approach, the participants would agree on where they want to go and a process for moving toward the identified objectives. "The commitment component relates participants to each other, while the pathway component relates decisions made at one point in the process to decisions made at other points in it." (at 304). This flexible approach recognizes the dynamic character of international competition law and is required in order to respect and accommodate the divergent interests involved.

The commitment pathway, in contrast to mere convergence, is in the form of an international agreement with four fundamental components (at 298-300). It must (1) adopt a set of objectives, (2) delineate the steps that are expected (note that Gerber uses the word "expected" instead of "required") to be taken toward those agreed goals, (3) agree on an obligation to support those steps (note that Gerber uses the word "support" instead of "implement") and (4) accept an obligation to engage in regular and extensive feedback and exchange with other participants along the pathway.

Because of the necessity to maintain a dynamic approach to global competition law and to accommodate the differences, Gerber suggests that this agreement need not be detailed and specific. "There is no need to specify an institutional arrangement or to establish specific sanctions for failure to meet obligations. Discussions of global competition law frequently assume the need for specificity and detail, but this tends to limit the options available for developing an effective strategy and to reduce its attractiveness for many." (at 298).

Although the commitment pathway agreement must identify the time dimension in which the obligations are to be met, Gerber advises that this does not necessarily have to be fixed dates. It could be tied to the occurrence of events. "Many discussions of international competition law assume that all obligations must become effective at the same time or at least at fixed times, but this obscures options that may well be a key to the effectiveness of a global competition law strategy" (at 300). Here again, this dynamic or flexible approach to international competition law is required out of recognition for accommodating the different interests involved. "National competition law goals would be expected to fit within a range of goals that narrows over time." . . . "The objective should be to articulate a set of goals that is specific enough to achieve a common commitment from states that prefer a narrow conception of goals, but broad enough to attract commitment from those who have a broader vision of goals" (at 309).

6 *Id.*

II. Challenges to the Commitment Pathway Approach

In an effort to stimulate discussion, and not out of disagreement with the proposals or conclusions reached in Global Competition: Law, Markets and Globalization, I would like to briefly discuss three challenges the commitment pathway will encounter.

1. Addressing the Political Value of Competition Law

One challenge the commitment pathway will encounter, and on which both Professors Waller and Guzman have written,[7] relates to the political value of competition law. Competition law is a form of market intervention employed to produce outcomes which market forces would not otherwise produce. In fact, the legitimacy of competition law lies in the recognition that markets are not entirely self-regulating. In a sense, the broad acceptance of competition law legitimizes state intervention in the market and enables states to intervene under the guise of competition law. This apparently legitimate intervention in the market to produce outcomes the market would not otherwise yield has a value to politicians and administrators which they are not going to relinquish easily. In fact, one could cynically hypothecate that the introduction of competition laws in many states in the last 20 years is due to the recognition of the political value of antitrust.

This is not a recent realization. The political value of competition law is a characteristic which has long been recognized as a challenge to international antitrust. Professor Guzman has similarly observed that the pursuit of individual interest makes international competition law difficult: "Imagine for a moment that all governments are motivated by a desire to maximize the overall welfare of their constituents. In a closed economy, then, the government pursues optimal policies. Once the economy is opened, however, states have an incentive to externalize costs while internalizing benefits. In this sense, states compete with one another. This competition can generate state incentives and policies that, from a global point of view, are inefficient and undesirable."[8] In an older but still relevant article, Professor Waller observed that: "Harmonization has succeeded where it has increased the power, prestige, and durability of national competition authorities and failed where the proposal would diminish rather than enhance the stature of national competition authorities."[9]

In my view, this is the greatest hurdle in achieving consensus on the commitment pathway. By definition, the commitment means relinquishing some sovereignty. Professor Gerber recognizes this

---

7 Andrew T. Guzman, *The Design of International Agreements*, 16 Eur. J. Int'l L. 579 (2005); Spencer Weber Waller, *Public Choice Theory and the International Harmonization of Antitrust Law*, 48 Antitrust Bull. 427 (2003).

8 Andrew T. Guzman, *Public Choice and International Regulatory Competition*, 90 Georgetown L.J. 971, 977 (2002).

9 Spencer Weber Waller, *Public Choice Theory and the International Harmonization of Antitrust Law*, 2003 Antitrust Bull. 427, 432 (2003).

challenge. His answer is to keep the commitment as flexible as possible in order to keep the costs of commitment low (at 305). Herein lies the key to the success of the commitment pathway approach. The participating countries need to relinquish some sovereignty in the area of competition law in order to make the system work. This makes it less attractive to the countries with developed competition law systems.

2. Detracting from the Legitimacy of Competition Law

According to Gerber, "in developing global competition law, a more dynamic view of law is necessary." (at 341). The legitimacy of any legal norm is dependent upon the perception that it is fair and objective and applied consistently. This is particularly true for legal norms regulating competition, which, by their very nature, rely on malleable concepts.[10] If one adopts a dynamic structure, which attempts to recognize and accommodate differences, one detracts from the legitimacy of competition laws from the perspective of the subjects of the law. A dynamic or flexible international competition law system, which attempts to accommodate differences runs the risk of undermining the legitimacy of competition law among businesses. The impetus for global competition law is the realization that markets have become global. If a market is truly global, it is difficult for a businessperson to understand why a particular practice is acceptable in one country but not in another country. Why, for example, are restraints on intra-brand competition illegal in one part of this global market but not another? I am frequently confronted with such questions from businesses. The answer tends to lie in the political realm. To accept and recognize the legitimacy of these differences detracts from the legitimacy of competition law. It is no coincidence that competition law enjoys the most legitimacy among businesses where it is consistently prohibited, i.e., naked price fixing.

According to Professor Gerber, "The goals of the project will have to be relatively general and flexible, becoming more specifically defined through experience along the pathway" (at 307). Gerber recognizes that "Flexibility provides its greatest potential value, but that flexibility may also be a major weakness" (at 304). The need for a dynamic international competition law system arises from the realization of different contexts, goals, norms, methods and institutions (at 262-265). As Gerber points out, and others participating in this seminar have pointed out,[11] competition and competition law operate in a particular economic, political and social context which helps to explain not only differences in the laws themselves, but also in the results of the application of those laws. One requirement of the commitment pathway is "that the agreed goals will have to be perceived as 'fair' by all types of participants." (at 307). My concern is with the dilutive effect this relativist approach will have on competition law.

It is interesting to note in this respect, that the legal norms do not differ between countries as much as one would assume. This is even recognized by Gerber: "The competition law norms articulated in statutes do not vary greatly. Most such statutes contain provisions prohibiting cartels and par-

10 *See* David J. Gerber, *Authority Heuristics*, 79 Chicago-Kent L. Rev. 959 (2002).

11 Michal S. Gal, Competition Policy for Small Market Economies (Harvard University Press 2003).

ticular forms of vertical agreements that allow more powerful firms to impede the competitive conduct of their distributors and suppliers. They also typically subject some kinds of mergers to some level of review and combat conduct of dominant firms that represents an abuse of that dominance. These basic categories have become standard." (at 265). I would agree with this assessment. The differences are mainly in the application of these legal norms.

3. Recognizing the Benefits of Unilateral Jurisdictionalism

Professor Gerber correctly identifies the inefficiencies associated with the current sovereignty-based system. Before discarding the sovereignty-based system, however, I think that it is important to recognize the benefits of such a system and account for them in any subsequent international competition law system. One benefit of the wide-spread reliance on the sovereignty-based approach combined with the acceptance of the objective territoriality principle is to address the national bias which occurs in the application of competition laws. According to Professor Guzman: "Agencies will be tempted to be lenient toward locals and tough on foreigners in this review process, even if no such double standard is called for in the relevant legislation."[12] The assumption here is that local competition authorities allow certain commercial transactions involving domestic firms which they should actually prohibit. One benefit of unilateral jurisdictionalism is that it provides a check on this bias. For example, if a competition law authority approves an otherwise anti-competitive domestic merger affecting global markets because of this bias, that same merger may be prohibited by competition authorities in other states. Professor Gerber holds out the abandoned merger of General Electric and Honeywell as an example of how a sovereignty-based systems leads to conflict (at 95-97). "Major public confrontations such as the GE/Honeywell case have highlighted the potential for disruption, uncertainty and economic waste inherent in jurisdictional conflicts" (at 116). Assuming, however, that the proposed merger was really anti-competitive (as the EU concluded),[13] and the U.S. Department of Justice approved the merger because of the bias of which Professor Guzman speaks, the extra layer of regulation resulting from the current sovereignty-based system actually worked effectively to prohibit a transaction that would have unjustifiably restrained competition. While I do not want to suggest that the inefficiencies of the current system should be ignored, they need to be weighed against the positive attributes and these positive attributes should be considered in any proposals to replace the current system.

12 Andrew T. Guzman, *The Case for International Antitrust*, 22 Berkeley J. Int'l L. 355, 356 (2004).

13 Eleanor M Fox, *Mergers in Global Markets: GE/Honeywell and the Future of Merger Control*, 23 U. Pa. J. Int'l Econ. L. 457 (2002).

Internal and External Factors Determining Latin American Developments

Javier CORTÁZAR-MORA

jcortazar@cortazarurdaneta.com

Professor, CESA University, Bogota

My presentation will be about the internal and external factors that have determined the developments of competition law in Latin America.

Since many constraints impeded any serious Latin American commitment to the idea of competition until the 90's, practically all the developments have arisen during the last 20 years. Even though I wish I could talk in more detail about all of them, logical time constraints only allow me to refer to what for me have been the recent years' most salient: a) The fight against hard-core cartels and, to some extent, against stern abuses of dominance, b) more serious advocacy efforts towards a more competition-friendly regulation, and c) the enhancement of the exogenous and endogenous internationalization of the still young Latin American experience.[1]

I. Developments in Corrective Antitrust Law

Beyond all the statistics and trends widely known by all the participants of this conference, the fight against hard-core domestic cartels is in the air of Latin American countries. During the last decade, for instance, Colombia has witnessed a handful of cases from financial and health care services to staples such as rice, sugar, chocolate, ethanol and cement. Even though all the powerful enterprises investigated did whatever was legally in their reach to avoid being fined as until then was usual, the authorities finally succeeded, orders to cease and desist were issued, and fines were imposed. As in Colombia, the trend can also be noticed all over the region. Chilean pharmacies, Argentinean cement companies, Peruvian transporters, and many more cases light the firmament of the enforcement of Latin American competition law. The list is huge, and according to what has

1 What I understand to be exogenous internationalization is all the international features related to competition and competition law outside the region and for endogenous internationalization the same features but within it. Participation of LA countries in the International Competition Network could be an example of the former and the Latin American Competition Forum of the latter.

been suggested by best practices manuals, mainly covers goods and services of high impact in terms of economic development. Brazil has been especially active. The tightening of the rules and the enhancement of its enforcement efforts led to numerous cases also affecting a wide range of goods and services.[2] Recently the Brazilian authority (CADE) imposed what, in my knowledge, is the harshest single case fine in Antitrust Law history of U.S. $1,3 billion to five companies involved in an industrial gases cartel.

With the exception of Brazil, the trend, however, is focused on domestic rather than international cartels, which is explained first by the raising dynamism of the aggregated domestic demand[3] and secondly by the still young international experience, especially in cooperation agreements, which have just began to gain pace.

In a recently published article, The Economist newspaper openly criticized the monopolistic or at least the highly oligopolistic structure of many of the Mexican markets and the rampant exploitative practices of the incumbents. It noted that a third or more of the Mexican household spending goes to the captive markets, which range from telecoms to air and land transport, financial services, utilities, etc.[4] Rather than the situation itself, which is not, to say, uncommon in Latin America, what grasped most of my attention was that all the data came from the Mexican Federal Competition Commission. This is good news as far as it is one of the hardest (and more dangerous) critics of the current state of the affairs of the Mexican economy and its competition shortcomings. Indeed, recently it finally managed to succeed in a case against América Móvil and its exploitative practices of abuse of dominance in the termination of phone calls, which in addition to the cease and desist orders, imposed a fine of U.S. $1 billion.

Even though in abuses of dominance there are not as many cases as there are in cartels, the kind of victory achieved by the Mexican authority is significant in the sense that it indicates that in spite of the hostile atmosphere for real competition law, at the end of the day competition authorities can prevail.

These advancements are the consequence of a series of developments and reforms of which—summarizing dangerously—the most salient are the introduction of leniency programs; the stiffening of sanctions, including the criminalization of cartel offenses; and the strengthening of the competition authorities' investigative powers.

In a survey carried out by the International Competition Network (ICN) about trends and developments in cartel enforcement, the Latin American countries that participated, Argentina, Brazil, Chile, El Salvador, Mexico, Panama, and Peru agreed that amongst all the different developments that have impacted the enforcement activities the most in the deterrence of cartels, the introduction of leniency provisions has played a crucial role. Indeed, barring Argentina, all the surveyed coun-

2 *See* Webcast, Oliver Antoine, Alfredo O'Farrell, Miguel del Pino, Ricardo Inglez de Souza & Amilcar Peredo, Recent Antitrust Enforcement in Latin America—What Every U.S. Company Needs to Know, 2011, *available at* http://webcasts.acc.com (last accessed on September 29, 2011).

3 United Nations Economic Commission for Latin America (Cepal), 2011 Estudio Económico de América Latina y el Caribe.

4 *See* Mexico's Economy—Making the Desert Bloom, The Economist (August 27, 2011).

tries have introduced leniency programs within their respective competition law systems. Many other Latin American countries have adopted such provisions, too; for example, Colombia, in 2009.

Regarding the remaining reforms, the current standard in Latin American competition law fines is its stringent level, which in countries such as Brazil can be up to 30% of the offender's revenue. As far as I know the only Latin American country that has had small fines has been Colombia until 2009, when the regime was amended, empowering the competition authority to impose fines up to 150% of the profits of the anticompetitive practice or 100,000 minimum monthly salaries (approx. U.S. $30 million), whichever was highest. For the staff involved, fines are up to 2,000 minimum monthly salaries (approx. U.S. $500,000.00), a fine that the enterprise cannot pay either directly or indirectly.

The last important factor that according to the survey played an important role in the trend is the strengthening of the competition authorities. Bittersweetly if, on one hand, the region's competition agencies have been organized with acceptable levels of political independence (barring Colombia and Argentina), on the other hand, they generally undergo lack of resources. During the last years and in some extent capacity has been enhanced with the adoption of manuals of best practices and guides and the improvement of the investigative powers of some agencies, allowing them to do things as dawn raids or question witnesses in situ instead of written statements and things like that.

Civil and criminal consequences of anticompetitive practices offer different scenarios. Private actions have not yet taken place in the region, as happens worldwide (apart from the U.S.). However, had there been more competition culture, the existing legal intricacies arguably could be viewed somewhat differently. In the case of Colombia, for instance, where since 1998 there has been the possibility of class actions in competition law (Law 472/1998), until recently it was assured and taken for granted that the only possibility was follow-on actions, an almost impossible path since they were easily blocked by procedural legalizes for decades. This was wrong. On the contrary, private actions have always been at the reach of the public. Additionally, since last year's amendment of the rules of civil procedure easing the rules of evidence for damages and shortening the timing of procedures, a case can last two or maximum three years, which is a reasonable time frame.

Criminalization of the most egregious antitrust offences gradually has been gathering pace in Latin America. Nowadays some important countries have established some anticompetitive offences as crimes, such as in Brazil, where various individuals have received sentences of up to five years although, as far as I know, nobody has yet done prison time. Mexico is on the way to criminalizing cartel offenses[5] and recently Colombia enacted a statute that criminalize bid rigging with a penalty of up to twelve years, which amongst other things means that offenders get prison sentences.

5 This paper was written on October 2011 when the bill criminalizing antitrust offenses was under discussion in the Mexican parliament. Currently the law was enacted.

II. Developments in Preventive Antitrust Law

Regulation has been the tool of excellence for the widely acknowledged Latin American distrust in the market forces and the economic dirigisme that has been so carefully detailed by all the academics interested in the region's competition law and policy. For centuries, regulation has been the instrument of excellence used by all kinds of governments to intervene in economic freedom and arguably obstruct competition even more than all the private anticompetitive practices together. The mere advancement over the last few years in the change of tide towards a more friendly approach to competition by regulators is in itself a significant development.

At the present time it is common to find competition advocacy provisions in the region's systems as a standard and more importantly the performance of real advocacy efforts by the competition authorities either in advocacy and society[6] or in advocacy in the regulatory process.[7]

Regarding the latter, the involvement of the competition agencies in the regulatory process has yielded sometimes noteworthy outcomes, especially in regulated industries such as the Brazilian deregulation of air transportation, or the more recent example of the Mexican authority involvement in the regulation of procurement of pharmaceuticals for the public social security system. However, on the other hand, successful advocacy has not been the rule as it has happened in the Mexican telecommunications market, the Chilean electric power market, or the Colombian transport services, just to mention a few. In sum, even though there have been many shortcomings in competition advocacy, there have also been some achievements.

III. International Developments

The last years have experienced an increase in both the exogenous and endogenous international activities of Latin American competition law. A good example of the former is the generalized inclusion of competition chapters in the numerous regional trade agreements (RTAs) that have flooded the region, following the 'spaghetti bowl' trend in international trade, in which Mexico and Chile have been especially active. The establishment of agreements in cooperation and technical assistance between some Latin American countries and external competition agencies, particularly from the U.S. and Europe, is another development worth a mention. Brazil has again been particularly active in this process.

Regarding the raising of intra-Latin American international activities, I'd like to refer to two good examples. One is that the increasing level of relationships has led to the beginning of what can now

6 That is to say all the non compulsory efforts developed by the competition authority to persuade society about the benefits of competition through for instance the media, seminars et al.

7 That is to say, the participation of competition agencies in the regulatory process issuing either compulsory or non compulsory opinions as well as other means.

be considered—paraphrasing Prof Gerber's term—an embryonic Latin American competition law community, especially amongst competition officials. Thanks to initiatives such as the Latin American Competition Forum organized by the OECD, since 2003 competition agencies and their staff have had the opportunity to officially gather on an annual basis. Beyond the entire official content of the meetings themselves, this constitutes a valuable opportunity to create closer ties (which for us Latin Americans is not difficult at all), facilitating the exchange of ideas and experiences of various kinds. In addition to this forum there are also other scenarios that facilitate experience-sharing and relations, such as increasingly numerous meetings and events—official as well as academic. There are for instance the ones sponsored by the UNCTAD, the ICN, and other international bodies and universities. The second example is the rising number of agreements of cooperation and technical assistance between different Latin American competition agencies, in which again Mexico and Chile have been especially active.

IV. Influences

Even though competition law varies throughout all countries, external influences somehow denote that ultimately it also has an ecumenical and international aptitude. This has fuelled both the trends towards convergence and the agreement alternatives for global competition law.

In this regard, Latin America has been essentially a follower up to the point that none of the referred developments have originated from within. Nonetheless this does not mean that Latin American countries simply have had to resort to the 'copy-paste' method referred to by Ms. Heba Shahein.[8] The influences have been more complex.

Dangerously trying to systematize them, I follow a two prong criteria. One is the origin or source of the influence, whether a country or an international organization. The second is the method of the influence, whether direct or indirect. This diagram illustrates the idea:

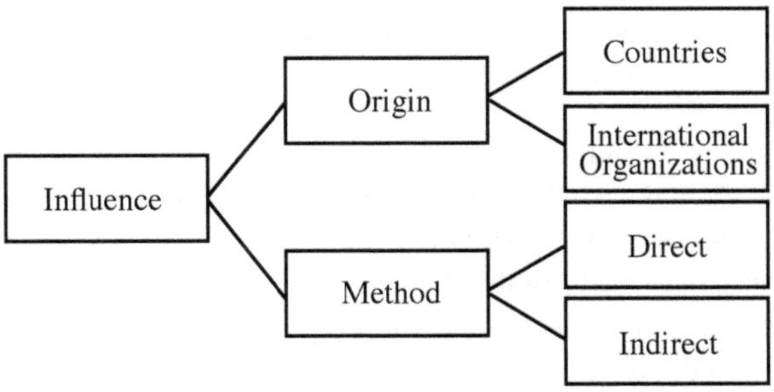

Since such variables are interwoven, a given country's influence, for instance, can be direct or indirect and so on. The interaction of these factors allows numerous possibilities, all present in the Latin American competition law scenario of influences.

8 Shagein Heba, Designing Competition Laws in New Jurisdictions: Three Models to Follow (2011), paper presented in the Sixth ASCOLA Conference, London, *available at* http://www.kcl.ac.uk/depsta/law/research/cel/events/2011/ascola/papers/HebaShahein.pdf (last accessed on October 18, 2011).

From the perspective of the origin, the countries that have exerted the most influences are the U.S. and the European Union. Notwithstanding the enormous differences between the predominantly private North American model and the more public (administrative) Latin American model, North American influence has been overwhelming. Mr. Bruce Owen, for instance, stated in an analysis of numerous Latin American cases he once made for an article that the outcome revealed that both North American competition agencies appeared to have taken jurisdiction, especially in mergers.[9]

European competition law is the second source of influence in Latin America. Some factors have eased the process. The legal Latin American culture stems from continental Europe, the region adopted the administrative model of control and last but not least one of the official languages of the EU is Spanish.

Regarding organizations, without going into too much detail, the more notorious influences have come from international organizations more involved in competition such as UNCTAD, OECD, The World Bank (WB) and the International Competition Network (ICN). Even though, strictly speaking, the ICN is not an international organization but an international semi-formal group, it has exerted a huge influence in various areas of Latin American competition law.

Direct influences, for example, diplomatic or economic impositions in exchange for assistance programs or lending money are less numerous, more manifest but less effective. The Argentinean case is illustrative. After 10 years following the adoption of the competition law amendments requested by the WB to lend the funds the country badly needed, the Tribunal for the Defense of Competition (Tribunal de Defensa de la Competencia) has not been organized yet. Among other things, this fact means that such an important country for the Latin American scenario is not occupying the place it is called to fulfill.

Indirect influences have been subtler but more effective. Such influences mainly have been materialized through academia. For the purposes of this presentation I understand the term to mean, on the one hand, all the teachings coming from the numerous North American and European programs of technical assistance and, on the other hand, university education. Each Latin American student of North American or European universities that ends up working in competition is a multiplier factor of the teachings received of incalculable consequences.

Given the burgeoning intra-Latin American relationships, it is worth opening a space for the intra-Latin American influences as well, in which we first have the Brazilian case. Two centuries ago and for three centuries all the Latin American countries, bar Brazil and some Caribbean islands, were part of a single nation, Spain. These circumstances made all the Hispanic American countries very similar practically in everything from language to religion, basic cultural values, habits, and traditions. This situation means that we can draw a dividing line between Hispanic American countries and Brazil. In terms of political traditions we have some things in common rooted in the lack of democracy that has affected the region throughout its history. However, there are also significant differences that set us apart (no one Spanish king, for instance, lived in any Hispanic American country, as happened in Brazil, and the processes of independency were quite distinct). Such dif-

9 *See* Owen Bruce, Competition Policy in Latin America, John M Olin Program in Law and Economics (Working Paper 268, 2003), *available at* http://papers.ssrn.com/paper.taf?abstract_id=45441 (last accessed October 18, 2011).

ferences are especially noteworthy in law, where contrary to what has happened with the Mexican, Argentinean, Chilean, and also Spanish law, the influence of Brazilian law in Hispanic America has been marginal. This is a cause for concern since it could difficult the spread the beneficial influence of the Brazilian competition law system, which is Latin America's most advanced.

Finally it is worth taking a look at the Mexican as well the Chilean and Spanish influences. Even though at first glance the latter may appear a little peculiar, this is not. It is important to bear in mind the fact that the Mexican, Chilean, and Spanish legal cultures have exerted deep influences in the whole Latin American legal development and, on the other hand, that they are the more advanced competition law systems within the Hispanic countries. Even though Mexico and Chile have been especially active players in the international scenario, Spain has been quite active too, mainly in the field of international cooperation. The country normally is engaged in various programs of technical assistance through its own institutions, such as the Spanish Agency of International Cooperation (Agencia Española de Cooperación Internacional) as well as through the international organizations where it is a member as the European Union and the OECD. Additionally, its presence is common in the Latin American Competition Law Forum, where, thanks to the enormous cultural empathy, it is quite easier for the Spanish representative to get into the Latin American officials' good books.

Given that it is not possible to cover the sun with one finger, overlooking the Spanish role could mean denying a factor that could potentially have a significant importance in the role that Latin America could play in the design and development of the future global competition law.

V. Additional Thoughts

Since the constraints and disadvantages that the idea of competition has faced within the region have not vanished—and will not at least in the foreseeable future—the region lags far from more desirable standards. As usual, things can be viewed as a half-empty or half-full glass. I see the latter.

Even though Latin America is part of the group of developing countries, it is distinguishable from the other developing countries by its cultural affiliation. Different from the Asian and the African contexts, Latin America is part of the western culture, which at the least allows us to consider that the factors that shaped competition ideas in the Western world have also the possibility of being replicated here; an issue about which I would like to give some additional thoughts.

First, and with all my respect, I do not agree with the kind of determinism generally accepted concerning the Latin American cultural inability to support the idea of competition. The difficulty does not stem from this reason but from the institutional weaknesses the region traditionally has suffered and that can be condensed in three words: lack of democracy. Not just elections, but true democracy built upon the rule of law and the system of checks and balances that makes societies more free and immune to the excesses of economic and political power.

Not long ago, perhaps just a few generations, all our ancestors lived in a world in which all kind of anticompetitive practices, powerful and arbitrary guilds, monopolies and regulatory privileges, were the rule, not the exception. In terms of economic thinking, I do not see for instance much difference between the Spanish colonial "encomienda" in which many academics have found a lot of Latin American deterministic opposition to the idea of competition and the European feudalism of the Middle Ages. In the same vein let us recall that the Latin American economic dirigisme has been inspired by the Colbertian dirigisme of unmistakeable French flavor.

One kind of tale tells that a well known Colombian armchair thinker of the XX Century, Mr. Absalón Fernández de Soto, used to say that "one thing is one thing and another thing is another thing." What distinguishes Latin America competition law development is not any inability to embrace the idea of competition, but rather the institutional obstacles that have impaired the progress of democratic economic freedom. The widely known characteristics of the Latin American context of unevenness, flaws of income distribution, vested interests of the elites, and erroneous economic theories so well depicted in Professor Gerber's book are rooted in the political and economic institutional feebleness that have shaped not only the panorama of competition but practically all the aspects of the Latin American economic way of life.

Widening the focus beyond competition, we can find for instance a parallelism which is worth taking into account between Latin American countries that are closer to true democracy and the development of competition law systems. In the Worldwide Governance Indicators[10] sponsored by the World Bank, for instance, we can see the Latin American countries with better governance indexes such as Brazil, Chile, and Costa Rica. It also happens that these countries have better competition policies and competition law systems as well.

The index also shows that the Latin American countries are situated at a medium level which, at the least, is promising given that the tendency is upwards. For instance, the infamous "caudillos" (dictators) that once seemed to be the perennial and most distinguishable characteristic of the Latin American political order are nowadays (almost) vanished specimens.

What distinguishes the Latin American countries in their advance towards the idea of competition and competition law is not any kind of political, economic, or cultural determinism, but the pace of the march and the dependency of competition and competition law to the more ample objective of democracy. If the region can maintain its tendency towards democracy, the idea of competition and competition law will also gather pace.

The future of competition brings many opportunities but also challenges. At the regional level, even though the omens are good (provided that the pace towards democracy is kept), some dark clouds such as protectionism appear on the horizon.[11] At the worldwide level, globalization has allowed the resurgence of China and India as world powers, the raising of others countries such as Brazil, the awakening of some surprising processes such as the Arab Spring, full of promises and uncertainties as well, and so on. This new world order however demands a law system benefiting all the stakeholders and the importance of factors such as blocks of countries is crucial. Notwithstanding all the region's differences and singularities, at the end of the day, for better or worse, Latin America is deemed to be a block. Such is its vocation. The question, however, is the direction it will take.

---

10 Daniel Kaufmann from the Brookings Institution, Aart Kraay from the World Bank Development Research Group and Massimo Mastruzzi, from the World Bank Institute, in http://info.worldbank.org/gobernance/wg/index.asp (last accessed on October 17, 2011).

11 *Protectionism in Argentina—Keep out*, THE ECONOMIST (September 24, 2011); *see also Protectionism in Brazil—A Self-Made Siege*, THE ECONOMIST, (September 24, 2011).

Structural Impediments to Global Antitrust Convergence: Lessons from China

Wentong ZHENG

wtzheng@law.ufl.edu

Assistant Professor, University of Florida Levin College of Law

In his groundbreaking book *Global Competition: Law, Markets and Globalization*, Professor Gerber convincingly laid out the limitations of relying on the voluntary convergence of national competition laws as the mechanism for forging a global competition regime.[1] Professor Gerber demonstrated that there is little basis to expect that extensive convergence will result from efforts to build consensus on competition law in the international antitrust community.[2] As an alternative to the current "jurisdictional" system, Professor Gerber proposed a "commitment pathway" as the way forward for establishing a global competition regime.[3]

In the space below, using China's experience in enacting and implementing its first antitrust law, the Antimonopoly Law (AML), I offer support for Professor Gerber's argument that extensive voluntary antitrust convergence is not likely. Drawing from my previous work on Chinese antitrust law, I argue that one of the crucial factors that prevents antitrust convergence is differences in the underlying political and economic structures of the different countries in the world. These structural impediments to antitrust convergence have important policy implications for how to best approach the global competition regime.

---

1 *See* David J. Gerber, Global Competition: Law, Markets and Globalization (Oxford University Press 2010).

2 *Id.* at 273-92.

3 *Id.* at 315-25.

I. Structural Impediments to Global Antitrust Convergence

In my 2010 article, *Transplanting Antitrust in China: Economic Transition, Market Structure, and State Control* (referred to as "*Transplanting Antitrust in China*" below),[4] I argued that several interrelated structural factors in China's economy—i.e., China's transition from a centrally planned economy to a market economy, China's lowly-concentrated market structures in most industries, and the extensive role of the Chinese state in key areas of the economy—prevented China from developing a Western-style antitrust jurisprudence despite the recent enactment of a Western-style antitrust law, the Antimonopoly Law (AML). As is widely observed, the AML incorporates most, if not all, of the major provisions of an antitrust law typically found in a market economy. But as I argued in that article, due to widespread distortions caused by those structural factors, China's economic conditions are fundamentally incompatible with the economic model embodied in the AML.

As I analyzed in that article, the incompatibility between China's underlying conditions and the AML can be seen in all three major areas of antitrust, namely, cartels, abuse of dominance, and merger review. First, with respect to cartels, the crucial assumption underlying rigorous cartel enforcement—the assumption that price competition enhances economic efficiency and consumer welfare—is violated in China as over-investment by the government, particularly local governments, through state-owned-enterprises (SOEs), leads to chronic excess capacities in many, if not most, industries. Because excess capacities routinely drive prices to abnormally low or even below-cost levels, more market competition could only lead to more SOE losses that are absorbed by the government or financed by loans from state-owned banks. As a result, the government often has to acquiesce or even actively participate in efforts to organize cartels as a way of limiting overproduction, despite the rigorous anti-cartel rules under the AML. Second, with respect to abuse of dominance, the AML contains stringent rules against abusive conduct by dominant firms to exclude market competition. In most of China's industries where there are dominant firms, however, the exclusion of market competition is done not by the dominant firms, but by the government through strict market access restrictions. As abuse of dominance in those industries is primarily of an exploitative, not exclusionary, nature, an antitrust law like the AML that focuses on exclusionary conduct only has limited relevance to abuse of dominance in China. Finally, with respect to merger review, the merger review regime under the AML presents a policy conflict with China's overall goal in SOE reforms. As part of its overall strategies for SOEs, China has been taking steps to strengthen large SOEs in key industries while privatizing or relinquishing control of small- and medium-sized SOEs. One of the most effective ways of accomplishing that goal is through government-initiated mergers and acquisitions among the largest SOEs. Given the priority accorded to SOE mergers, it is highly doubtful that the merger review provisions of the AML will be meaningfully applied to domestic mergers involving large SOEs.

Transplanting Antitrust in China was written and published at a time when a key structural problem discussed in the article—the excess capacity problem—was masked by China's unprecedented

4 Wentong Zheng, *Transplanting Antitrust in China: Economic Transition, Market Structure, and State Control*, 32 U. Pa. J. Int'l L. 643 (2010).

housing and infrastructure booms in 2008-2010 that resulted largely from China's four-trillion RMB stimulus program in response to the 2008-2009 global financial crisis. The rising construction activities at the time artificially boosted demand for industrial outputs, muting the excess capacity problem to some extent. But since 2011, amid cooling housing and infrastructure construction and lagging export demands, the excess capacity problem has been becoming more accentuated in many of China's key industries. China's steel industry, for example, saw industry-wide profits plunge nearly ninety-six percent in the first half of 2012 as compared to a year earlier, with more than twenty large- or medium-sized steel mills reporting losses due to excess capacities.[5] For another example, after explosive growth in 2009-2011, China's polysilicon industry is teetering on the brink of bankruptcy thanks to staggering excess capacities, which in 2011 accounted for eighty percent of the excess capacities worldwide.[6] For yet another example, excess capacities in China's cement industry also reached dangerous levels, with production capacity forecasted to exceed demand by more than thirty percent by 2013.[7]

The responses of China's antitrust regulators to the excess capacity problem illustrate the paradoxical situation they find themselves in. To use the cement industry as an example, in 2011, eleven major cement producers in Liaoning province, China's key province for cement production, agreed to jointly suspend production for two months after the entire cement industry in Liaoning suffered losses for two consecutive years in 2009 and 2010.[8] As a result of this production cartel, cement prices in Liaoning stabilized, at least temporarily. But the Liaoning provincial office of the State Administration for Industry & Commerce (SAIC), which is charged with investigating cartels that do not involve pricing, imposed large sums of fines on members of the cartel for violating the AML's prohibition against horizontal agreements. This move perplexed the cement industry as to why the government wanted to punish the industry for doing the only thing that could alleviate the excess capacity problem and save the industry from bankruptcy. Interestingly, the national level SAIC kept silent on the Liaoning cement cartel, as did the SAIC offices in other provinces where similar cement cartels were organized. Those SAIC offices perhaps better understood the policy dilemma they were facing: On one hand, the production cartel was strictly prohibited by the AML, but on the other hand, the production cartel was a rational, welfare-enhancing response to the excess capacity problem that was caused by the distortive role of the government in the investment process. If the government could not address the over-investment that is at the root of the excess capacity problem, it will be logically inconsistent, as well as welfare-reducing, to require the antitrust regulators to take a firm stance on cartels.

As a matter of fact, not only is the government not taking steps to address the excess capacity problem, but it is taking steps that have the effect of aggravating the problem. Since early 2012,

---

5 *See Shiye kunju jiaju, gangtie ye da kui* [Economy Gets Worse; Steel Mills Reporting Big Losses], CHINA TRADE JOURNAL (find at http://finance.sina.com.cn/hy/20120816/103912867072.shtml).

6 *See Fengguang xin nengyuan shen xian channeng guosheng; hangye jutou duo binlin pochan* [Clean Energy Firms Deeply Trapped in Excess Capacities; Most Industry Giants on Brink of Bankruptcy], CHINA NEWS NET (find at http://kfq.people.com.cn/n/2012/0814/c54918-18741744.html).

7 *See* http://money.163.com/12/0330/06/7TQTRI1G00253B0H.html.

8 *See Duodi shuini weigui shangma, hangye channeng guosheng binlin bengkui bianyuan* [Cement Plants Established Against Government Orders in Various Localities; Cement Industry Near Collapse Due to Excess Capacities], *available at* http://money.163.com/12/0813/07/88P6680N00253B0H.html?from=money.

in efforts to stave off a possible hard landing for the economy, local governments in China have unveiled new stimulus programs that, again, rely heavily on government investment in infrastructure and manufacturing.[9] These investment measures may temporarily lift market demand, but the resulting additional capacities will undoubtedly further contribute to the structural imbalance of China's economy.

As seen in the area of cartels, China faces steep structural impediments to implementing the AML. Arising primarily from the extensive—and distortive—role of the government in the economy, these structural impediments go towards the core of China's political-economic system and are beyond the control of the antitrust regulators. China may have nominally converged to the global antitrust norm by adopting the AML, but true convergence in terms of developing a substantively similar antitrust jurisprudence will be an improbable task as long as the structural impediments are present. Until and unless those structural impediments are removed, antitrust will be a sideshow in China despite the nominal significance of the AML.

II. Policy Implications

The experience in China has important implications for global antitrust convergence. The international antitrust community, as represented by the International Competition Network (ICN), has invested huge amounts of resources in promoting antitrust "best practices" across the globe. The premise of such efforts is that an antitrust rule or practice function equally well under different political and economic conditions. This premise, however, does not necessarily hold in every jurisdiction, as not every jurisdiction possesses the same political and economic structures on which the "best practices" are based. The structural impediments to global antitrust convergence call for a more nuanced approach, one that tailors the "best practices" to the political and economic environments in which antitrust is embedded.

China's experience also calls for a reevaluation of the basic approach to technical assistance by advanced antitrust jurisdictions such as the United States and the European Union. The United States and the European Union have in the past been very active in training foreign antitrust officials, judges, and other legal professionals on technical antitrust issues. But in providing technical assistance, antitrust experts from advanced antitrust jurisdictions need first be "reversed trained" on the political and economic parameters of the host country in order for the technical assistance project to be even relevant. For example, does it truly matter to China whether and how it should implement a "leniency program" for cartels when it is not even clear whether cartel enforcement is desirable in the first place? In light of the structural factors that affect the design and implementation of an antitrust regime, technical assistance should be a two-way, instead of one-way, exchange.

---

9 *See Gedi wen zengzhang jihua luxu chulu; defang si wan yi touzi yin danyou* [Growth Packages Unveiled Across the Country, New "Four-Trillion" Stimulus by Local Governments Cause for Worry], *available at* http://finance.gucheng.com/201208/2065736.shtml.

Interfacing the "Local" with the "Global": A Developing-Country Perspective on "Global Competition"

Mor BAKHOUM

mor.bakhoum@ip.mpg.de

Senior Research Fellow,
Max Planck Institute for Intellectual Property and Competition Law, Munich, Germany

I. Introduction

"Global competition"[1] does not deserve the criticism of not taking into account a new reality in international antitrust: *diversity*. The early debates and attempts to capture and regulate international related antitrust matters were limited to the circle of the advanced jurisdictions.[2] The situation has now changed dramatically. "New players," especially developing jurisdictions,[3] have now entered the "game" and have their say in the future of international antitrust.[4] The fall of the Berlin Wall, which marked the triumph of the market economy, was followed by the emergence and diversification of competition laws, especially in developing countries. Since then not only has there been an increase in the number of jurisdictions that have enacted competition laws, but the approach of those new legislations, especially in developing jurisdictions, diverge, sometimes, from the mainstream approach in developed jurisdictions. The language of development, which encompasses specific goals (not only economic goals), norms and expectations, has started to

1 David J. Gerber, Global Competition, Law, Markets and Globalization (Oxford University Press 2010).

2 *Ibid.,* at 19 & seq. on the evolution of international antitrust.

3 We paraphrase Gerber, who refers to the "other players" such as developing jurisdictions. *Ibid.,* p. 205.

4 *See* Josef Drexl, *International Competition Policy after Cancún: Placing a Singapore Issue on the WTO Development Agenda*, 27(3) World Competition 435 (2004) (discussing the reasons for the opposition of developing countries to the EU proposals for a WTO multilateral framework on competition policy).

emerge.[5] This new reality adds another layer of complication to the discussions on a multilateral framework for competition law. Diversity is a fact that a multilateral framework has to deal with. Professor Gerber has taken into account this new reality.

In Sub-Saharan Africa, the 1990s witnessed an upsurge in the number of jurisdictions that enacted competition laws.[6] Some jurisdictions refined their pre-existing interventionist competition laws to make thme "fashionable" and more in conformity with the international standards, which advocate less state and more market.[7] Yet, the African continent, with of course the exception of South Africa,[8] is still lagging behind in competition law development. This thin experience at the continental level has consequences on the "African voice" on the issue pertaining to an international framework on competition law. Professor David Gerber has brilliantly highlighted the main reasons why African countries have taken the back seat in the development of competition at the continental and international levels.[9]

Yet, the benefits and relevance of competition law for the African countries are unquestionable.[10] As Gerber points out:

> *The potential benefits of competition law are particularly significant for Africa, and thus there are potentially strong incentives for competition law development. In addition to the generic benefits of reducing prices, enhancing consumer choice and providing a more flexible and efficient economy, competition law in Africa can help address the fundamental issue of economic diversification. By most accounts the most significant problem facing many African countries is the lack of diversity in their economies. The colonially imposed and state-controlled economic model has proven difficult to change, but without such structural changes the countries of Africa will be left exposed to the vagaries of the world markets that have periodically devastated their economies.*[11.]

---

5 *See in general*, for a discussion of competition law and policy from the perspective of developing countries, Eleanor M. Fox, *Economic Development, Poverty and Antitrust: The Other Path*, 13 SW. J. L. & TRADE AM. 213; Mor Bakhoum, *A Dual Language in Modern Competition Law? "Efficiency Approach" versus "Development Approach" and Implications for Developing Countries*, 3, 34 WORLD COMPETITION LAW AND ECONOMICS REVIEW 487 (2011). *See also* ELEANOR M. FOX, *Competition, Development and Regional Integration: In Search of Competition Law Fit for Developing Countries*, in 273 & seq. COMPETITION POLICY AND REGIONAL INTEGRATION IN DEVELOPING COUNTRIES (Josef Drexl, Mor Bakhoum, Eleanor M. Fox, Michal S. Gal & David J. Gerber eds., Edward Elgar 2012).

6 For a general overview of the competition regimes in Sub-Saharan Africa, *see* African Competition Forum (ACF), Full Needs Assessment Report, Final 1, February 24, 2011.

7 In Senegal for instance the first competition Act entered into force already in 1965. It was modernized in 1994 with a more liberalized approach. *See* Loi 94/63 sur les prix, La Concurrence et le contentieux economique, *available at* http://www.globalcompetitionforum.org/regions/africa/senegal/Loi%2094-63.pdf.

8 South Africa is considered very advanced in terms of competition law enforcement and the sophistication of its institutions.

9 *See* GERBER, *op. cit. supra* note 1, at 248-258.

10 *See* GERBER, *op. cit. supra* note 1, at 248-258. On the relevance of competition law in Sub-Saharan Africa, *see* Josef Drexl, *Perspectives européennes sur la politique de la concurrence dans l'espace OHADA*, 30 REVUE INTERNATIONALE DE DROIT ECONOMIQUE 284-289 (2011).

11 *See* GERBER, *op. cit. supra* note 1, at 258 (emphasis added).

Despite this potential, Gerber raises a burning question: *Is competition law and policy in Africa a short story or a preface?*[12]

Judging only by the number of African countries that have enacted competition laws over the past two decades, one could contend that a great success has been achieved in diffusing the competition principles in Sub-Saharan Africa. Having a kind of competition law and creating an enforcement authority is now considered part of good governance. As a consequence, competition laws are enacted on a grand scale, cartels are prohibited, mergers are regulated and states must be kept out of business. They have to be neutral in the market.

In a perfect world where the competition values and principles were embedded in the society, the business community, the states, and the consumers, together and on their respective sides, would ensure an effective enforcement of competition law. In the advanced jurisdictions, competition law and policy has, over time, become a value which is protected by all stakeholders.

In developing countries, the picture is very murky when it comes to the enforcement of those competition laws. The environment suitable for an effective enforcement has yet to be created. This is especially true about West Africa.

This contribution is based on first-hand experience in the environment in which competition authorities in West Africa operate. Over the past months, I had the opportunity to visit eight (8) French-speaking West African states: Mali, Senegal, Ivory Coast, Niger, Burkina-Faso, Guinea Bissau, Togo and Benin.[13] I reviewed their competition laws and institutional enforcement framework and discussed with all the stakeholders; consumer associations: the business community, and people in academia. I would like to pass on some preliminary insights from this "competition round trip" in West Africa. This contribution is very practically oriented; it draws from and reports experiences I gained from my trip, things I have seen and learned that convince me that the challenges of developing countries, especially those faced by the West African states that I have visited, are different from the challenges of the developed countries. This convinces me that it would be a great mistake to force the developed-country competition law model on developing countries.

These local pre-conditions, experiences and challenges facing a competition authority somewhat determine its stand on the debate on an international framework. This thin local experience will be interfaced by the global debate on an international framework. The objective is to showcase how local experience interfaces with global experience. Hence the title of this contribution: interfacing the *"local"* with the *"global."*

Considering the global aspect, this contribution retraces the role, if any, of African competition authorities in the debate on an international framework for competition law. It identifies the factors that justify the "low African competition voice" in the international arena. Some comments will be

12 *See* Gerber, *op. cit. supra* note 1, at 257.

13 This research trip was conducted in the framework of a study on the reform of the institutional framework of the West African Economic and Monetary Union (WAEMU): Mor Bakhoum, *Étude sur la révision du cadre institutionnel de mise en œuvre des règles de concurrence de l'Union Economique et Monétaire Ouest Africaine (UEMOA)*, forthcoming.

made on the commitment pathway proposal developed by Professor Gerber from the stand point of African countries and, by extension, developing countries.

The first section deals with the issue raised by David Gerber: Competition law and policy in Sub-Saharan Africa: a short story or a preface? Section 2 discusses Africa's place in the global competition law debate. Section 3 comments on the commitment pathway proposal.

II. Competition Law and Policy in Sub-Saharan Africa: A Short Story or a Preface?

A couple of remarks related to the political, legal, institutional and cultural and dimensions of competition law and policy in West Africa will briefly be discussed.

1. The Historical and Political Dimension of Competition Law and Policy: *The Process*

1.1. The Historical Dimension

The development of competition laws and policies in the advanced jurisdictions is the result of a process which came to maturation over time. The initial objectives and the challenges have shaped not only the goals of their competition laws, but also the way they are enforced.[14] In the case of Sub-Saharan African countries they have almost overnight been "blessed" with a competition law that they are required to apply.[15] Hence, the enactment of competition laws in Sub-Saharan African countries does not result from an internal *process* which takes into account the local characteristics and needs. In some cases, it was dictated from the outside, by the financial institutions, as part of the liberalization process.

In Sub-Saharan Africa, historically, the states have been big players in the "regulation" of competition in the market. The opening up of their economies to market principles did not put an end to the interventionist policy of the states. In West Africa, after becoming independent in

---

14 For the development of competition law in Europe from a historical perspective, *see* David J. Gerber, Law and Competition in Twentieth Century Europe: Protecting Prometheus (Oxford University Press 1998).

15 *See* on this aspect, tracing the development of competition law in Africa, M.M. Salah, *La problématique du droit économique dans les pays du Sud (première partie)*, Revue Internationale de Droit Economique 19 (1998); M.M. Salah, *La problématique du Droit Economique dans les Pays du Sud (deuxième partie)*, Revue Internationale de Droit Economique 165 (1998).

the 1960s, the then-young independent states had the challenging task not only to construct their political and administrative institutions, but also, and more importantly, to build their new and weak economies.[16] Of course, building sound institutions is intertwined with the economic dimension. As a consequence, states were vested with the power to intervene in the market, to ensure the supply of public goods and to control prices. It was a period of great interventionism. This was normal at that time for the newly independent states, since interventionism was also how business was conducted by the former colonizer, France. Professor Gerber has highlighted the interventionist character of some European countries, including France, at that time.[17] Even the institutional orientation, and especially the administrative model, inherited from colonial France, have influenced the way enforcement institutions are shaped today.[18]

It may sound odd, considering the newness of competition laws in developing countries, but some states in West Africa had a "competition law" as early as the 1960s. In Senegal, for instance, the first Competition Act was enacted in 1965. Benin has had legislation regulating competition and prices since 1967[19] and the law regulating prices and competition in Niger entered into force in 1992.[20] These different pieces of "competition laws" have a common feature. They reflect a great deal of state interventionism in the market. The entry into the market is regulated, prices are controlled, some sectors are exempted from competition; governments have the leeway to intervene in the market.[21] This is in part inherited from French law, which in the colonial period was very interventionist.

This colonial legacy is not a past and forgotten history. It still influences the perception and the orientation of competition laws in many African countries. It is common in these legislations that after reaffirming the principle of free competition the state creates a loophole in the legislation which allows it to intervene and unilaterally fix prices in "exceptional circumstances,"[22] when the market conditions so require. Despite the recognition of the principles of competition, prices are still regulated to a large extent. This pattern is noticeable in the competition legislations of West African countries. In Senegal, for instance, the competition law gives the government the power to unilaterally fix the price of certain goods. Prices of goods, such as oil-driven products and gas, are unilaterally fixed by the government. Prices of pharmaceutical products, sugar, flowers, and bread have to be authorized by the government. There is a price ceiling for those products.[23]

---

16 *Ibid.*, at 21. *See also* KEBA MBAYE, *Sources et evolution du droit africain*, in 354 L'ETAT MODERNE, L'HORIZON 2000; ASPECTS INTERNES ET EXTERNES, MÉLANGES OFFERTS À P.F. GONIDEC (IGDJ, Paris 1985).

17 *See* GERBER, *op. cit. supra* note 1, at 175-180.

18 Most African competition laws still rely on the administrative model with the enforcement powers vested in the executive, generally the ministry of trade. In countries with an "independent" administrative authority, the executive is represented, e.g., by the commission or the executive has review power over the decision issued by the competition authority.

19 *See* Ordonnance n° 20/PR/MFAEP du 5 juillet 1967 portant réglementation des prix et des stocks.

20 *See* Ordonnance n° 92-025 du 7 juillet 1992 portant réglementation des prix et de la concurrence.

21 *See*, for instance, Articles 42 and 43 of Regulation 1994/63, which provides for the possibility to unilaterally set the prices of products and services if the economic circumstances require it.

22 *See* Article 43 of Regulation 1994/63.

23 *See* Décret 2006-1246 du 14/11/2006 modifiant l'article 3 du décret n° 95-77 du 20 janvier 1995 portant application des articles 44 et 64 de la loi n° 94-63 du 22 août 1994 sur les prix, la concurrence et le contentieux économique, JORS du 15/11/2006. Arrêté du 15/11/2006, portant application des dispositions de l'article 1 du décret n° 2006-1246 du 14 novembre 2006 modifiant l'article 3 du décret 95-77 du 20 janvier 1995 sur les prix, la concurrence et le contentieux économique, JORS, du 15/11/2006.

In the case of Ivory Coast, the prices of certain staples, such as rice or sugar, are determined by the government in collaboration with the business corporations.[24] The same patterns are noticeable in Benin and Niger. In Niger, for instance, there is a Commission comprised by the agent of the ministry of trade and the business community that determines the prices of staples.

Government price control is a common and accepted practice in West African states. The business community accepts it and the consumers recognize themselves in the price control schemes. They are more comfortable if the prices are fixed with the involvement of the government. In line with these practices, the government agents in charge of applying the "competition law" are vested with the power to make sure that the predefined prices are respected. In their understanding, they apply a kind of competition law.

As to the economic structure of the economies in West Africa, David Gerber has highlighted how colonial rule has shaped the economic structure of those markets then and now.[25] These economies are concentrated in the hands of a few, they are oriented toward exportation, they lack diversity, local entrepreneurship is poor and south-south trade does not exist. This legacy is reflected in the present economic structure of West African states. It creates specific competition law challenges.

1.2. The Political Dimension

The political dimension[26] of competition law and policy is also of paramount importance in the enforcement of competition laws in developing countries. A given competition law does not get off the ground spontaneously, enjoying acceptance and application. It needs political support. This support is lacking in West African states. There are a number of reasons for this.

The process of introducing competition laws in those countries did not stem from a perceived and accepted need to protect free competition in their markets. It is rather the result of a top-down process: international lending institutions required them to introduce competition law as part of a "development package." Of course the states enacted competition laws without the required political support for the new legislation. The consequence of this legislative approach is that in the book the law is perfect, but in practice, little attention is paid to enforcing this legislation. As a consequence, enforcement authorities are given little or no means at all to do their job. The lack of resources in developing countries is very well documented. In West Africa the situation is the same.[27] The enforcement institutions (often an office within the ministry of trade) are unfunded. Their personnel also lack training in competition law.

---

24 These developments are based on an interview conducted with the competition authority of Ivory Cost in 2011 in the framework of a study on the reform of the institutional framework of the WAEMU competition policy. *See* Bakhoum, *op. cit.* (note 13).

25 *See* Gerber, *op. cit. supra* note 1, at 248 & seq.

26 For discussion of the political dimension of competition law and policy from a regional integration perspective, *see* David J. Gerber, *Regionalization, development and competition law: exploring the Political Dimension*, in 253 & seq. Competition Policy and Regional Integration in Developing Countries, *supra* note 5.

27 For an overview of the situation in West Africa, *see* Bakhoum, *op. cit. supra* note 13.

South Africa, which is by far the most advanced jurisdiction in Sub-Saharan Africa, evidences that if the political leadership believes in the value of having a strong competition law and policy, they will support it by providing independence and resources to the enforcement authorities. In West Africa, political and economic power is intertwined. Political leadership provides economic power, and economic power secures political influence. In the current rent-seeking situation, the close link between political power and economic power in the hand of few political leaders precludes the establishment of competition law as a value that deserves protection. It is therefore not a surprise if the political support for the introduction of strong competition law regimes is lacking in West African states.

Politics *stricto sensu* also has a great impact on the functioning of the competition authority and the way the law is applied. Competition law is not only a legal tool used to achieve economic results. It could also be used as a political tool.

It is reported in Ivory Coast that, due to political turmoil since 2002, the competition agency is no longer functioning.[28] The constant changing of the minister of trade, who is in charge of the renewal of the members of the Competition Commission, has created a deadlock in the functioning of the Commission. Since 2002, new members of the Commission have not been appointed. The political instability the country is undergoing has a great impact on the functioning of the institutions in general and the competition authority in particular.

Competition law can also be used for a politico-economic purpose. Ivory Coast, again, has just come out of a very chaotic social crisis following the contested presidential election in November 2011. The socio-political situation is getting more stable as the country is healing its wounds. On the economic front also, the new rulers are redefining the rules of the game. It has been reported that the new authorities already have in their radar the big businesses that used to benefit from undue privileges from the previous government, which they financially supported during the crisis. The new authorities have launched an inquiry into the alleged dominant position of some companies in the importation of rice, for instance, with the aim of breaking the businesses in the sector that were connected to the previous regime. This is done by using their competition law.

28 This is based on an interview conducted with the competition authority of Ivory Coast in 2011 in the framework of a study on the reform of the institutional framework of the WAEMU competition policy. *See* Bakhoum, *op. cit. supra* note 13.

2. The "Legal" Dimension *Stricto Sensu:* Poorly Drafted Competition Laws

By legal dimension, I refer to the competition laws as enacted: the provisions as they stand in the books, the goals as they are set and the basic prohibitions as they are framed.

Cartels are harmful in every jurisdiction, regardless of whether it is developed or less developed. In this respect Michal Gal contends that competition law is a discipline that can "fit all formulation." However, some areas still raise tension given the fact that the structure of the market of the hosting jurisdiction should influence the way those prohibitions are applied. If we take unilateral conduct rules for instance, it is very debatable to contend that prohibitions should be framed in the same way. Dominance is no longer an issue in advanced jurisdictions. The perception of dominance does not necessarily hurt competition. As a consequence, unilateral conduct rules are more permissive. This is the case of the approach toward predatory pricing in the United States.[29] In contrast, in developing jurisdictions dominance is still a big competition concern. In Sub-Saharan African economies, for instance, the economies used to be, and still are, very concentrated. A handful of people, often connected with the states, enjoy economic privileges and monopoly positions. Economic and political powers are intertwined. States are still big economic players. In these conditions, competition law prohibitions should focus on fighting dominance effectively and dismantling economic concentrations. Achieving economic atomization and providing economic opportunities to citizens, thereby protecting their very economic freedom, could be achieved by specific enforcement of the rules on dominance.

Very often, the existence of a large so-called informal economy in developing countries is acknowledged. In West Africa, for instance, a large part of the economy is informal.[30] Competition law has not so far given a sound orientation on how to deal with the anticompetitive practices taking place in such informal markets.

3. The Institutional Dimension

By institutional dimension of competition law and policy I refer to two aspects: the first is the intrinsic side of the institutions, which means the *enforcement mechanisms* set forth in order to enforce the competition law. The extrinsic aspect of the institutional dimension refers to the *broader*

---

29 Commenting on the U.S. Supreme Court's approach toward predatory pricing, Eleanor Fox contends that the Court has repeatedly declared that predatory pricing rarely occurs and is even more rarely successful. She continues, "on that premise, combined with the aim to give consumers the benefit of low prices and the fear that courts will protect inefficient firms, the U.S. Supreme Court has formulated a rule of law that makes it nearly impossible for a plaintiff to win a predatory pricing case." She questions the suitability of this approach in markets dominated by state-owned firms and characterized by dominance. *See* Fox, *Competition, development and regional integration*, *op. cit. supra* note 5, at 279-280.

30 *See*, for an extended discussion of the informal or popular economy, D´une économie populaire à une économie fiscalisée; INEADEC-Actes du colloque international de Kinshasa du 19 septembre 2008, Grégoire Bakandeja wa Mpungu, Bernard Remiche (dir.), Larcier, 2010.

framework in which competition authorities operate. Building strong enforcement institutions is crucial for a competition law to be effective. This is a great challenge in developing countries.

3.1. Two Dimensions: Enforcement Institutions and Political Institutions

The enforcement powers and the procedural rules of a given competition authority, including the inquiry powers, the independence of the competition authority and the private right of action, are amongst institutional preconditions that determine the success of that competition authority. Extensive work has been done on the subject that highlights the importance of having strong institutional enforcement, especially in the context of developing countries.[31]

In practice however, enforcement mechanisms are not always suitable to an effective enforcement. In Ivory Coast, for instance, which had a very well-functioning competition authority—the Competition Commission—from 1992 to 2002, before the political crisis, the Commission had only the power to conduct the inquiries and to deliver an opinion on the case. The decision-making competence was exclusively vested in the minister of trade, who had the power to follow the opinion or to overturn it. Private right of action was not initially recognized by the competition act. It was only later that the private parties were allowed to bring actions before the Commission.[32]

National competition commissions, in the states where they exist, do not enjoy the independence their work requires. They are influenced by the government, which provides them with funding and monitors their actions. This is the case in Senegal, Burkina Faso and Mali. In Niger a competition commission is theoretically created by the law but it has only advisory power. In Benin, Togo and Niger it is a government office under the umbrella of the ministry of trade, which is in charge of enforcing their competition laws.[33]

At the regional level, the enforcement institutions are poorly designed. In the case of the West African Economic and Monetary Union (WAEMU) for instance, the regional office in charge of applying the regional law does not have the leeway to take strong enforcement actions.[34] Some flaws in the design of the regional enforcement institutions undermine the efficiency of the actions of the Commission. It is required to inform the companies before conducting inquiries. It is not allowed by law to conduct surprise, or "dawn raids," and it has to inform the member state of all

31 *See* William E. Kovacic, *Getting Started: Creating New Competition Policy Institutions in Transition Economies*, 23 Brook. J. Int'l L. 403 (1997-1998); William E. Kovacic, *Institutional Foundations for Economic Legal Reform in Transition Economies: The Case of Competition Policy and Antitrust Enforcement*, 77 Chi.-Kent L. Rev. 265 (2001).

32 *See* Bakhoum, *op. cit. supra* note 13.

33 *See* Bakhoum, *op. cit. supra* note 13, for the enforcement framework of the competition law in Benin, Togo, and Niger.

34 *See* on this aspect Mor Bakhoum, L'articulation du droit communautaire et des droits nationaux de la concurrence dans l'Union Economique et Monétaire Ouest Africaine (UEMOA) 157 & seq. (Bruylant, Stämpfli, 2007). *See also* Bakhoum, *op. cit. supra* note 13.

inquiries conducted at the national level. A strong centralization of the enforcement powers also limits the effectiveness of the regional law.

Institutions also include strong consumer associations or a bar association to foster private enforcement. These institutions, if they exist, are not aware of the competition issues.

Political institutions, such as a well-functioning judiciary system or a non-corrupt and well-functioning administration, are also crucial in the operation of a competition authority.

4. The "Cultural" Dimension

Competition law and policy is not an abstract concept or a legal construction that is effectively enforceable regardless of whether the businesses and consumers identify with it or not. In an environment where the competition culture is weak, businesses and states do not spontaneously follow the competition principles. Acceptance of competition principles by a society is a precondition of their spontaneous and effective application.

In the advanced jurisdictions, competition law and policy is embedded in the society. It has become over time a societal value that is accepted and protected by all stakeholders. States interfere less with free competition, businesses integrate competition principles in their transactions and consumers are aware of the benefits of competition law. Those combined factors make enforcement easier.

In developing countries, however, and in Sub-Saharan Africa in particular, competition and competition law are not embedded in the society as a value that has to be protected. In this vein, Professor Gerber contends that, in the context of Africa, competition law is "alien" or competition law is "not African."[35] This is true in a sense. Hence, in a society where cooperation is valued socially and in business, "open" competition is not necessarily viewed as positive. This shows the disconnection between the economic behavior valued by the society and the values and rationale of competition law. In a society where community and common behavior used to be the rule, valuing a competition law, which is based on individual economic decisions in the market, is not an easy task.

Not surprisingly, a strong focus is placed on building a strong "competition culture" in developing countries. This is the crux of the agenda of competition law experts and technical assistance institutions. The often-heard mantra in the framework of the capacity building programs is that the competition law culture must be diffused in the society. The aim of this endeavor is to make the stakeholders integrate, accept, and recognize themselves the values of competition and spontaneously follow competition principles, or at least initiate legal action when the law is violated. Building a "culture" and building a competition law culture is not an easy task. It raises challenges. In the process of creating a competition culture in developing countries, quite often the focus is on groups of people who are a bit knowledgeable on competition principles. The target is on official and enforcement authorities. However, potential violators of the very basic principles of competition law are not educated on the principles of competition law. In Mali, for instance, the

35 Gerber, *op. cit. supra* note 1, at 254.

president of the consumer association with the highest number of members is not even aware of the existence of a competition law which they could invoke against anticompetitive practices.

In addition, in West African people still rely on the government. When the prices are high they complain before the government, not the competition authorities. This is justified by the fact that governments used to be, and still are, to a certain extent, providers of economic welfare. It is common in West African states that demands for lower prices and quality products are directed toward governments that, in fact, are still controlling the prices. The governments are still considered by the consumers as the legitimate and the only authority capable of providing fair prices and quality products. Competition authorities, where they exist, are not perceived as providers of economic welfare.

Moreover, the legitimacy of a decision from a competition authority is sometimes questioned by the business community and the citizens. In Niger, for instance, I learned that an independent competition authority in the form of a commission, not connected to the administration and the government, is not viewed as a credible authority or a legitimate entity that could take sanctions. The idea and perception is that if a sanction is to be binding, it has to come from a state authority. It is only the state that should be vested with the authority to take sanction. This raises serious issues regarding the acceptance and the legitimacy of decisions made by the competition authority.

These examples show that the perception and the acceptance of competition principles and enforcement institutions are crucial for the success of a competition authority. This requires education in the competition principles.

III. Africa and the Global Competition Law Debate

1. Retracing the African Countries' Role in the Debate on a Global Competition Law

Apart from South Africa, whose competition law is developing increasingly with well-functioning institutions, competition law experience in African countries is still very meager. The increase in the number of countries that have adopted competition policies evidences the awareness and willingness of African countries to rely on competition law enforcement as a development tool. However, different factors render this endeavor very challenging. There is still, for different reasons, a wide divide between the laws in the books and the law in action. This meager experience in competition law enforcement has an impact on the African presence in the international arena and its position in competition-related matters.

This part of the contribution retraces the role, if any, of the African countries in the debate pertaining to a global competition law. Three aspects will be considered: the multilateral level, the bilateral level and the convergence approach.

1.1. The Multilateral Level

African countries were absent in the early efforts to create a multilateral framework on competition law. During the colonial period, there was a quasi-absence of competition laws in the African countries. In countries that did have a sort of competition law, such as Senegal, which enacted its first competition law in 1964, these legislations were influenced by the French interventionist approach. Being under colonial rule, their economies and legal institutions were basically following the interest of the colonial ruler. However, the interests of developing countries were not totally ignored during the negotiation of a multilateral agreement in the International Trade Organization (ITO). As pointed out by David Gerber, during the negotiation of the ITO, significant changes were made to the proposal in order to accommodate the interests of developing countries.[36]

The developments at the international level from the post-war period also witnessed limited participation of the African states. In general, their interests have been taken into account by the instruments developed, and certain organizations are devoted exclusively to the interests of developing countries. The U.N. set of principles for the control of restrictive business practices[37] developed in the framework of the United Nations Conference on Trade and Development (UNCTAD) takes into account the interests of developing countries with regard to cartels. However, its recommendations are not binding and it has limited influence on the behavior of transnational companies.

UNCTAD is taking a stand for developing countries by promoting an agenda that takes their interests into account. But apart from reinforcing the technical capacities of developing countries on competition law and policy, it does not have the mandate to represent developing countries.

It was only during the 1990s, especially during the debate for a potential international framework on competition law in the WTO, that African countries started to have their voice heard. With other developing countries, under the leadership of India, they opposed the proposal of the EU.[38]

The African stand on the negotiations at the international level is summarized by David Gerber as follows:

> *Africa has generally played at best a marginal role in global competition law development until very recently, but several factors suggest that that role may increase. African states were not yet independent during the early efforts to develop a transnational competition law, and even during the negotiations over the set in the early 1980s, they showed relatively little interest. During the discussions concerning inclusion of competition law in the WTO, however, African countries generally backed Brazil, India and other opponents of the proposal.*[39]

36 Gerber, *op. cit. supra* note 1, at 44-45.

37 *See* UNCTAD, Set of Multilaterally Agreed Equitable Principles and Rules for the Control of Restrictive business practices, *available at* http://r0.unctad.org/en/subsites/cpolicy/docs/cpset/cpset.htm.

38 *See* on this aspect Drexl, *op. cit. supra* note 4, at 435-437.

39 Gerber, *op. cit. supra* note 1, at 257 (emphasis added).

The development of competition law in West Africa is hindered by an array of challenges. As we have seen, the countries face different challenges that their competition law orientation should take into account. Economic concentration, lack of economic diversity, a poor institutional framework, corruption, strong state involvement, and poor education on competition law are amongst the competition constraints African countries are dealing with. These local characteristics should have an impact on their competition law orientation, which is still not clearly defined. This lack of a clearly articulated African competition law vision has an impact on how they approach international competition issues. Apart from South Africa, which has its own competition law orientation tailored to its specific needs, African states are still in search of their competition law model. Developing countries have not yet formulated a clear vision on an international framework that takes their own interests into account. They rather take a defensive stand, claiming that an international framework should not merely be used as a market access tool and that they need flexibilities.

With the increased development of competition law in Sub-Saharan Africa, the increased political support of its enforcement, and the leading position of South African competition authorities, one could expect an increased role of African authorities in the international arena. Their presence in the different international for a—the International Competition Network (ICN) and UNCTAD—which gives them exposure to the international issues, could, in the long run, help them identify and defend their own interests. Efforts undertaken on the continental level through the African Competition Forum (ACF) as well as at the regional level should certainly augment their role.

1.2. The Bilateral Level

Given the hurdles in setting an international framework that would define the guidelines for competition enforcement in global markets and the potential conflicts that unilateral jurisdictionalism embodies, states have turned to bilateral cooperation in competition law enforcement. Antitrust cooperation agreements aiming at facilitating exchange of information have been signed by competition enforcers, especially among developed countries' competition authorities. The United States and the European Union are using this approach in order to identify potential anticompetitive conduct having an effect in their markets.[40]

When dealing with anticompetitive practices induced by international firms, access to the relevant information is often a major issue for a competition authority in a developing country. Yet, accessing such information is still a big challenge. Cooperation agreements that involve close enforcement cooperation and exchange of sensitive information are only available in developed countries' competition authorities. Developing countries in general and African competition

40 The first cooperation agreement between the U.S. and the EU was signed on September 23, 1991. It involved notification of enforcement activities, exchange of non-confidential information, cooperation and coordination activities, etc. *See* Agreement between the European Communities and the Government of the United States of America regarding the application of their competition laws, *available at* http://ec.europa.eu/competition/international/legislation/usa01.pdf. *See also* U.S.-EU Merger Working Group, Best Practices on Cooperation in Merger Investigations, available at http://ec.europa.eu/competition/international/bilateral/eu_us.pdf.

authorities are excluded[41] from this closed enforcement cooperation, although it would help them deal with enforcement issues resulting from the global markets. Why this exclusion of developing and African competition authorities?

A bilateral cooperation agreement can be motivated by the desire to avoid the risks of jurisdictional conflicts and clashes of decisions between two competition authorities. This risk of conflict is likely to appear when two competition authorities have respective jurisdictions over a merger, for instance, and diverging solutions would create a clash. Cooperation at the early stage would help avoid conflicts. This risk does not exist if the case involves a competition authority in a developing country. For instance, a merger authorized in the U.S. or the EU would certainly not be prohibited by a competition authority in a small African state. The exterritorial reach of a competition law of a developing country is inexistent, although in theory their laws have an extraterritorial reach. An African competition authority would not have the tools to discover and sanction anticompetitive practices initiated abroad. *For a bilateral cooperation to be relevant, the risk of conflict of jurisdiction has to exist.* This is not the case between a competition authority of a developed country and a competition authority in a developing country. A real potential of extraterritorial enforcement that would threaten an enforcement orientation of a given competition authority has to exist for a bilateral cooperation to be relevant for a competition authority in an advanced jurisdiction.

Exchanging enforcement in order to detect potential violation requires some preconditions. The cooperating competition authorities involved should be at the same level of sophistication and enforcement of their competition laws and be able to satisfy enforcement requests from the signatory parties.[42] The two parties should also be trustworthy regarding the information they receive, and the legal system should provide sound guarantees that the information exchanged would not be used for other purposes.[43] This sophistication and trust does not yet exist between the competition authorities of developed countries and developing jurisdictions. A U.S. or EU competition authority would not necessarily trust sensitive information to an African or developing-country competition authority.

Those elements that justify a country's willingness to enter into bilateral agreements do not exist in developing countries. There is no risk of extraterritorial application of their competition law, their credibility is limited and their competition law is still at a nascent stage. They are unable to capture the behavior of foreign firms based in the United States and the European Union.

Some bilateral agreements involve enforcement issues but are not directed to information exchange or the need to deal with cross-border anticompetitive practices. They take the form of technical assistance and knowledge development of national competition authorities. In Africa, the South African competition authority is increasing its cooperation with some African competition

41 Recently, on September 27, 2012, the Competition Commission of India (CCI) signed a Memorandum of Understanding (MOU) with the U.S. FTC and DOJ with the objective to increase technical cooperation in enforcement, including exchange of information. *See* the press release at the following link http://www.ftc.gov/opa/2012/09/indiamou.shtm?goback=.gde_1903800_member_169600958.

42 *See* on this aspect Diane Wood, *Soft Harmonization Among Competition Laws: Track Records and Prospects*, Antitrust Bulletin, Summer 2003, 313.

43 *Ibid.*, at 316.

authorities in the form of training of competition officials. The newly created African Competition Forum (ACF) is also starting to be active in training competition authorities.

Another type of agreement is the bilateral trade agreement, which encompasses competition law elements that are not directed to protection of free competition as such. Bilateral agreements are turned toward diffusing competition law principles of the advanced jurisdictions into developing ones. This is evidenced by the EU-CARIFORUM agreement, which requires CARIFORUM member states to adopt competition laws that are market-access oriented.[44] The same approach is undertaken by the EU in its ongoing negotiations for free-trade agreements (FTAs) with some African states.

2. Potential of the African Countries to Strengthen Their "Voice" at the International Level

Two aspects that have the potential of strengthening the African "voice" in the international arena will be discussed: the regional integration process in competition law and the African Competition Forum (ACF).

2.1. The Regional Integration Process and Its Potential

Regionalizing competition policies in a regional trade agreement or common markets has the potential to help developing countries overcome the enforcement challenges they face. Pulling the limited resources together at the regional level, it is often contended, would foster enforcement. In addition to the common and classic benefits associated with regional competition law (protecting free competition in the common market, efficiently fighting international cartels, fostering interstate trade by reducing national barriers and state involvement), regional integration has the potential to connect developing countries with each other and help them become integrated in the global economy.[45] Several regional integration initiatives with a competition law component have been undertaken in Africa. These include WAEMU, COMESA, SADC and ECOWAS, which is in the

44 For a discussion on the issue, *see* South Centre, Competition Policy in Economic Partnership Agreements (CARIFORUM text), April 2008, available at:http://www.southcentre.org/index.php?option=com_content&view=article&id=607%3Afact-sheet-nd8-competition-policy-in-economic-partnership-agreements-cariforum-text&catid=101%3Aeconomic-partnership-agreements-epas&lang=fr; *see also* Mor Bakhoum, *Commerce International, Politique de Concurrence et Accords de Partenariat Economique, Réflexions sur les Enjeux et Perspectives d'un Tryptique*, GLOCAL 2, Revue Africaine sur le Commerce et le Développement, octobre 2010, at 3 & seq.

45 *See* Josef Drexl, *Economic integration and competition law in developing countries*, in 231 Competition Policy and Regional Integration in Developing Countries, *op. cit. supra* note 5.

process of creating a regional competition framework.[46] Although the promises are many, different challenges render the endeavor difficult. Limited interstate trade, lack of national cooperation, poor regional institutional design, different levels of economic development, and a lack of political will are amongst factors that slow down the dynamics of regional competition law.

If the regional process runs smoothly, it will be a useful tool to fight international anticompetitive practices. A threat of strong enforcement from a regional competition authority against a firm that has interests in a regional market would be more credible than an enforcement threat from a national competition authority. The chances of a strong regional competition authority getting information from its counterpart in a developed country are more likely than cooperation with a national competition authority.

The regional process holds a lot of promise. However, it has to overcome a lot of challenges before delivering its potential.

2.2. Networking: The African Competition Forum (ACF) and Its Potential

A recent initiative, and one that is very unique in terms of its goals and the context in which it was created, deserves some reflection as to its potential in taking into account the interests of some developing countries in the current international framework. The mechanisms to set up the African Competition Forum (ACF) were discussed at the African Stakeholder Workshop (ASW) held in Nairobi, Kenya, in March 2010. It was agreed during that meeting that the ACF would be run as a virtual network. This calls to mind the ICN. . . .

The network was officially launched at the first conference of the ACF held in Nairobi on March 3, 2011. One of the rationales and core objectives of the ACF is to *"promote the adoption of competition principles in the implementation of national and regional economic policies of African countries, in order to alleviate poverty and enhance inclusive economic growth, development and consumer welfare by fostering competition in markets, and thereby increasing investment, productivity, innovation and entrepreneurship*."[47] It follows from this statement that growth should be based on market-oriented principles and include participation. This approach clearly shows a focus on the issues of development and inclusion in economic growth.

Three functional objectives guide the actions of the ACF:

I) "Encourage and assist African countries that do not have a competition law to adopt one";

II) "Help build the capacity of existing and future African competition agencies: this includes human resources, budget and institutional structure through training, exchange and funding";

---

46 On regional competition policies in developing countries, *see generally* COMPETITION POLICY AND REGIONAL INTEGRATION IN DEVELOPING COUNTRIES, *op. cit. supra* note 5.

47 Thula Kaira, The Possibility of Establishing an Africa Competition Forum, Presentation Prepared for the Workshop on Competition Law and Policy in African Small States, July 26-27, 2010, Windhoek, Namibia (emphasis added).

III) "Increase the awareness of the benefits of implementing competition laws among governments, the general public and stakeholders."

A steering committee created at the launch of the forum is in charge of coordinating the activities of the forum. In preparation for the first ACF conference in Nairobi, a need assessment survey was conducted, which resulted in a report providing an overview of the different competition laws in Africa as well as the functioning of the different African competition agencies.[48] The report provides a wealth of information on different countries' competition laws.

The network is too recent to allow a full analysis of its potential for putting forward an African agenda on competition law. However, the future design of the ACF, its rationale, and its objectives provide some hints on how this "kind of African ICN" would work.

The ACF, which is "African driven," has the primary objective to help African countries "identify and address obstacles to fair competition." As to its potential, the ACF "would facilitate exchange of information, dissemination of knowledge and experience, building staff and institutional capacities through provision of technical assistance, conducting various studies and related programs to promote the development and strengthening of competitive markets."[49]

As to its relationships with existing forums, the ACF aims at enhancing participation of member countries in various international forums "to represent and put forward 'African' points of view."[50]

The initiative to launch an African forum is very promising. However, the ACF will have to overcome a number of challenges to be successful. The network needs strong leadership. The presence of members of relatively advanced competition authorities in Africa, South Africa, Zambia, and Egypt in the steering committee is certainly a positive factor for the success of the initiative.

The network takes advantage of the international events to meet regularly. Members often meet during the UNCTAD meetings. They also met this year at the ICN annual conference in The Hague. Under the intellectual leadership of David Lewis, this initiative should certainly help African countries strengthen their voice at the international level.

---

48 ACF Full Needs Assessment Report, *op. cit. supra* note 6.

49 Kaira, *op. cit. supra* note 47.

50 *Ibid.*

IV. Commitment Pathway and the Integration of Africa in the Global Competition Law Dynamic: Promises and Challenges

This part of the contribution shares some reflections on the commitment pathway proposal[51] developed by Professor Gerber from the standpoint of the African countries, and developing countries in extrapolation. Would the commitment pathway approach take account of developing countries' need to have a competition law tailored to their system? Does it respect these countries' right to choose their own "blend" of competition law? Would the proposal help address restrictions of competition resulting from global markets? What are the chances to have developed countries commit, given the trend of shifting to bilateral cooperation agreements and FTAs? This part of the contribution briefly addresses those issues.

1. "Agreement" and "Commitment": A Beneficial Approach for Developing Countries

The current approaches in dealing with enforcement issues of practices having cross-border effects do not involve shared obligations through a multilateral framework. The difficulties in reaching a multilateral agreement on competition law cast some shadow on the prospect of reaching an agreement.[52] Bilateral enforcement cooperation, trade-related agreements dealing with competition matters, convergence,[53] and more recently competition provisions in the FTAs[54] offer the current solutions in global markets. Although those different alternative tools offer transitory solutions, they do not reflect the interest of all stakeholders, and their effectiveness depends on the level of sophistication of the competition laws of the parties involved. Convergence does not, as such, address restrictions of competition in global markets. The primary focus of this approach is to strengthen the enforcement capacities of competition authorities, and to reduce the gap between different national competition approaches. Although they have the potential to foster enforcement capacities, they do not directly deal with restrictions of competition in global markets. Their objective is not to protect free competition at the international level. As to cooperation agreements on enforcement, they are limited to the competition authorities of developed countries. Developing countries are seeing their markets become more and more open while their protection from anticompetitive practices remains weak.

---

51 *See* GERBER, *op. cit. supra* note 1, at 293 & seq.

52 Drexl, *op. cit. supra* note 4.

53 *See generally* Eleanor M. Fox, *Linked-In: Antitrust and the Virtues of a Virtual Network*, 43 INTERNATIONAL LAWYER 151 (2009).

54 *See* South Centre, *op. cit. supra* note 44.

Experience has revealed that it is difficult to reach an international agreement on competition law that would put binding obligations on members. However, from the standpoint of developing countries in general, such binding commitment is necessary to address international restrictions on competition effectively. If, as suggested by David Gerber, the pathway strategy addresses cartels, parties would be required to take action against anticompetitive acts that affect international markets. Similar proposals have been made in the literature.[55] This would give a developing country, for instance, the right to request enforcement action from a developed country's competition authority for practices affecting the former's market. The current strategies do not include such obligations. Given the limited discovery capacities of the competition authorities in developing countries, an agreement that would allow them to request enforcement action would be more effective. This is especially true of African countries.

Given their limited capacities to apply their laws unilaterally to cross-border anticompetitive practice affecting their markets, African countries would certainly benefit from a multilateral agreement giving them the possibility to pursue cartelists in an international forum. Similar benefits would also stem from a requirement to prohibit export cartels initiated in developed countries. These obligations could be driven from within a multilateral framework. Similar proposals have been made in this regard in the scholarship that meets the interests of African countries in a multilateral framework dealing with competition law. It has even been asked in this regard if developing countries did not act against their interest by refusing to enter into a multilateral agreement on competition law in the framework of the WTO.

The pertinence of this approach is supported by the fact that alternative solutions based on cooperation in enforcement are one-sided.

From a political economy perspective, contrary to the past, the recent developments in competition law in Sub-Saharan Africa provide a prospect for more influence of African countries in the debate pertaining to a multilateral framework. Hence, the regionalization of competition policies in the framework of regional integration groups is a tool to get more influence on the international level. Moreover, the newly created ACF has the potential to put forward an African agenda at the multilateral level. These developments give African countries stronger and more coordinated voices on the international level.

2. Commitment Pathway and Diversity: Integrating a New Reality

Over 100 jurisdictions have competition legislations. This could be considered a success if we only consider the number. However, in countries with limited resources to enforce their legislation, the real benefits of having competition policies have yet to be seen. From an international perspective, this new reality creates new challenges, especially in the prospect of creating a multilateral framework dealing with international competition matters. Although developed countries' competition policies tend to be closer in their objectives and enforcement approaches, the "new players"

55 *See* Drexl, *op. cit. supra* note 4, at 451, proposing, for a multilateral agreement, the ban of export cartels and the evaluation of the effects of a practice worldwide.

have a different vision and different expectations of their competition policies. They not only speak the language of economics and efficiency. Should efficiency triumph over inclusiveness and the integration of the majority into the economic channels? How to use their competition law in order to achieve their development concerns matters for them. This dual language would have to be taken into account in any international initiative. A clear framework of a competition law and policy is not formulated yet, but the "dissenting voices" that question a competition law modeled only on the western competition laws are calling for a competition law adapted to the context of developing countries. The debate around issues such as the economic and non-economic goals of competition law, dominance from the standpoint of developing countries, public interest and competition law, employment saving and competition law, industrial policy and competition law is known. Should unilateral conduct rules be less permissive in the context of developing countries, where economic concentration and abuses resulting from it is a looming issue? Those different perceptions, orientation and expectations of competition law have to be taken into account for an international framework to succeed.

The early initiative for an international framework on competition law and even the EU initiative in the framework of the WTO have been tainted and strongly influenced by the developed models. Rightly, developing countries feared that a potential international framework would constitute an additional market access tool. The future initiative will have to be different.

The commitment pathway takes account of this new reality. Goals of competition, as envisioned by Gerber, should be "shared" or "sharable" and "fair" for all participants. The approach is sound. But given the trend in advanced jurisdictions toward narrowing down the goal of competition law to efficiency and consumer welfare, as showcased by the more economic approach in the EU and the simultaneous broadening of its goals in developing jurisdictions, reaching "shared," "sharable," and "fair" goals will be problematic. Achieving the same goals, over the time, such as consumer welfare in all participants, entails an assumption that new jurisdictions' competition laws will grow and become mature enough not to take into account non-economic goals. This is very uncertain.

From the Sub-Saharan African countries' perspective, competition law and policy are still in their infancy. A model of competition law that fits their development need is still being sought. This newness is taken into account in Gerber's gradual approach. It respects African countries' limited experience in competition law enforcement and the need of their competition laws to develop.

The phasing out of the norm settings proposed by Gerber reflects diversity as well. Agreement on the core and shared aspects that are relevant and accepted in every competition law would respect diversity; the right of nations to choose. This approach, which is very developing-country sensitive, would certainly be difficult for advanced jurisdictions to accommodate.

3. The Time Dimension and the Learning Necessity for Developing Countries

In the process of setting a multilateral framework on competition law, time may be an ally for developing countries. It may also be an enemy. Their experience in dealing with competition matters is still very limited. Let us recall that one of the reasons for the opposition of developing countries to the EU-proposed framework at the WTO is that they did not have enough experience in dealing with competition law matters and their experience with the TRIPS Agreement was still fresh in their memories. They seek an agreement that would take into account their own interest in term of competitiveness of their own firms and flexibility to pursue their own goals. They do not want a competition law which would be an additional market access tool. Flexibility and exceptions were also among the concerns raised by developing countries. Yet, a general framework outlining a competition law and policy is not defined. Perhaps this is impossible since developing countries have different competition constraints that have to be taken into account in their competition policies. Finding the appropriate blend of competition law requires time. This time dimension is fully taken into account by Gerber's proposal. It allows developing countries to be committed to the aspects they are comfortable with before strengthening the commitments.

The competition law and policy landscape is still taking shape in Africa. South Africa's competition law features concerns of including SMEs and integrating previously disadvantaged black people into economic channels. The regional dimension is being explored and seems to be advisable for African countries. It would allow them not only to benefit from the regional markets, but also to gain from the globalization of the markets.

4. Commitment Pathway Strategy and the Shift toward Bilateral Cooperation: Multilateral Approach *versus* Bilateral Approach

The benefits of a multilateral agreement dealing with restrictions of competition on global markets are unquestionable. Yet, such an agreement would be difficult to achieve. The current shift toward the bilateral approach in dealing with competition matters renders the prospects of reaching an agreement unlikely. Developed countries such as the United States and the European Union are strengthening their cooperation in antitrust enforcement. At the same time, they are pushing for more harmonization of competition laws worldwide. The ICN, which manifests this approach, is achieving results in narrowing down the gaps between competition laws. The FTAs that encompass competition rules also support the EU competition agenda. The EU-CARIFORUM Agreement and the ongoing negotiations with the African states evidence this approach.

Given their success at the bilateral level, would developed countries be willing to enter any kind of multilateral agreement that, although flexible like the commitment pathway, would create commitments?

CONTRIBUTORS' BIOS

David J. Gerber, Distinguished Professor of Law and Co-director of the program in International and Comparative Law at Chicago-Kent College of Law, teaches and writes primarily in the areas of international and comparative law, comparative law, and antitrust law. He holds a Bachelors degree from Trinity College, a Masters degree from Yale University, and a law degree from the University of Chicago. He has also received an Honorary Doctor of Laws degree from the University in Switzerland. He was formerly associated with the Frankfurt, Germany law firm of Peltzer and Riesenkampff and the New York law firm of Casey, Lane and Mittendorf. Prof. Gerber has taught law at the University of Pennsylvania, Northwestern University and Washington University in the United States as well as at the Universities of Stockholm and Uppsala in Sweden, and the Universities of Freiburg and Munich in Germany. He is a titular member of the International Academy of Comparative Law and vice-president of the American Society of Comparative Law. His book LAW AND COMPETITION IN 20TH-CENTURY EUROPE was published by Oxford University Press in 1998 (paperback 2001). Prof. Gerber's most recent book is GLOBAL COMPETITION: LAW, MARKETS AND GLOBALIZATION (Oxford University Press 2010, paperback 2012).

Sungjoon Cho is Professor of Law at the IIT Chicago-Kent faculty and teaches courses in international law, international trade law, international business transactions, and comparative law. He is Professor of Law and Norman and Edna Freehling Scholar and teaches courses in international law, international trade law, international business transactions, and comparative law. He earned his LLB from Seoul National University in 1989. From 1994 to 1996, before coming to the United States, Professor Cho represented the government of the Republic of Korea in negotiations under the World Trade Organization (WTO) and the Organization for Economic Cooperation and Development (OECD). In 2002, he received his SJD (Doctor of Juridical Science) degree from Harvard Law School. He is a member of the bar of the state of New York. He also holds a license to practice law in Korea. Professor Cho served as a Co-Chair of the International Economic Law Interest Group of the American Society of International Law from 2011 to 2013. He has recently been appointed member of arbitration panel roster under Chapter 14 (Dispute Settlement) of the Korea–European Union Free Trade Agreement. Professor Cho is also advising the government of the Republic of Korea under various capacities. He was appointed a Visiting Professor of Law in many institutions, including Northwestern University School of Law, Fordham University School of Law, and Seoul National University School of Law. He has published numerous articles and op-ed pieces related to international trade and domestic politics, including those published at Financial Times and Wall Street Journal. His works and comments have been cited by many institutions, including the U.S. Department of Commerce, the Law Library of Congress, and Voice of America. His new book, THE SOCIAL FOUNDATIONS OF WORLD TRADE: NORMS, COMMUNITY, AND CONSTITUTION, will be published by Cambridge University Press in 2014.

Eleanor M. Fox is the Walter J. Derenberg Professor of Trade Regulation at New York University School of Law. Before joining the faculty of NYU Law School, Fox was a partner at the New York law firm Simpson Thacher & Bartlett. She has served as a member of the International Competition Policy Advisory Committee to the Attorney General of the U.S. Department of Justice (1997-2000) (President Clinton) and as a Commissioner on President Carter's National Commission for the Review of Antitrust Laws and Procedures (1978-79). She has advised numerous younger antitrust jurisdictions, including South Africa, Egypt, Tanzania, The Gambia, Indonesia, Russia, Poland and Hungary, and the common market COMESA. Fox received an honorary doctorate degree from the University of Paris-Dauphine (2009). She was awarded an inaugural Lifetime Achievement award in 2011 by the Global Competition Review for "substantial, lasting and transformational impact on competition policy and/or practice." Her books include THE COMPETITION LAW OF THE EUROPEAN UNION (West 2009), GLOBAL ISSUES IN ANTITRUST AND COMPETITION LAW with Dan Crane (West 2010), READINGS ON DEVELOPING COUNTRIES AND COMPETITION with Abel Mateus (Elgar 2011), and the new third edition of U.S. ANTITRUST LAW IN LAW IN COMPARATIVE CONTEXT (West/Reuters 2012).

William E. Kovacic is currently a professor of Global Competition Law and Policy at George Washington University, where he is also director of the Competition Law Center. Before joining the GW Law School in 1999, he was an FTC Commissioner from January 2006 to October 2011 and served as chairman from March 2008 until March 2009. Previously, Professor Kovacic was the FTC's general counsel from 2001 through 2004, and also worked for the Commission from 1979 until 1983, initially as a staff attorney in the Bureau of Competition's Planning Office and later as an attorney advisor to former Commissioner George W. Douglas. Before he became a Commissioner, Kovacic was the E.K. Gubin Professor of Government Contracts Law at George Washington University Law School, where he began teaching in 1999. He had taught at the George Mason University School of Law since 1986, after practicing antitrust and government contracts law for three years at Bryan Cave's Washington, DC, office. Earlier in his career, Kovacic spent one year on the majority staff of the U.S. Senate Judiciary Committee's Antitrust and Monopoly Subcommittee. Since 1992, Kovacic has been an adviser on antitrust and consumer protection issues to the governments of Armenia, Benin, Egypt, El Salvador, Georgia, Guyana, Indonesia, Kazakhstan, Mongolia, Morocco, Nepal, Panama, Russia, Ukraine, Vietnam, and Zimbabwe. Kovacic received a bachelor degree from Princeton University in 1974 and a law degree from Columbia University in 1978.

David A. Hyman is considered to be one of the country's top health law scholars. Professor Hyman, the H. Ross & Helen Workman Chair in Law, teaches civil procedure and health care regulation. His principal research interests are the regulation of healthcare financing and delivery and empirical law and economics. Professor Hyman has published articles on a wide range of subjects, including medical malpractice, managed care, consumer protection, narrative, professional responsibility, tax exemption, and civil procedure. Professor Hyman was named the Galowich-Huizenga Faculty Scholar in November 2005 and serves as the director of the Jon David and Elizabeth A. Epstein Health Care Law and Policy Program. Professor Hyman is responsible for a portfolio of path-breaking work on medical malpractice, health law and policy, professional responsibility, and tax exemption. Professor Hyman has been a visiting professor at the University of Texas and George Washington University Schools of Law, and a professor at the University of Maryland School of Law. He is a member of the American Law Institute and was the chair of the section of law and social sciences of the American Association of Law Schools. Professor Hyman served for three years as special counsel to the Federal Trade Commission, where he was responsible for coordinating hearings and a major report on health care and competition law and policy. He is on the editorial board of the American Journal of Law & Medicine and is an adjunct scholar at the Cato Institute. He is admitted to practice before the 6th, 7th and 10th Circuit Courts of Appeal and the United States Tax Court and is a member of the Illinois Bar. Professor Hyman earned a BA, MD, and JD from the University of Chicago. His 2006 book, Medicare Meets Mephistopheles, was named to the U.S. Chamber of Commerce/National Chamber Foundation's Top Ten Books of 2007, a list of books by leading think tanks, business leaders, and policy experts that the U.S. Chamber recommends to industry leaders. In March 2005, Professor Hyman, along with three co-authors, released the research paper, "Stability, Not Crisis: Medical Malpractice Claim Outcomes in Texas, 1988-2002," which received national media coverage in outlets including The New York Times, Associated Press, Reuters, and the Washington Post. The paper was subsequently published in the Journal of Empirical Legal Studies. Follow-up papers have been published or accepted by the Journal of Legal Studies and the Journal of Empirical Legal Studies.

Xiaoye Wang is professor and director of Law, Chinese Academy of Social Sciences. Professor Wang holds a bachelor's degree of philosophy from Inner Mongolian Normal University (1981), an LLM from Renm in University of China (1984) and a Doctor Juris degree magna cum laude from the University Hamburg (1993). Since 1984, she has been working at the Institute of Law, Chinese Academy of Social Sciences (CASS). From 1988 to 1993, she studied in Germany based on Max-Planck Institute for Comparative Private Law. Professor Wang works in the areas of economic law, international economic law, and focuses on competition law. Professor Wang has served as vice president of National Association for Economic Law of China, the head of the Consultant Committee for WTO Trade and Competition Policy of the Ministry of Commerce, and member of the Expert Advisory Board for Anti-Monopoly Legislation of the State Council and the National People's Congress.

Laurence Idot, Docteur en droit (1981), Agrégée des Facultés de Droit (1982), has taught EC andCompetition Law for post-graduate students at University Paris I Panthéon-Sorbonne (1993-2007) and University Paris II Panthéon-Assas (since 2007). Her other fields of interest include arbitration law and private international law, and their interaction with competition law. She is also co-director of the monthly review Europe (1991), director of the scientific committee of the review Concurrences (2004), and a member of advisory boards of several reviews, such the Common Market Law Review. She has an active role in many academic associations and is the president of the French Association on Competition Law (AFEC) as well as one of the French NGA for the ICN. These last five years, she has devoted quite a few articles as well as a book (Bruylant, 2004) to European competition reform. Ms. Idot has also experience as a practitioner, a consultant, and an arbitrator. She was appointed as a member of the Autorité de la concurrence early 2009.

Spencer Weber Waller is Professor and Director of the Institute for Consumer Antitrust Studies of Loyola University Chicago School of Law where he teaches antitrust, procedure, and international business courses. Professor Gerber served as a staff law clerk law clerk for the U.S. Court of Appeals for the Seventh Circuit. He also worked for the U.S. Department of Justice, first as a trial attorney in the Foreign Commerce Section of the Antitrust Division and later as a special attorney in the Chicago Strike Force of the Criminal Division. He then practiced at the Chicago firm of Freeborn & Peters. He was a full-time faculty member at Brooklyn Law School for ten years until joining Loyola in 2000.

André Fiebig practices in the area of corporate and antitrust law with a particular emphasis on mergers and acquisitions, international joint ventures, international antitrust and competition law and commercial law. Mr. Fiebig assists clients doing business internationally and foreign clients doing business in the United States. He advises on mergers and acquisitions as well as on commercial transactions. He also provides advice on antitrust and competition law matters and obtaining merger clearance for transactions both in the United States and abroad. Mr. Fiebig previously practiced law in Germany and Belgium. Since 1997, Mr. Fiebig has served as an adjunct professor at Northwestern University School of Law where he teaches Mergers & Acquisitions and European Business Law. He is also a member of the advisory board of the Institute for Consumer Antitrust Studies at Loyola University Chicago School of Law. Mr. Fiebig is an officer of the ABA Section on Antitrust Law and a Member of the Steering Committee of the European Law Committee of the ABA Section on International Law and Practice.

Javier Mora-Cortázar, lawyer from the Universidad Javeriana of Bogota, is the most prolific Colombian legal writer in competition law. He is one of the founders of the Colombia's only academic law journal in international law (International Law–Revista Colombiana de Derecho Internacional), lecturer in various Colombian universities in competition law and also a practitioner. Mr.

Cortázar is a member of the Academic Society for Competition Law (ASCOLA) and the International Law Association (ILA).

Wentong Zheng has worked as an assistant professor at the University of Florida Levin College since 2011. His teaching and scholarship activities mainly focus on International Trade, International Business Transactions, Antitrust and Competition Policy, Chinese Law, Commercial Law, Law and Economics. He also worked in the private sector at Steptoe & Johnson LLP (Washington, DC, 2005-2009). Professor Zheng holds a JD, Stanford Law School, a PhD. in Economics, Stanford University, and a MA, Renmin University of China BA, Renmin University of China.

Mor Bakhoum is a senior research fellow at the Max Planck Institute for Intellectual Property and Competition in Munich, Germany. He has an international education and graduated from three different Universities. From the University of Saint-Louis he holds a master degree in Economic and Business Law which he completed top of the class with honors. From the University of Lausanne (Switzerland) he holds an LLM in European and International Economic Law as well as a Certificate in International Comparative Arbitration. In 2006 Mor Bakhoum successfully defended his PhD in competition law at the University of Lausanne with the distinction summa cum laude and was awarded the 2008 prize of the city of Lausanne for the best PhD in human sciences. Mor Bakhoum holds an LLM in International Intellectual Property Law from Chicago-Kent College of Law which he completed in 2008 with high honors and ranked top of the class. He received in addition the Cali award for the best antitrust paper as well as the Cali award for the best LLM thesis at Chicago-Kent. Mor Bakhoum was the lead expert of the reform of the West African Economic and Monetary Union (WAEMU) reform project of its regional institutional framework for the application of its competition law. He is currently in charge of coordinating the Max Planck Institute project on "Competition Law in Developing Countries." He has extensively published and talked on competition law and international related aspects of IP. Mor Bakhoum is proficient in French, English, Wolof, and has basic knowledge in German.

INSTITUTE of
Competition Law
Antitrust databases and resources

The Institute of Competition Law

The Institute of Competition Law is a think tank, founded in 2004 by Dr. Nicolas Charbit, based in Paris and New-York. The Institute cultivates scholarship and discussion about antitrust issues through publications and conferences. Each publication and event is supervised by editorial boards and scientific or steering committees to ensure independence, objectivity, and academic rigor. Thanks to this management, the Institute has become one of the few think tanks in Europe to have significant influence on antitrust policies.

Aim

The Institute attracts government, business and academic attention to a broad range of subjects relating to competition law, regulations and industrial economics.

Boards

To maintain its unique focus, the Institute relies upon highly distinguished editors, all leading experts in national or international antitrust: Bill Kovacic, Mario Monti, Eleanor Fox, Barry Hawk, Laurence Idot, Fred Jenny, etc.

Authors

2,500 authors, from 55 jurisdictions.

Partners

- Universities: University College London, King's College London, Queen Mary University, Paris Sorbonne Panthéon-Assas, etc.

- Law firms: Allen & Overy, Cleary Gottlieb Steen & Hamilton, Hogan Lovells, Jones Day, White & Case, Kinstellar, Vogel & Vogel, etc.

Events

More than 130 events since 2004 in Brussels, London, New York, Paris, and Washington DC,.

Publications

The Institute publishes Concurrences Journal, a print and online quarterly peer-reviewed journal dedicated to EU and national competitions laws. Launched in 2004 as the flagship of the Institute of Competition Law, the journal provides a forum for both practitioners and academics to shape competition policies. The Institute also releases e-Competitions Bulletin, the first online database that features more than 9,000 case summaries from 1,900 experts in 55 countries. In addition to Concurrences Journal and e-Competitions Bulletin, the Institute publishes two series of books. The e-Competitions series comprises an annual Competition Digest, in US and EU versions, and Festschrift or Mélanges. The Concurrences series comprises the proceedings of the annual conferences, the Concurrences Award thesis, and books by academics and practitioners.

Website

Concurrences website provides all articles published since its inception, and about 1,000 articles published online only, in the electronic supplement.

Concurrences
Competition Laws Journal

Concurrences Journal

Concurrences is a print and online quarterly peer reviewed journal dedicated to EU and national competitions laws. It has been launched in 2004 as the flagship of the Institute of Competition Law in order to provide a forum for academics, practitioners and enforcers. The Institute's influence and expertise has garnered interviews with such figures as Christine Lagarde, Doug Melamed, Bill Kovacic, François Hollande and Nicolas Sarkozy.

Contents

More than 8,000 articles, print and/or online. Quarterly issues provide current coverage with contributions from the EU or national or foreign countries thanks to more than 800 authors in Europe and abroad. Approximately 25 % of the contributions are published in English, 75 % in French, as the official language of the General Court of justice of the EU; all contributions have English abstracts.

Format

- In order to balance academic contributions with opinions or legal practice notes, Concurrences provides its insight and analysis in a number of formats:

- Forewords: Opinions by leading academics or enforcers
- Interviews: Interviews of antitrust experts
- Trends: 4 to 6 short papers on hot issues
- Law & Economics: Short papers written by economists for a legal audience
- Doctrines: Long academic papers
- Case Summaries: Case commentary on EU and French case law
- Legal Practice Short papers for in-house counsels
- International: Medium size papers on international policies
- Books Review: Summaries of recent antitrust books
- Articles Review: Summaries of leading articles published in 45 antitrust journals

Boards

The Scientific Committee is headed by Laurence Idot, Professor at Panthéon Assas University. The International Committee is headed by Frederic Jenny, OECD Competition Comitteee Chairman. Boards members include Bruno Lasserre, Mario Monti, Richard Whish, Wouter Wils, etc.

Online version

Concurrences website provides all articles published since its inception, in addition to selected articles published online only in the electronic supplement.

- Interviews: Interviews of antitrust experts
- Trends: 4 to 6 short papers on hot issues
- Law & Economics: Short papers written by economists for a legal audience
- Doctrines: Long academic papers
- Case Summaries: Case commentary on EU and French case law
- Legal Practice Short papers for in-house counsels
- International: Medium size papers on international policies
- Books Review: Summaries of recent antitrust books
- Articles Review: Summaries of leading articles published in 45 antitrust journals

IIT Chicago-Kent
College of Law
ILLINOIS INSTITUTE OF TECHNOLOGY

Chicago-Kent College of Law

IIT Chicago-Kent College of Law, the law school of Illinois Institute of Technology, is nationally recognized for the scholarship and accomplishments of its faculty and student body. The second oldest law school in the state of Illinois, Chicago-Kent has a history marked by innovation and excellence. Chicago-Kent has always emphasized professional responsibility in the broadest sense, encompassing intellectual discipline, careful analysis, comprehensive research, and sensitivity to the needs of clients and the context in which the law operates.

Chicago-Kent's growth has been spurred by a number of factors: an innovative and dedicated faculty, constantly upgraded facilities, and an outstanding student body. Chicago-Kent's law library, one of the largest among law schools in the nation, provides resources that enhance the educational process. Chicago-Kent is nationally recognized for offering the most comprehensive research and writing program of any law school in the country. In addition, its extensive clinical and trial advocacy programs help to sharpen students' practice skills. The Law Offices of Chicago-Kent, which supervises the clinical program, is the first fee-generating law firm to operate as part of an American law school. The Programs in Business Law, Criminal Litigation, Environmental and Energy Law, International and Comparative Law, Intellectual Property Law, Litigation and Alternative Dispute Resolution, Labor and Employment Law, Public Interest Law, and the Center for Law and Computers underscore Chicago-Kent's commitment to curricular innovation to better prepare lawyers for the demands of practice in a complex society. All of these programs contribute to the essential task of the law school, which is to teach its students to think like lawyers. Faculty members continually pursue this fundamental goal, whether by exploring the theoretical justification for a rule of law in traditional Socratic fashion or by helping a student fashion a complaint on behalf of a client in the Law Offices of Chicago-Kent. The faculty distinguishes itself in legal scholarship in areas ranging from international business to environmental law.

From the initial gathering of law students in judges' chambers, Chicago-Kent has grown to a current enrollment of over 1,000 students, a large full-time faculty and an adjunct faculty made up of practicing attorneys and members of the judiciary.

Chicago-Kent College of Law is accredited by the American Bar Association (1936) and is a member of the Association of American Law Schools (1951) and the Order of the Coif (1989).

www.ingramcontent.com/pod-product-compliance
Lightning Source LLC
LaVergne TN
LVHW081519300926
849161LV00006B/1223